MALE HOMOSEXUALITY IN FOUR SOCIETIES

Brazil, Guatemala, the Philippines, and the United States

Frederick L. Whitam
Robin M. Mathy

PRAEGER SPECIAL STUDIES • PRAEGER SCIENTIFIC

New York • Philadelphia • Eastbourne, UK
Toronto • Hong Kong • Tokyo • Sydney

Library of Congress Cataloging-in-Publication Data

Whitam, Frederick L.
   Male homosexuality in four societies.

   Bibliography: p.
   Includes index.
   1. Homosexuality, Male-Cross-cultural studies.
2. Transvestism—Cross-cultural studies.   I. Mathy,
Robin M.   II. Title.
HQ76.W45   1985   306.7′662   85-16752
ISBN 0-03-004298-4 (alk. paper)

HQ
76
.W45
1985

Published in 1986 by Praeger Publishers
CBS Educational and Professional Publishing, a Division of CBS Inc.
521 Fifth Avenue, New York, NY 10175 USA

6789 052 987654321

Printed in the United States of America on acid-free paper

INTERNATIONAL OFFICES

Orders from outside the United States should be sent to the appropriate address listed below. Orders from areas not listed below should be placed through CBS International Publishing, 383 Madison Ave., New York, NY 10175 USA

Australia, New Zealand
Holt Saunders, Pty, Ltd., 9 Waltham St., Artarmon, N.S.W. 2064, Sydney, Australia

Canada
Holt, Rinehart & Winston of Canada, 55 Horner Ave., Toronto, Ontario, Canada M8Z 4X6

Europe, the Middle East, & Africa
Holt Saunders, Ltd., 1 St. Anne's Road, Eastbourne, East Sussex, England BN21 3UN

Japan
Holt Saunders, Ltd., Ichibancho Central Building, 22-1 Ichibancho, 3rd Floor, Chiyodaku, Tokyo, Japan

Hong Kong, Southeast Asia
Holt Saunders Asia, Ltd., 10 Fl, Intercontinental Plaza, 94 Granville Road, Tsim Sha Tsui East, Kowloon, Hong Kong

Manuscript submissions should be sent to the Editorial Director, Praeger Publishers, 521 Fifth Avenue, New York, NY 10175 USA

For my parents and for Bob and Mary May.

Frederick L. Whitam

For Caryl Ainley, Ronald "Tune" Eastin, and my father.

Robin M. Mathy

ACKNOWLEDGMENTS

An investigator whose field research extends intermittently over a decade and several countries is likely to encounter many more helpful persons than he has space to name. In any event, I would like to single out a few persons who have been especially helpful to me during the course of this project.

In Guatemala: I would like to thank the Latin American Teaching Fellowship Program for the opportunity to teach at the Universidad Del Valle and conduct research in Guatemala City in 1975 and 1976. I would also like to thank Hector, Marco Tulio, and Miguel for their assistance in interviewing.

In Brazil: I am grateful to João Rezende and Domingo Montalban of São Paulo for their assistance in the summer of 1977. In Bahia, for their help in the summer of 1984, I want to thank Maria de Lourdes A. Motta, Angelica Oliveira Madureira, Luiz Mott, Professor of Anthropology, and Aroldo Assunção, graduate student in Anthropology, both of the Universidade Federal da Bahia. I am especially grateful to all the members of the Grupo Libertário Homossexual and the Grupo Gay da Bahia for their valuable co-operation and assistance.

In the Philippines: I would like to thank the late Donn Hart, at the time, Director, Center for Southeast Asian Studies, Northern Illinois University. In Cebu itself, I am grateful for the unsurpassed Philippine hospitality of Resil Mojares, Director, Cebuano Studies Center; Fr. Theodore Murnane, Presidential Assistant for Research and Faculty Development; Fr. Joseph Fertal, Department of Psychology; Zeniada Uy, Chairperson, Department of Sociology and Anthropology; and Lapulapu Nacua, my student assistant, all of the University of San Carlos. I also thank Pepe Tiu for his advice and assistance.

In Thailand: I would like to thank Chawiwan Prachuabmoh, Professor of Sociology and Anthropology of Thammasat University, and Songkram Nutjaras, also of Bangkok, for their valuable help and guidance.

In the United States: I would like to thank Jim Magary, Joe Harry, Jack Coates, Steve Dawson, Chuck Springfield, Fred Myers, Frank Westie, and Mary Hotvedt, for their support and encouragement. I am grateful to Milton Diamond of the Department of Anatomy and Reproductive Biology, John A. Burns School of Medicine, University of Hawaii, for his many kindnesses and stimulating conversations during my sabbatical leave there in the fall of 1979.

I am indebted to several graduate students who worked through sections of this material in connection with their Masters' theses and who contributed greatly to the analysis of these data: Mary Jo Dizon, Ruben Martinez, Michael Zent, and Gloria Milton. I am grateful to Fred B. Lindstrom and Leonard Gordon, former chair and present chair respectively, of the Sociology Department at Arizona State University for their support and assistance. I thank my own university, Arizona State University, for a grant from the Faculty Grant-in-Aid Program during the summer of 1979, for a sabbatical leave in the fall of that year, and for a travel grant in the summer of 1984.

I am grateful to my office staff, Peggy Cowan, Rose Ingram, Sandra Woodard, and Debbie Sult for assistance with the manuscript itself.

Frederick L. Whitam

Several professors at Arizona State University have given me invaluable support and encouragement during my participation in this project, each of whom deserves a special thank you: Leanne T. Nash, Department of Anthropology; Mark Harris and Thelma J. Shinn, Department of English; B. Richard Burg, Department of History; Nancy Eisenberg, Department of Psychology; Ronald A. Hardert and George M. Thomas, Department of Sociology. In addition, I sincerely appreciate the many hours of intellectually and emotionally stimulating discussion with Caryl Ainley. Kathleen Fairman provided assistance in the operation of computer systems, without which the analysis of data would have been a significantly more time-consuming task, and for this and her continued friendship a simple thanks is not enough.

Robin M. Mathy

FOREWORD

There are several questions in the field of sex research which hold special prominence. Among the more significant is: what factors are involved in whether an adult will engage in heterosexual or homosexual activities? With this are the concomitant questions of how these preferences might be predicted in a youngster and what behaviors other than genital activities might be related. Using the unique investigating technique of conducting personal interviews about contemporary and retrospective behavior among different cultural groups, it is nothing less than these questions that Fred Whitam and Robin Mathy set about to answer.

Fortunately, the senior author is eminently qualified for the task. He is a sociologist who has been active in the field of sex research for more than ten years. In addition to gathering research responses in Arizona, Hawaii, and the Philippines, he conducted his own interviews in Spanish and in Portuguese in Guatemala and Brazil. To use the same set of interview questions among individuals of different language groups is itself sufficiently unique to merit our attention. For the same investigator to do so is even more unique and valuable in ensuring the validity of the findings. There is no other instance of such research that I know of in the literature. This rare technique which, in and of itself bears our understanding and appreciation, has proven quite revealing. It has demonstrated that there are certain childhood behaviors and adult activities strongly and significantly correlated with homosexual and heterosexual behaviors, that these behaviors can be recognized cross-culturally, and that these childhood activities appear to develop spontaneously enough to be considered innate; that is, more of biological than sociological origin.

When in 1965 I wrote that sexual behavior and gender role were not neutral at birth but biased to interact with social forces (Diamond 1965) my thinking was based mostly on genetic and endocrine research, less on psychological and social data. Little did I suspect this cross-cultural interview technique specifically, and sociological studies in general, would be among those most significant in augmenting the correlation. The Whitam and Mathy research is consistent with that of Bell, Weinberg, and Hammersmith (1979), which showed that no strong evidence could be found demonstrating social or familial influences in the origin of homosexual or heterosexual partner preference. They similarly follow in the tradition of the longitudinal studies of Richard Green and his colleagues, showing that nongenital childhood behaviors are strongly predictive of adult sex partner preferences. These cross-cultural studies possess their own value among strong company.

The inductive method of science benefits most from a large mass of data being available before conclusions are drawn. This publication represents such an accumulation of data. But the book does much more. It presents a wealth of personal anecdotes and first person accounts which enrich the scientific story and add a measure of human understanding otherwise unavailable.

The book also has another strength. It touches on sigficant issues of the sociopolitical ramifications of homosexuality as well as the use of scientific findings which bear on homosexuality. I particularly welcome such color and perspective because the respondents to the questionnaires become people as well as subjects and statistics, and the topic becomes more contemporary and relevant.

To the science and data, the authors also add a good measure of speculation and hypothesis. Not everyone will appreciate this departure from the data nor agree with the conclusions or theories extrapolated. But it is as legitimate to do so from these data as has traditionally been done with the social data used in similar discussions in the past. The data and ideas presented here will have to be seriously considered in any future discussion of the origins of heterosexual and homosexual behavior.

While Fred Whitam is well known in the area of sex research, the coauthor, Robin Mathy, is less known. They also serve who . . . don't go in the field but remain back at the university helping to analyze and organize data and write results. So it is with Robin. For the past several years he has worked with Fred in such an arrangement. The results of their collaborative efforts are now apparent.

I am pleased the authors have asked that I write this foreword. It gives me the opportunity to personally recommend this book for its thought-provoking content, interesting perspective, and enlightening insight into important aspects of sexual development. It also allows me to emphasize the value of a standard research instrument being used cross-culturally. It is thus a book from which one can gain pleasure as well as intellectual benefit.

Milton Diamond

Honolulu, Hawaii

PREFACE

Since the publication in 1935 of Margaret Mead's Sex and Temperament in Three Primitive Societies, social scientific opinion has been enamored of the notion that all aspects of sex and gender are highly variable culturally and are largely products of cultural definitions. Although Margaret Mead (as well as many of her contemporary anthropologists) had little to say on the subject of homosexuality, by extrapolation from the widely accepted concept of cultural relativity, homosexual orientation has come to be regarded as derived from culture and social structure.

During the 1920s Freud and his followers profoundly influenced social scientific conceptions of homosexuality—especially in applied areas such as psychiatry and social work. The most influential interpretation of homosexuality which emerged from the psychoanalytic school was that homosexuality resulted from aberrant early childhood interaction between parents and children. The configuration of the dominant mother and passive father became the most popular version of psychoanalytic interpretations. While more sophisticated and more empirically derived formulations were available both before and during the Freudian period in the work of Havelock Ellis, John Addington Symonds, and Magnus Hirschfeld, ideas emerging from social anthropology and psychiatry became the most important determinants of contemporary views of homosexuality.

Social-anthropological and psychoanalytic formulations—so often at odds—converged in the 1930s to produce a social-deterministic view of homosexuality which has continued almost intact into the 1980s as the most influential social-scientific and the most popular public interpretation of that subject. It is only now, a half century later, that these deeply entrenched notions are being questioned, albeit tentatively.

The subject of homosexuality cross-culturally remains oddly cloaked in numerous misconceptions. Despite the fact that we live in an age of rapid communication and easy travel, little empirical cross-cultural work on homosexuality has been done in the past decades. Most discussions still rely on older secondary sources, such as Ford and Beach (1951), a work itself derived from cross-cultural area files which reflect material that is highly fragmentary and in which homosexuality was generally treated as an incidental aspect of studies of kinship, marriage, or other aspects of non-Western societies.

The sexuality of all societies seems to be characterized by a core of culturally invariable elements that appear regard-

less of culture and social structure. Most obvious of these
elements is a heterosexual axis upon which all societies rest.
A fact not so widely accepted is that this culturally invariable core of sexuality also includes a continuum of persons of
variant sexuality: homosexuals, transvestic homosexuals (a
subgroup within homosexual communities), and transsexuals.
These persons predictably appear in all societies. It is commonly assumed by many social scientists as well as lay persons that the "natural world" includes only heterosexual males
and females, with other variations in sexual orientation being
temporary, accidental, or aberrant. In reality the world of
sexual orientation is quite complex and homosexuals as well as
heterosexuals appear "in nature." Insofar as these groups
emerge in the context of different cultures, their outward expression may vary somewhat from society to society. Societies
only react to homosexuals who emerge spontaneously and perhaps at random; they do not create them. Not only does sexual orientation itself appear to be determined by nonsocial
factors, but specific behavioral elements occur with such pre-
dictability in homosexual populations in different societies with-
socialization into these patterns as to suggest that certain
elements of gender-related behavior similarly may be determined by nonsocial factors. In short the theme of this book is
that homosexuals are a permanent manifestation of human sexuality found at about the same rates in all societies. Homosexuals in different societies are characterized by similar patterns
of psychosexual development. An important aspect of this development is the similar patterns of cross-gender behavior
which are apparent in childhoods of most prehomosexual children. Regardless of culture, prehomosexual boys exhibit similar interests in cross-dressing, playing with girls' toys and
hobbies, and other activities more typical of the opposite sex.
In adulthood these patterns of cross-gender behavior, which
in many societies are disparaged and punished, are transmuted
as adults into socially useful behavior having to do with dance,
fashion, entertainment, the arts of embellishment, and related
activities. Male homosexuals in all societies manifest striking
similarities in such behavior and produce similar social institutions despite different cultural contexts.

By virtue of their sexual orientation and the behaviors
linked to that orientation, homosexuals perform valuable functions for society which are often unrecognized. One of the
principal themes of this book is that while one's sexual orientation is only one dimension of complex human sexual behavior,
it is a very significant dimension, having important implications
for both the homosexual's personal existence and for the society at large. Despite the fact that it is quite common in social
scientific circles to assert that homosexuality refers merely to
sexual behavior, it appears likely that there is considerable
behavior which is linked to sexual orientation. Stated another

way, homosexual orientation is not merely sexual; certain forms of nonsexual behavior seem to be intrinsically linked to sexual orientation. It is one of the fundamental aims of this book to delineate those behavioral elements which appear to be related to homosexual orientation and in so doing to sketch out the unique functions which homosexuals perform for society.

CONTENTS

LIST OF TABLES

INTRODUCTION

In January of 1975, under the auspices of the Latin American Teaching Fellowship Program, I went to Guatemala to teach. Soon after my arrival there I began interviewing homosexuals, having decided to give cross-cultural emphasis to my research, which had begun as an exploration of childhood cross-gender behavior. Guatemala is a small Central American country of about 5 million people, half of whom are Indians, speaking Mayan dialects and, to a large extent, living in nearly intact traditional societies, wearing colorful, handwoven clothing. Guatemala City is an outwardly placid capital of some 1 million people, and it is the major urban area in the country. While half the population is regarded as Indian and the other half Ladino (of Spanish descent), there has been considerable intermarriage between Indians and Ladinos. Moreover, many Indians have moved to the city and become ladinoized, so that many gradations exist between pure Indian and pure Ladino.

Because practically all of the interviewing was done in Guatemala City, most of the persons interviewed are either Ladino or urbanized Indians. In some cases, respondents themselves had been raised in traditional Indian societies, having moved as children or young adults with their parents into Guatemala City. In a few cases, respondents were living close to, if not actually in, traditional Indian societies. For example, one Indian respondent living in Quezaltenango, the largest urban area in the predominantly Indian altiplano, had a lover, and the two of them, without any contact with the homosexual lifestyle in the capital, thought they were the only homosexuals in Guatemala. They were surprised to learn that there were many other homosexuals in the capital and even more surprised to hear that there were places such as bars where groups of homosexuals gathered.

Data collection in Guatemala was done through personal interviews, most of which were conducted in Spanish by myself. Toward the end of the Guatemala project, a Guatemalan university student assisted me in interviewing. One hundred thirty-two interviews with homosexuals, bisexuals, and heterosexuals were conducted, although tabular data presented comparing heterosexual and homosexual responses are based upon questionnaires from 36 heterosexual and 54 homosexual respondents. Actual contact with the homosexual community in Guatemala City was relatively easy. The rigid social stratification of Guatemalan society and the sharp distinctions between the middle and upper classes on the one hand, and the lower classes on the other, were reflected in the homosexual community. The distinctions were so sharp, in fact, that at times it seemed I was simultaneously conducting research with two different communities. As an outsider and researcher, my activity was not restricted to either group, and I had equal access to and movement within both social classes.

For both homosexual and heterosexual lower class youths, social life took place in the streets, and contact with them was quite easy. The center of their social life was the central plaza (Parque Central) and the main avenue of the city (Sexta Avenida). In a country where official minimum salaries were at that time $40.00 a month, and the unemployment rate of adult males was as high as 35 percent, there was, needless to say, a large group of "street youth," many unemployed, with considerable time on their hands. The homosexual youths were often cruising the plaza for amusement or seeking sex. The heterosexual youths were "hanging around" on Sexta Avenida, hoping to borrow money from acquaintances to buy a hamburger in the late-night Fu-Lu Shoo Chinese restaurant or to go to a movie. After initial conversations and friendships were established on the Avenida, I located two youths, Hector and Marco Tulio, the former heterosexual and the latter homosexual, to help me with the research. Hector and Marco Tulio explained the project to their friends and provided me with introductions. Interviews were usually conducted in restaurants and bars. Pollo Campero, the Guatemalan version of Kentucky Fried Chicken, was the inevitable favorite spot, with my treating the entire table, respondents and assistants alike. While Hector or Marco Tulio helped set up the interview situation, they were instructed not to interfere with the interview and hence usually wandered off to a bar for a beer, and returned at the end of the interview. My assistants were not paid on a commercial basis, but from time to time they requested and received "loans" or other favors. Some interviews were conducted with lower-class respondents without the help of Hector or Marco Tulio. However these assistants provided extremely valuagle services in the Guatemalan phase of the project.

While homosexual social activity in Latin American countries does not take place in bars primarily, some bar life occurred as a weekend activity in two bars located in lower-class neighborhoods. One rather typical bar was run by a family, with children helping behind the bar. Homosexuals as young as 13 or 14 danced, tables of <u>locas</u> (effeminate homosexuals) with painted nails, eye shadow, and rouge chatted while neighborhood <u>machos</u> (heterosexual males) drank, watched and sometimes danced with the <u>locas</u>. Public sexual activities took place in two inexpensive <u>movie</u> houses and two bathhouses which were primarily used on the weekends by lower-class heterosexual men to relax, bathe, and drink beer.

While middle- and lower-class homosexuals sometimes mixed, often clandestinely for sexual purposes, the middle- and upper-class group kept itself rigidly separated from the lower-class street boys in their public social contacts. The middle- and upper-class homosexuals did not generally frequent Sexta Avenida, except for ordinary business purposes during business hours. Even if acquainted through sexual liaisons, middle-class homosexuals did not generally acknowledge lower-class acquaintances publicly by speaking or talking on the streets, and under no circumstances would they share coffee or <u>merienda</u> (afternoon snack) in public places. Not only did social class and educational barriers separate the two groups, but family presence was strongly felt. Since everyone sooner or later traversed Sexta Avenida to shop, work, and run errands, middle-class homosexuals could not risk being seen in public with lower-class street boys. Not only would class lines be violated, but perhaps more importantly, an uncle or a cousin would inevitably ask why "Carlos" was having coffee in a restaurant with a street boy. In the case of Guatemala, and the rest of Latin America, for that matter, suspicions of homosexuality are easily aroused. Whereas an American homosexual in the same situation might fabricate a plausible and socially acceptable excuse, Latin Americans are not so easily deceived. They seem to be much more aware of the existence of homosexuality than Americans and their suspicions are more easily aroused. The social activities of the middle-class homosexuals took place in private homes, an "exclusive" (memberships required) American style disco, and a couple of mixed discos.

Almost no one in Guatemala (except foreigners) lives away from home unless he or she is married. This custom applies to homosexuals as well. Some of the wealthier families, in order to keep their bachelor sons happy and at home, provided them with complete apartments within the compound of the family home, permitting them to come and go as they liked and to entertain their friends. Their activities sometimes consisted of homosexual parties and even sexual relations, but parents rarely inquired into the exact nature of the activities.

My entry into the middle-class homosexual world was facilitated by Miguel, a university student and Psychology major who had wide contacts in both the homosexual and heterosexual worlds. Miguel, himself well-educated and sophisticated in the social sciences, was of great help with obtaining middle-class respondents of both sexual orientations, and toward the end of the project he also interviewed some respondents. Not all interviews with middle-class respondents were obtained through Miguel, however, and other Guatemalan friends were willing to help with the project and offered me introductions.

Toward the end of my time in Guatemala, I began to think of the possibility of working in still another Latin American country, perhaps one of the larger, more highly urbanized and industrialized countries which would offer a contrast with Guatemala. After my two-year teaching fellowship in Guatemala ended, I had the opportunity to travel in most of the rest of Central and South America where, equipped with letters of introduction, names of bars and other meeting places, and international gay guides, I visited and investigated to some extent, depending upon time and circumstance, homosexual life in nearly all the countries of Central and South America. It should be noted that in all countries of Latin America there are people who are exclusively or near-exclusively homosexual in their sexual orientation, who form homosexual subcultures of varying sizes and complexities. The size and complexity appear to be closely related to the size and complexity of the society itself. Small, nonurbanized countries like Honduras tend to have relatively small, simple homosexual subcultures. Large urban countries, like Brazil, have large and highly developed subcultures. In most of Latin America, there is little effort made to control homosexual populations in the way in which they are controlled in North America, and there is little moral repugnance and outrage exhibited by the populace as in the English-speaking world--points that will later be discussed at greater length in Chapter 6.

A major exception to this Latin tradition of tolerance was Argentina, which I visited in December of 1976, where I talked with, among others, the remnants of Argentina's homosexual liberation front. The surveillance and repression of Buenos Aires's homosexual community by the government were so intense that meetings and interviews had to be arranged and carried out covertly. Many homosexuals had been jailed and many, especially intellectuals, were at that time making arrangements to emigrate to Spain, Canada, or Australia. In Argentina political repression came not so much because of homosexuality per se, but because the Argentine homosexual liberation organizations had taken a leftist turn. Argentina, then, where I had considered working, was out of the question. All homosexual bars, restaurants, and clubs were closed, and contact would have been exceedingly difficult and even dangerous.

In 1977 upon returning to the United States I began interviewing and administering an expanded version of the questionnaire to heterosexual males in a university setting and to homosexual males in the gay community of Phoenix, primarily through personal contacts and gay bars. This longer version of the questionnaire was administered to 36 homosexual and 58 heterosexual respondents, mainly in the Phoenix area. Because some items were added to the questionnaire after returning from Guatemala, these responses are not available for some items. Phoenix samples are included throughout the text in the tables showing American responses.

Although the Phoenix area encompassed over a million people during the 1970s, it was not a city which, like San Francisco, New York, or Los Angeles, had special appeal to homosexuals, and it therefore had a relatively small and rather quiet homosexual population. The homosexual population tended to be, like the city itself, primarily middle-class and white-collar. Until recently there were relatively few upper-middle class professional gay people such as doctors and lawyers. For example, in the mid-seventies Phoenix there was no doctor with a gay clientele, as is frequently found in San Francisco, New York, or Los Angeles. Although there were a few gay lawyers, none were openly gay, a fact which may have contributed to the traditional lack of strong gay political organizations in Phoenix. Arizona is not a consenting-adults state, and Phoenix is not known as a particularly receptive community for gay people. The city has an active vice squad, which maintains surveillance of the bookstores, public restrooms, and bars.

With an increase to about 1.5 million in the Phoenix population in the late 1970s and early 1980s, the gay and lesbian community of the Phoenix area experienced a corresponding growth and proliferation of bars and other organizations. By mid-1984 the Phoenix area had 23 gay bars, four of which were primarily for lesbians, three gay restaurants, two Metropolitan Community Churches, several gay groups affiliated with major churches and denominations, the Arizona Lesbian and Gay Task Force, the Lesbian and Gay Academic Union, Parents and Friends of Gays, Western Express (a biweekly newspaper), at least two theater groups, a men's chorus, a square dance club, a gay band, and several social clubs, the most influential of which is the Camelback Business and Professional Association. Thus by 1984 the homosexual community of Phoenix had organizationally come to resemble those of most American cities with similar populations.

Like gay communities elsewhere, the Phoenix gay community reflects the ethnic composition of the area, having a predominance of Anglos, significant numbers of Hispanics and

Native Americans, and a relatively small number of blacks. The gay community of Phoenix presently resembles those of cities such as Denver and San Diego, rather than those of large metropolitan areas with extensive and complex gay sub-cultures, such as New York, San Francisco, and Los Angeles.

Brazil became the logical choice for a third country in which to work, and in the summer of 1977 I returned to São Paulo to conduct interviews. Brazil, an enormous country of some 120 million, is also the most economically developed in Latin America. Of all homosexual communities in the Western hemisphere, the Brazilian is in many ways the freest. São Paulo, a city of some 12 million, has produced the largest and most public homosexual community in Latin America. In the Largo Do Arouche area of São Paulo, there are as many, or more, homosexual men on the streets as in the Castro Street district of San Francisco or Christopher Street in New York. Many of the restaurants and bars in this area of down-town São Paulo become entendido (homosexual) during the weekends as the entendidos (homosexuals) flood the streets to walk, cruise, or meet friends. In São Paulo there are even several lesbian bars and restaurants, quite rare in Latin America.

Social activity is generally limited to weekends due to financial considerations. Even Brazil's middle class, faced with enormous annual inflation rates, are hard-pressed to find money for bars and restaurants. Homosexual life is austere by U.S. standards. In homes coffee is generally offered in the place of liquor, and to avoid waste it is cus-tomarily placed in a thermos after being made. The apex of public homosexual life are two elegant clubs, Medieval and Nostro Mondo, famous for their elaborate musical productions. These clubs, while quite expensive, are frequented by middle- and upper-class homosexuals when finances allow, and serve as focal points for gossip in the homosexual community. Brazil's famous carnaval is of great interest to homosexuals, and this four-day period of dancing, drinking, and frenzied sexual activity is the high point of the year's social activities.

Rather than try to interview in all segments of the large and complex homosexual world of São Paulo, I decided to focus my attention intensively upon a single friendship net-work of 23 middle-class homosexual men, hoping to thereby achieve a somewhat different perspective than I had in Gua-temala, where I tried to interview in all segments of that homosexual community. During the summer of 1977, I lived in downtown São Paulo, in a building which was nearly half occupied by homosexual men and lesbians. The apartment of two friends and informants in this building served as a focal point for the social activities of this friendship network of homosexual men. Some of the men lived in other apartments in the building or in nearby buildings. Others lived with their families or in other parts of São Paulo. The two owners of the focal apartment, Domingos and José Roberto, held informal open house during the weekend, when friends and acquaintances dropped by. In addition to interviewing members of this network personally, I also was able to observe at close range the social interaction, conversations, and activities of the group.

Despite the fame of Brazil's favelas (slums), São Paulo is actually a prosperous middle-class city, the commercial and financial hub of Brazil's coffee industry, and the center of a highly developed industrial region. The state of São Paulo, as large as France, in many respects resembles more closely an industrialized European nation or a state like California than it does many other parts of Latin America. The population of the city of São Paulo contains many persons of European origin--Spanish, Italian, Portuguese--in addition to large numbers of Brazilians who have migrated to São Paulo from smaller Brazilian cities and towns. While no single friendship group is representative of such a large homosexual population, the group I observed is certainly not atypical. Most of the men worked in banks, automotive companies (Ford has a huge plant in São Paulo), and other white-collar jobs. Most of them were in their middle or late 20s and 30s, and in addition to holding full-time jobs during the day many attended classes at night, hoping to protect or improve their economic situations in an economy hard-pressed by inflation and political uncertainty. The comparative heterosexual group in São Paulo consisted of 16 students in a college of Business Administration who voluntarily filled out a Portuguese translation of the questionnaire.

In the summer of 1984, I returned to Brazil for six weeks, spent mainly in Salvador, Bahia, famous as the old colonial capital of Brazil, conducting interviews with Brazilian lesbians and initiating an exploratory cross-cultural study of paraphilic behavior. My initial impressions of Brazilian tolerance for homosexuals were confirmed by my stay in Bahia, where despite widespread poverty, high unemployment, and inflation rates of 300 percent annually, an extensive homosexual subculture flourishes without scapegoating of homosexuals and with little attention from law enforcement agencies.

Sexual law and custom seem to be related to what may be called "erotic traditions" or geographic and cultural areas where sexual attitudes appear to be somewhat similar. For example, sexual laws and attitudes seem to be somewhat similar in the Southern European countries and Latin American countries, forming what might be called the Latin erotic tradition. Attitudes toward homosexuals in a particular erotic tradition consequently tend to be similar. The United States is part of the Anglo-Saxon erotic tradition, which includes Great Britain, Canada, Australia, and New Zealand. Thus the United States represents the Anglo-Saxon erotic tradition, whereas Guatemala and Brazil are both variations within the Latin erotic tradition.

During my sabbatical leave in 1979, I decided to investigate a fourth society representative of the Southeast Asian erotic tradition. If what I had read about the sexuality of the Philippines was true, it represented a very different erotic tradition than either the Anglo-Saxon or the Latin. While many people are under the impression that the Philippines is thoroughly hispanicized after 400 years as a Spanish colony or thoroughly Americanized through 50 years as an American "commonwealth," the Philippines is neither Spanish nor American, but is instead a westernized Asian nation, regarded by anthropologists as a distinct cultural area. The extent of Spanish influence in the Philippines is somewhat superficial. While most Filipinos have Spanish surnames, these names were taken from civil lists of Spanish cities and arbitrarily conferred by the Spanish colonial administrators. The widespread occurrence of Spanish surnames typically is not the result of intermarriage of indigenous Filipinos with the Spanish colonial administrators, who never really cared much for the Philippines and regarded it as an undesirable appointment. The Spaniards never constituted more than 1 percent of the total Philippine population, nor was Spanish ever spoken by more than 10 percent of the population. While educated Filipinos speak English as a second language, as a first language Filipinos speak indigenous Filipino languages such as Tagalog or Cebuano, not English or Spanish.

Cebu City was chosen as a research site partly because of its size of about 1 million persons, which was similar to that of Phoenix and Guatemala City (thus making comparisons easier), and partly because I was invited to conduct my research at the University of San Carlos, the principal university in Cebu and one of the most important universities in the Philippines. Cebu is itself the second largest city in the Philippines and the principal urban area of the Visayas, an important group of islands south of Luzon and north of Mindanao, where Cebuano is spoken. Contacts with the Cebuano bayot--the most commonly used Cebuano term for homosexual --were initially made through bayot students at the University of San Carlos. A bayot student who was a sociology-anthropology undergraduate became my paid research assistant and conscientiously leading me through the world of the Cebuano bayot in November and December of 1979.

I returned to Cebu in the summer of 1981, to finish my research on male homosexuality and initiate research on the lesbian community in Cebu. Like all homosexual communities, Cebu's bayot community contains both masculine and feminine homosexuals. Unlike American homosexual communities, however, it is the effeminate or transvestic homosexuals who dominate the social organizational aspects of homosexual life in Cebu. It is this group to which Laps (my research assistant) belonged, and where most of the interviewing was done. The Cebuano sample therefore probably over-represents feminine or transvestic homosexuals, though some masculine homosexuals were also interviewed.

Interviewing was initially done by myself with a few bayot who were fluent in English, with the help of my research assistant. Because relatively few of the bayot were sufficiently fluent in English, most of the 34 interviews with bayot eventually were conducted in Cebuano by my research assistant alone or with myself present. The comparative sample of 30 heterosexuals was obtained from students at the School of Engineering of the University of San Carlos.

In addition to extensive observation and interviewing in the four societies which are the focus of this work, I have had the opportunity to observe homosexual subcultures which are not reported upon extensively here. In the summer and part of the fall of 1979 I spent my sabbatical leave in Hawaii at the John A. Burns School of Medicine, University of Hawaii. With the help of my host, Dr. Milton Diamond, I was able to conduct some interviews and obtain some questionnaires from native-born Hawaiian homosexuals, including transvestic homosexuals and female impersonators. This work proved to be difficult and slow, perhaps because the native-born population has been over-studied by social scientists. The small sample of some 12 native-born respondents has not been included in this analysis. Observation of native-born homosexuals or mahu as they are traditionally called, proved useful ethnographically.

In 1980 I spent the summer in Guadalajara, Mexico, where an active homosexual subculture exists, resembling that in Guatemala City or smaller cities of Brazil. For seven weeks in 1982, in connection with another research project, I had the opportunity to observe at close range the black male homosexual community of San Francisco. That same year I spent part of the summer in Scandinavia, where I observed in Stockholm the Swedish "Gay Pride" week. In the summer of 1983, in connection with an attempt to assess the incidence of homosexual orientation in non-Western societies, I collected data from Thai students and administered a very abbreviated version of the questionnaire to homosexuals and heterosexuals in Thailand. This work is not yet complete. While quantitative data on these societies are not available, it should be pointed out that the homosexual subcultures in these groups or societies tend to resemble those in the four societies reported upon in detail. Generalizations about male homosexuals, such as those having to do with the incidence of homosexual orientation, early cross-gender behavior, interest in dance and entertainment, relative lack of interest in athletics, and the presence of transvestic homosexuals, appear to be applicable to these subcultures as well as the four reported upon in detail.

A Methodological Note

I have used a questionnaire in this study either as such or as an interview schedule, a favorite tool of sociologists, and thus have amassed considerable data. All the field research was done by the senior author between 1975 and 1984. In 1983, the junior author joined the project, contributing primarily to writing, editing, and analysis of data.

It should be emphasized that the questionnaire itself did not come ex nihilo; rather, it was a result of my attempt to test previously published findings or to explore dimensions of homosexuality which appeared to me to be theoretically interesting or important. For example, questions about athletics did not proceed from so called stereotypes but from conversations with homosexuals about their attitudes toward sports. I had for some time been struck by the lack of interest in organized sports by homosexual men. Items were dictated either by the literature or by experiences with homosexuals themselves. It should be said that I regard the qualitative aspects of this research as important as the quantitative.

Human sexuality is exceedingly complex behavior which does not always lend itself to quantitative analysis. When I offer qualitative analysis or interpretation, they are based on what I have seen or heard. If such interpretations do not always serve as the final word on a topic, then let these become points which can be checked by other investigators. Throughout the several years of this research, I kept notes and diaries, recorded parts of conversations, sometimes reconstructing an entire evening's conversations, and jotted down anecdotes and gossip. Completed questionnaires represent only a small number of people with whom I have talked and a small part of the information compiled.

Throughout the course of this research project, I have tried to proceed with an attitude of openness and flexibility as to the nature of the homosexual world. I have tried to follow the data and to be led by what I actually saw and heard rather than by preconceived theoretical schemes or rigid hypotheses to be proved or disproved. If what I observed conflicted with ideas which I had held, as sometimes happened, I was determined to go with the observation, rather than force my observations to fit preconceived ideas. For example, my initial research interest was in the childhood aspects of homosexuality. I was under the impression, having talked to many homosexuals about their childhoods, that what is called "early cross-gender behavior" was characteristic of all homosexuals in childhood. This idea soon had to be revised on the basis of the data, and out of this has come a more complex but more accurate description of early cross-gender behavior. These ideas are incorporated in Chapter 2. For example, in Guatemala I was puzzled by the frequency of sexual contacts between the heterosexual and homosexual men. At first I was incredulous that such extensive contacts existed, tending to believe that the relationships between heterosexual and homosexual men in Guatemala were probably much the same as in the United States, where such contacts are much less frequent. Only after extensive discussion of this point with many persons, both homosexual and hetero-sexual, did I feel that I had come to something of an under-standing of this complex relationship. What I was seeing was actually something quite common throughout the world--the use of homosexuals by heterosexuals as a secondary form of sexual release. Because such activity is so repressed in the Anglo-Saxon societies, it was difficult for me to come to understand it.

If I have learned nothing more in the past several years, I have learned that the sociology of homosexuality suffers from the lack of a cross-cultural perspective. I have spoken with intelligent sociologists, for example, who do not believe that homosexuality as a sexual orientation exists outside the United States and Western Europe. Sociologists, while railing against ethnocentrism, often perpetuate the notion that homo-sexuality is the peculiar product of North American or West-ern European industrialized societies. Anthropologists often regard homosexuality as a unique creation of a particular primitive or traditional society.

As is true of all behavior, homosexuality is acted out in a cultural setting. The culture in which homosexuality is enacted, therefore, determines the outward form which cer-tain elements of homosexual behavior take. There are, how-ever, many important elements of homosexuality which appear to be the same in all societies. These differences and similar-ities in widely varying cultural settings are of critical impor-tance to an adequate sociological understanding of homosexu-ality. Moreover, their implications, however they may impinge upon existing models and theories of homosexuality, must be taken seriously. Real behavior is far more interesting and ultimately far more important for social scientists than is philosophical speculation.

Frederick L. Whitam

All statistics were initially computed manually by various graduate students. These results were verified or altered as necessary by using an INSTANT-SC program (by Michael Aiken) on an IBM PC computer. These results were then re-checked, with 100 percent consistency of findings, using SPSSX on an IBM MVS operating system. All symmetrical (2 by 2) tables were assessed to determine exact expected frequencies and the appropriate usage of Yates' Correction for Continuity by performing the calculations with Microsoft Multiplan on an IBM PC computer. All symmetrical tables with at least one expected frequency value of 5.0 or less indicate Yates' Correction. All tables in which statistics were computed by eliminating one category also show the statistics with the category included in computation. Some Gamma and Pearson's r tests have been included to indicate strength of ordinal-, interval-, and ratio-level data.

Robin M. Mathy

1

UNIVERSALITY OF HOMOSEXUALS
IN PLACE AND TIME

The existence of homosexuality has puzzled mankind for centuries, and for the past 100 years it has evoked an enormous amount of research and speculation from social scientists of various disciplines. Despite serious social-scientific efforts given to the understanding of homosexuality over the past century, many fundamental questions remain unanswered. There is still widespread disagreement among experts and misunderstanding among the general public about such questions as whether homosexual persons exist in all societies, what "causes" homosexuality, who is a homosexual, and what homosexuals do in and for societies. Despite thousands of articles, books, and expensive research efforts, there seems to be more misunderstanding of homosexuality than almost any other topic in the social sciences.

One of the principal themes of this book is that while one's sexual orientation is only one dimension of mankind's complex behavior, it is a very significant dimension, having important implications for both the homosexual's existence and for the society at large. Despite the fact that it is quite common in social scientific circles to assert that homosexuality refers merely to sexual behavior, and despite the fact that homosexuals also share much in common with the rest of the human race, there is considerable behavior that is linked to sexual orientation. Homosexual orientation is not merely sexual; rather, certain forms of nonsexual behavior seem to be intrinsically linked to it. One of the fundamental aims of this book is to delineate those behavioral elements that appear to be related to homosexual orientation, and in so doing to sketch out the unique functions that homosexuals perform in society. Despite significant evidence of the presence of homosexuals in all places and times, most contemporary social scientists have been reluctant to accept as fact the universal

1

appearance of homosexuals in all human societies, thus fostering the impression that homosexual orientation is aberrant and accidental rather than an intrinsic and socially useful variation of human sexuality.

WHO ARE HOMOSEXUALS?

Homosexual persons may be defined as those who are exclusively or nearly exclusively sexually attracted to persons of the same sex. In this work, the terms "homosexual persons" or "homosexuals" usually refer to males who are exclusively or nearly exclusively sexually attracted to other males. The term "homosexual" is generally used rather than "gay" because of the cross-cultural nature of this analysis. The term "homosexual" or its cognates is widely used and understood in most countries of the world. The term "gay" is of English origin and is widely used in the English-speaking world. While the term "gay" has recently become known in other than English-speaking countries, it is used in general conversation almost exclusively in the English-speaking world. Moreover, the term "gay," which for many years was used synonymously with "homosexual," has in the past decade acquired a political and psychological meaning which goes beyond the descriptive term "homosexual." Because "homosexual" is widely used and understood by homosexuals themselves, as well as by social scientists and the educated public in most of the world, "homosexual" is preferable to "gay" or other similar terms. In this work, "gay" is sometimes used when referring to American homosexuals, but usually only when the context is appropriate. While, technically speaking, lesbians are homosexual in that they prefer same-sex partners, the term "lesbian" has a long history of usage in the English-speaking world and seems to be preferred by lesbians themselves. It is also widely used and understood by social scientists and the educated public in most of the world. In this work, "lesbian" is generally used to refer to females who prefer same-sex partners.

In his now famous studies, Kinsey measured sexual orientation on his well-known seven-point scale. Persons who were exclusively heterosexual were designated as zero; persons exclusively homosexual as six. For our purposes, homosexuals are "Kinsey fives" and "Kinsey sixes," that is, persons who exclusively or nearly exclusively prefer partners of the same sex for most of their adult lives. Many persons who are predominantly heterosexual have had some homosexual contacts at some point in their lives, most commonly during adolescence. Similarly, many homosexuals have had heterosexual sexual contacts, often at adolescence. However, it is "Kinsey fives" and "sixes" who form the core of the

homosexual world. Since we are interested in the social creations of homosexuals in that world, it is persons who are
exclusively or nearly exclusively homosexual who are of primary concern to us. The "Kinsey four"--a predominantly
homosexual individual with significant heterosexual experi-
ences--might also be regarded as a homosexual since his
orientation is more homosexual than heterosexual. However,
the "Kinsey four" tends to be ambivalent about the homosexual world, moving in and out of it, frequently marrying and
leading a publicly heterosexual lifestyle. Somewhat the same
may be said for the "Kinsey three"--equally homosexual and
heterosexual--and "Kinsey two"--predominantly heterosexual
with more than incidental homosexual interest--who may from
time to time enter the homosexual world to seek sexual relations.

Persons in these bisexual categories are usually aware of
the homosexual world, but generally are not a permanent
part of it. "Kinsey zeros" and "Kinsey ones" form the core
of the heterosexual world, which obviously is much larger
than the homosexual world. Most people in the world are
heterosexual, as are most of the dominant structures and
institutions in all societies. "Kinsey ones" are predominantly
heterosexual persons with incidental homosexual experience,
perhaps in adolescence or in adulthood in occasional or special circumstances. In American society, homosexuals are
generally not used for sexual outlet as is common in some
societies. The use of homosexuals by heterosexuals for secondary sexual outlet is quite common in Latin American
countries, North Africa, and many parts of Asia.

While it is generally accepted by sex researchers (for
example, Churchill 1967) that males in many societies exhibit
homosexual behavior under certain circumstances, what is
not established and remains controversial (and is the main
theme of this chapter), is the concept that all societies have
populations of homosexual persons, that is, persons who are
exclusively or nearly exclusively homosexual in sexual orientation. Not only do all societies have homosexual people,
but all societies that have reached a certain size and degree
of urbanization tend to produce homosexual subcultures, and
these subcultures, found in disparate societies, are remarkably similar in certain aspects. Regardless of other manifestations of homosexuality, such as ritualistic homosexuality or
secondary sexual activity, populations of homosexual persons
emerge in all societies and the rates of these homosexual
populations tend to remain small but stable over time, and
about the same in all societies.

HOMOSEXUAL ACTS AND HOMOSEXUAL PERSONS

There is an important distinction between homosexual persons and homosexual acts. In regard to homosexual acts, there seems to be considerable cultural variability which has given rise to the notion that some societies have more homosexuals than other societies. The incidence of homosexual acts on the part of men who are heterosexual or bisexual varies considerably with culture or circumstance. Many cultural traditions define the use of homosexuals, especially as the passive partner in anal intercourse, as an acceptable sexual outlet, provided there is no emotional involvement. Quite common in Latin America, North Africa, and Asia, homosexuals in such activity are regarded much the same as prostitutes or otherwise as objects to be used for secondary sexual outlet. In the Philippines, there has evolved a rather complex call-boy system wherein heterosexual males are paid to have sexual contact with homosexuals. Thus, the incidence of homosexual acts varies for these and other societies primarily for cultural reasons. Despite cultural variations in the extent of homosexual acts, groups of persons who are exclusively homosexual emerge in every society, and the emergence of groups of homosexual persons is independent of whether societies define homosexuals as appropriate for secondary sexual contact. Unlike Latin America and the Philippines, Anglo-Saxon societies such as the United States, Great Britain, Canada, and Australia do not define homosexuals as appropriate for secondary sexual outlet. In fact, while such contact does occur in these societies, it is widely regarded as morally repugnant.

Persons of homosexual orientation emerge regardless of the normative structure in a given society. Homosexuals appear in every society, with equal frequency, regardless of whether or not the society tolerates or represses homosexuality. If homosexual acts are punished severely enough, the total number of homosexual acts is minimized and the homosexual subculture is attenuated. For example, this seems to be the case in the Soviet Union, where homosexuality is severely punished and homosexual bars and meeting places are almost nonexistent. Social norms may serve to reduce the overall incidence of homosexual outlet. In the Soviet Union and Cuba, where deliberate attempts have been made to eliminate homosexuality as a symptom of bourgeois decadence, the total incidence of homosexual outlet is probably reduced, yet reports from these countries suggest that homosexuals continue to emerge, although their social organization is greatly reduced. Throughout the nineteenth and early twentieth centuries, debate existed among sexologists as to whether Paris or London had the most homosexuals. If was generally concluded that the homosexual populations were

about the same, despite the fact that since the late eight-
eenth century France had decriminalized homosexuality while
England retained severe penalties until 1967. Well-to-do
English homosexuals in the nineteenth century often fled to
France to live when threatened with criminal prosecution.

Attitudes and normative-legal systems vary greatly in
regard to homosexuality. In all societies, a small population
of homosexuals emerges in the midst of a predominantly heterosexual population which controls the normative-legal structure. All societies formulate policies toward homosexuals that
range from extreme repression to good-natured tolerance.
Among the most repressive major societies in the world at
present are the Soviet Union, Cuba, and Iran. Relatively
little is known about homosexuals in the Soviet Union, since
they officially do not exist. However, several articles written
by Soviet homosexuals or western observers have appeared
in the homosexual press in the United States and Australia
(Schuvaloff 1976; "G" 1980; and Phillip 1980). These articles
attest to the existence of homosexuals in all parts of the
Soviet Union despite official repression, surveillance, and
elimination of social-organizational forms of homosexual life,
such as bars, restaurants, or clubs. For example, the anonymous writer "G" states that "there are gays in every city,
in every small town. They were in my village in Siberia. They
always find each other ("G" 1980, p. 16).

The Spartacus International Gay Guide (1979), intended
for use by gay people traveling abroad, lists gay bars, organizations, and meeting places in 113 countries, practically
every country in the world. In Table 1.1 the number of
homosexual places refers to the number of homosexual bars,
restaurants, baths, clubs, and organizations mentioned in the
guide for each country. The number of homosexual persons
cannot be inferred from the number of homosexual places,
because societies vary widely with respect to the way homosexual life is organized. For example, much of the third world
social organization is relatively loose, and contact among homosexuals often takes place in public places, such as plazas and
streets, reflecting the general ambiance of these societies. In
the United States and Western Europe, homosexual contact
often takes place indoors in bars and clubs and, more recently, through specialized homosexual organizations such as "alternative life centers." In some societies, such as the Soviet
Union or Argentina, homosexual places are explicitly prohibited, although homosexual persons exist in these societies. Despite criminal laws prohibiting same-sex acts in much of the
Anglo-Saxon world, homosexual meeting places are allowed to
exist, although tacit approval by and understandings with the
police are often necessary.

Spartacus International Gay Guide has been published
for 12 years by John Stamford, who lives and works in Am-

sterdam. It is revised annually on the basis of traveling by the publisher and his assistants, as well as 12,000 letters received annually from readers (Stamford 1982, p. 12). Information in the Guide tends to be most accurate for Western European countries and certain third-world countries, such as the Philippines and Tunisia, which are popular with homosexual travelers because of tolerant attitudes toward homosexuals. Information about more remote, isolated third-world countries, those in the midst of political turmoil or those countries which restrict tourist travel, are naturally much less complete (see Table 1.1).

TABLE 1.1 Number of Homosexual Places in Countries of the World

Country	Number of Homosexual Places	Country	Number of Homosexual Places
Aden	3	Finland	21
Afghanistan	1	France	521
Algeria	18	French Guyana	3
Antigua	7	Germany (East)	67
Argentina	96	Germany (West)	790
Australia	166	Gibraltar	16
Austria	75	Greece	97
Bahamas	14	Grenada	3
Bahrain	3	Guatemala	16
Barbados	13	Guyana	8
Belgium	176	Holland	239
Bermuda	6	Honduras	16
Brazil	187	Hong Kong	24
Bulgaria	34	Hungary	18
Burma	3	Iceland	3
Cambodia	5	India	25
Canary Islands	15	Indonesia	17
Chile	57	Iran	3
China	3	Iraq	2
Colombia	60	Israel	17
Costa Rica	10	Italy	403
Cuba	7	Ivory Coast	6
Curaçao	4	Jamaica	9
Cyprus	9	Japan	128
Czechoslovakia	51	Kenya	24
Denmark	51	Laos	4
Dominican Republic	13	Lebanon	19
Ecuador	12	Libya	10
Egypt	18	Luxembourg	8
Fiji Islands	5	Madeira Islands	5

Country	Number of Homosexual Places	Country	Number of Homosexual Places
Malaysia	18	Senegal	3
Malta	15	Singapore	18
Mexico	90	Somalia	2
Monaco	6	South Africa	106
Morocco	59	South Korea	4
Mozambique	14	Spain	244
Nepal	2	Sri Lanka	7
New Caledonia	4	Surinam	5
New Guinea-Papua	13	Sweden	112
New Zealand	58	Switzerland	160
Nicaragua	12	Syria	1
Nigeria	10	Tahiti	7
Norway	27	Taiwan	4
Pakistan	6	Tanzania	8
Panama	25	Thailand	28
Paraguay	4	Trinidad/Tobago	15
Peru	15	Tunisia	20
Philippines	31	Turkey	28
Poland	41	United Arab Emirates	2
Portugal	66	United Kingdom	926
Portuguese Timor	1	U.S.S.R.	28
Puerto Rico	74	Uruguay	5
Rhodesia	4	Venezuela	14
Rumania	12	Vietnam (South)	7
Spanish Sahara	2	Virgin Islands	23
El Salvador	3	Yugoslavia	38
Santa Lucia Islands	8		

Source: Based on John D. Stamford, ed., *Spartacus International Gay Guide* (Amsterdam: Spartacus, 1979). Originally published in Frederick L. Whitam, "Culturally Invariable Properties of Male Homosexuality," *Archives of Sexual Behavior* 3 (1983):211-13.

Omission of countries does not mean that homosexuals do not exist there, but that the editors do not have sufficient information for inclusion. In addition to the listing of homosexual meeting places, the guide presents a summary of what is known of laws and local attitudes toward homosexuality. Not only does this guide suggest that homosexuals exist everywhere, but it probably is the single most important sociological resource bearing on this topic.

The United States and Canada are not included in this guide because these countries are fully covered in other guides. In a few cases (such as the Canary Islands) places listed as countries are not independent political entities.

It is astonishing that sociologists have not made more use of such resources produced by homosexuals themselves. There is an unfortunate tendency among sociologists to reject out-of-hand the observations of homosexuals. For example, Schur claims that estimates by individual homosexuals are not likely to be accurate, because many homosexuals "have a psychological stake in exaggerating their number" (Schur 1965, p. 75).

In a recent revision of their textbook on deviant behavior, Clinard and Meier repeat such arguments against using material from the gay community as they write: "To date, estimates as to the incidence, prevalence, and increase of homosexuality, have been based on inadequate and unrepresentative data, often accompanied by fallacious reasoning" (Clinard and Meier 1979, p. 30). They conclude that one of the main problems has to do with the unreliability of reports by homosexuals themselves. While random samples and comprehensive standardized studies of the sex life of every society in the world would be of enormous help to sex researchers and other social scientists, they unfortunately do not exist. In their absence, evidence derived from many sources, including homosexual sources, is valuable source material.

It should be noted that in listing 113 countries, the Spartacus Guide does not limit its observations to Western European countries, where the guide is published but gives information on homosexual life in countries as culturally different as Saudi Arabia, Senegal, Singapore, Somalia, South Africa, South Korea, Sri Lanka, and Surinam. This evidence suggests that homosexual persons and homosexual subcultures (of varying degrees of elaborateness) occur in every country in the world. The existence of elements of a homosexual subculture is strong evidence for the existence of homosexual persons, since it is unlikely that homosexual social organization can persist without the presence of a homosexual population to sustain it. In small capitals, such as those in the Caribbean Island-Nations, social organization is quite simple, often consisting of a single bar or promenade. In larger societies, such as the United States, Brazil, or West European societies, the organizational forms tend to be quite extensive and complex.

THE SIZE OF HOMOSEXUAL POPULATIONS

In contemporary societies, it is of course very difficult to estimate the size of homosexual populations. However, the homosexual populations of cities of similar size, unless there are special reasons why this should not be the case, tend to be similar. While the particular social-organizational forms of homosexual communities in Guatemala and the United States differ, the homosexual population of Guatemala City, a city of a million people, appears to be similar to that of Phoenix, Arizona, a community of similar size. In turn, the homosexual population of Cebu, Philippines, a city of one million, also appears to be about the same as in Phoenix or Guatemala City. There are cultural differences in the way in which the homosexual communities in these three cities are organized, yet the homosexual populations do not appear to exceed 5 percent in any of the three cities.

The homosexual population of São Paulo is much larger --the city has some 12 million inhabitants. In the Largo Do Arouche area of São Paulo, homosexual men are to be seen promenading in much the same way and in similar numbers as on Christopher Street in New York City. San Francisco, whose homosexual population is one-fourth of the city's total (Arizona Gay News 1980), has long drawn homosexuals from all over the United States. Unless special circumstances prevail, as in the case of San Francisco, there tends to be a general correlation between city size and size of the homosexual population.

Table 1.2 graphically shows that the size of homosexual populations tends to be a function of the size of cities. As has been suggested, it is difficult to infer the size of homosexual populations from the number of homosexual bars, cafes, meeting places and other organizations to compare across cultural boundaries. However, general inferences may be made about the size of homosexual populations from the number of places within a single society or perhaps similar societies. In Table 1.2 the number of homosexual places listed in the 1981 Spartacus International Gay Guide have been juxtaposed with the population of German cities for about the same time. Germany was selected because the information in Spartacus for Germany is regarded as particularly accurate and because German law is uniform with respect to homosexuals in that it does not vary from state to state. In 1967, Germany adopted a consenting-adults law applicable to homosexuals. By examining this table it may be seen that, in general, the number of homosexual places, and by inference the size of homosexual populations, follow the size of cities. Exceptions to this pattern tend to consist of university cities such as Heidelberg, where there are unusually large numbers of young single males or resort areas such as Westerland-Sylt, sometimes called the "Fire Island" of Europe, which is a summer resort very popular with German homosexuals.

Everywhere in the world, homosexual populations appear to comprise no more than 5 percent of the total population. There are no countries which appear to have an inordinate percentage of homosexuals in comparison with heterosexuals, and all societies are predominantly heterosexual. This is true despite reports of a primitive society in the jungles of Peru where everyone is homosexual. These reports are derived

TABLE 1.2 Number of Homosexual Places and Population of German Cities

City	Population	Homosexual Places	City	Population	Homosexual Places
Berlin (West)	1,898,900	130	Witten	106,000	2
Hamburg	1,648,800	96	Bergisch-Gladbach	101,400	3
München	1,298,900	73	Erlangen	100,900	3
Köln	976,800	69	Ulm	100,600	4
Essen	650,200	33	Wilhelmshaven	99,300	2
Frankfurt am Main	629,200	63	Kaiserslautern	98,800	7
Dortmund	609,400	25	Trier	95,300	6
Düsseldorf	592,200	48	Marl	89,500	4
Stuttgart	582,400	27	Lünen	85,900	2
Duisburg	558,700	19	Ludwigsburg	81,400	1
Bremen	555,700	21	Neumünster	80,200	2
Hannover	535,100	27	Castrop-Rauxel	79,100	1
Nürnberg	483,900	13	Villingen-Schwenningen	79,000	4
Bochum	402,000	6	Minden	78,000	2
Wuppertal	393,800	11	Marburg	75,300	1
Bielefeld	312,600	5	Worms	73,500	1
Gelsenkirchen	305,600	3	Celle	72,800	1
Mannheim	303,600	15	Tübingen	72,400	9
Bonn	287,100	10	Bamberg	72,000	4
Wiesbaden	273,000	10	Bayreuth	70,300	2
Karlsruhe	270,800	15	Herten	69,300	2
Münster	267,600	5	Konstanz	68,300	3
Braunschweig/Brunswick	261,500	7	Detmold	67,200	1
Mönchen-Gladbach	258,000	6	Lüneburg	62,100	1
Kiel	250,400	12	Aschaffenburg	59,200	1
Augsburg	246,600	12	Cuxhaven	58,800	1

City	Population	
Aachen/Aix-la-Chapelle	242,700	6
Oberhausen	229,300	3
Krefeld	223,400	3
Lubeck	221,100	12
Hagen	220,100	5
Kassel	195,500	10
Saarbrucken	193,700	13
Mainz	186,700	6
Herne	183,000	2
Mühleim/Ruhr	182,100	2
Freiburg im Breisgau	173,600	9
Hamm	171,600	1
Leverkusen	161,500	1
Ludwigshafen	160,300	11
Osnabruck	157,800	18
Neuss	144,300	1
Bremerhaven	138,900	5
Darmstadt	138,300	4
Oldenberg	136,400	7
Heidelberg	131,900	10
Regensburg	131,800	2
Göttingen	128,500	6
Würzburg	127,900	8
Recklinghausen	119,600	3
Bottrop	114,600	2
Koblenz	113,900	4
Siegen	112,500	1
Heilbronn	111,500	5
Offenbach	111,200	3
Paderborn	109,600	1
Troisdorf	58,100	1
Kempten	57,400	1
Schweinfurt	52,700	4
Goslar	52,700	3
Neunkirchen	52,200	1
Emden	51,500	3
Rosenheim	51,400	2
Bad Homburg	51,000	4
Passau	50,500	1
Neustadt	50,400	2
Baden-Baden	49,200	4
Albstadt	48,300	2
Weinheim	41,800	1
Böblingen	41,300	1
Bad Kreuznach	41,200	1
Soest	40,500	1
Rendsburg	32,500	1
Nordenham	30,400	1
Kehl	29,900	1
Garmisch-Partenkirchen	27,800	8
Rinteln	26,000	1
Altenau	24,000	1
Lindau	24,500	1
Husum	24,400	3
Eckernförde	23,100	1
Alfeld	22,500	2
Bad Kissingen	22,300	2
Zindorf	20,800	4
Bad Berleburg	20,200	1
Bad Tölz	less than 20,000	1

Table 1.2 (continued)

City	Population	Homosexual Places
Brak	less than 20,000	1
Brunsbuttelkoog	"	1
Giessen	"	3
Herrischried	"	1
Metzingen/Neuhausen bei Reutlingen	"	4
Norddeich	"	3
Norderney	"	1
Otzenhausen	"	1
Punderich	"	2
Reydt	"	2
Schollnach	"	1
Schonwald	"	1
Seeg	"	1
Sierksdorf/Ostsee	"	1
Southofen	"	1
Vilshofen-Albersdorf	"	1
Westerland-Sylt	"	12
Wolfratshausen	"	1

Sources: Statistisches Bundesamt/Wiesbaden, 1981, Statistisches Jahrbuch für die Bundersrepublik Deutschland. (Stuttgart: W. Kohlhammer, 1981); and John D. Stamford, ed., Spartacus International Gay Guide (Amsterdam: Spartacus, 1981).

from the work Keep the River on Your Right (1969) by Tobias
Schneebaum, which was introduced into the sex research
literature by Tripp (1975) as a serious work in the anthropology of sex. Since the publication of Tripp's work,
Schneebaum's "homosexual tribe" has captured the imagination
of many undergraduates, and even appears to be making its
way into the serious social science literature. For example,
Mehan and Wood make use of Schneebaum in a work in ethnomethodology (1975). Schneebaum, a painter, went to Peru
on a Fulbright fellowship in 1955 and describes his alleged
experiences some 15 years later. While in Peru, he went into
the jungles near the point where the borders of Bolivia and
Brazil join that of Peru. He reached a very remote mission,
the name of which has been changed by the author, who also
changes the names of the tribes themselves and the "names
of a few places that would pinpoint the mission" (Schneebaum
1969). These names have been changed, presumably to protect these indigenous people from any further corruption by
westerners. At this point-furthest-out mission, which serves
the "Puerangas," themselves quite primitive, the narrator
hears of an even more remote, primitive, and dangerous
tribe never visited by a white man, called the "Akaramas."
Schneebaum reports that he travels along through the jungle,
"keeping the river on his right," and after a week finds the
Akaramas, not knowing whether they will kill him or celebrate
him. They follow the latter course, greeting him gleefully,
stripping him naked, and treating him as one of them. He
participates fully in their existence, becomes fluent in their
language, immediately practices cannibalism without flinching,
and after seven months returns to the mission.

The book, dedicated to Carlos Castaneda and written in
a mystical, poetic style suggestive of Castaneda's works, is
not regarded by anthropologists as authentic field work, but
rather of the same genre as that of Castaneda. Murray (1979)
has criticized Schneebaum's work from an anthropological
point of view.

It is sometimes alleged that the child-rearing practices
and socialization patterns which take place on the Israeli
kibbutz produce populations free of homosexuals. Material in
both the Spartacus guide and an article in QQ, a defunct
travel magazine for homosexuals, debunks this notion. Lorrimer (1975) documents extensively the presence of homosexual
activity and the presence of male homosexuals and lesbians in
the life of the Israeli kibbutzim. Examination of material for
Israel in the Spartacus International Gay Guide attests to the
presence of homosexuals in all parts of Israel. It should be
noted that Israel, sometimes regarded as an exemplary democ-
racy, does not have consenting-adults laws, and homosexual
acts, regardless of age, are criminalized in Israel.

THE PRESENCE OF HOMOSEXUALS
IN NON-WESTERN SOCIETIES

The view that homosexual persons exist in all societies is not inconsistent with previously published reports. The best known, of course, is the analysis of Ford and Beach (1951), which is sometimes regarded as evidence for the absence of homosexual persons in some societies. In a widely quoted passage, these researchers write: "In twenty-eight of the seventy-six societies for which information is available, homosexual activities on the part of adults are reported to be totally absent, rare, or carried on only in secrecy. It is to be expected, however, that the estimate would run considerably below actual incidence, since this form of sexual expression is condemned in these societies" (p. 129). Closer scrutiny raises doubts as to whether these reports can be used as evidence for the lack of homosexual persons in these societies. Ford and Beach write: "Holmberg, who lived with a band consisting of about 100 Siriono natives, found no instances of overt homosexual behavior. One bachelor appeared to show some homosexual tendencies, but he was never seen to make overt sexual advances toward other men" (p. 130). Thus, while this society is classified as a society where homosexuality is rare or absent, there does appear to be one possible homosexual male. It should also be emphasized that if it is true that the number of homosexual persons increases as the population increases, it might be quite possible to find a very small society such as that of the Siriono where homosexuality is rare or perhaps even nonexistent at a particular point in time.

Ford and Beach report on the observations of an ethnographer who "had described an 18-year-old Goajiro boy who insisted upon dressing like a girl and working with the women" (p. 129). While the Goajiro are classified by Ford and Beach as a society where homosexual activities on the part of adults are "totally absent, rare, or carried on only in secrecy," the report of a young man who dresses like a girl and works with the women strongly suggests the appearance of a transvestic homosexual or transsexual.

Haiti is similarly listed by Ford and Beach as a society where homosexuality is absent, rare, or carried on only in secrecy. However, according to the Spartacus International Gay Guide, while homosexuality is not mentioned in Haitian law, there is a rather complex and well-established homosexual "scene" in Haiti, which includes guest houses, bars, and clubs (Stamford 1982, pp. 338-42).

Similarly, Tonga is listed as a society where homosexuality is absent, rare, or carried on only in secrecy, yet according to the Spartacus International Gay Guide, "Local queens are called fakalady" and there is "Lots of gay action despite many official rules" (1982, p. 617). Thus, in Tonga there appears to be an indigenous group of homosexuals, including effeminate or transvestic homosexuals, as well as indigenous terminology for this group.

Ford and Beach report on 76 societies for which information is available. Although 28 of these societies are regarded as societies where homosexual activities are totally absent, rare, or carried on only in secrecy, many of these societies are very small societies of two or three hundred persons, or perhaps even fewer, where the number of homosexual persons relative to the population is quite small or perhaps even non-existent at the time of observation; yet even in some of these societies evidence suggests the likelihood of some homosexual persons. Contemporary sources such as the Spartacus International Gay Guide suggest not only the existence of homosexual persons, but even elements of homosexual subculture in some of these 28 societies.

In sum, there is nothing in Ford and Beach's analysis which definitively contradicts the notion that homosexuals appear in all societies. While such interpretation is sometimes given to the Ford and Beach analysis, this does not appear to have been the intent of these authors, who conclude that: "The cross-cultural and cross-species comparisons presented in this chapter combine to suggest that a biological tendency for inversion of sexual behavior is inherent in most if not all mammals including the human species. At the same time we have seen that homosexual behavior is never the predominant type of sexual activities for adults in any society or in any animal species" (p. 143). Of the total 76 societies reported on by Ford and Beach, 49 (or 64 percent) approve of some forms of homosexuality.

One of the few reliable estimates of the percentage of homosexuals in populations of contemporary traditional societies comes from the field work of Donn Hart (1968), who worked in a village 35 miles southwest of Dumaguete on the island of Negros Oriental, Philippines. In the Barrio Caticugan with a population of 729 persons, Hart found six male homosexuals, about 1 percent of the total population. Although there were no known lesbians in this village, there were lesbians in the larger poblacion of Siaton, with a population of 2,862, there were 12 male homosexuals, about .5 percent. In the larger town of Dumaguete, with a population of 18,000, there were 70 openly homosexual males and 58 lesbians, nearly 1 percent of the total population. If these figures are doubled or trebled to allow for the fact that there were probably covert homosexuals who may not have been identified by the researcher, an estimate of 2 or 3 percent of the total population is consistent with estimates of 2 to 4 percent obtained in early nineteenth century European populations and the 4 percent figure used by Gebhard for American society.

Moreover, Hart's figures suggest that the lesbian population is smaller than that of male homosexuals, a finding also consistent with Gebhard's estimates. These estimates further suggest that the percentage of homosexuals does not increase in societies like the Philippines, which are extremely tolerant of homosexuality. Even making liberal allowances for undercounting of the homosexual population, the percentage of homosexuals in the total population stays well under 5 percent. These figures also suggest that like populations of European homosexuals, the larger the population in general, the larger the population of homosexual persons.

Despite the fact that there is significant evidence to support the idea that homosexual persons exist in every country of the world and some evidence that suggests that the rates of homosexuals are similar in all societies, there is a curious resistance in the social sciences to accepting this idea. We will probably never have complete data on homosexuality in all societies, as we will similarly never have complete data on incest in every society; yet few social scientists question the universality of the incest taboo. Data suggesting the universality of the incest taboo are no more complete than data on homosexuality, perhaps less so.

Clearly, the problem lies elsewhere. Resistance comes from other sources, and these sources are primarily political, not scientific. Some observers are reluctant to give the same status to homosexuality as to heterosexuality. But more importantly, perhaps, the universal occurrence of homosexuality, cross-culturally and historically, suggests a very different explanation of homosexuality than those which now prevail in the sociological literature. The universal, parallel development of homosexual populations points to an explanation in terms of biology, rather than the social-construction, role-modeling, and social-learning concepts which now dominate social scientific explanations of the origins of sexual orientation.

THE PRESENCE OF HOMOSEXUALS IN HISTORICAL CONTEXT

Having stated that homosexuals exist everywhere in the world at about the same rate, we shall go on to say that this has probably always been the case. It is, of course, even more difficult to demonstrate this point than the universality of homosexuals in contemporary societies. We cannot go back in time to investigate the sexuality of societies which no longer exist, nor even to investigate the sexuality of societies extant a hundred years ago. Even so, there exists considerable data that bear upon the universal occurrence historically of homosexuality. For example, there is ample documentation of the existence of homosexuals in the ancient world--in Babylonia, Egypt, Greece, and Rome (for example, Bullough 1976; Karlen 1971). Similarly, there is a considerable evidence which suggests that homosexuals existed in European countries during the Middle Ages (Bullough 1976; Karlen 1971; Goodich 1979; Boswell 1980).

Much has been made of the case of the Greeks. While there is not complete agreement among the scholars as to the sexuality of the Greeks, it is clear that ancient Greece was no means a homosexual society, as is sometimes thought; nor were all Greeks bisexual. Conversely, many persons are under the impression that there were no exclusively homosexual persons in ancient Greece. Yet, Karlen (1978, p. 224) points out: "Juvenal and other ancient writers described parts of Athens and Rome where long-haired depilated boys cruised the streets and worked in brothels . . . The Roman drag queen's cosmetics and the less overt homosexual's signals (wearing certain colors and clothes, strolling certain paths) are almost unchanged today."

The mention of depilated boys working in brothels suggests the presence of transvestic homosexuals in much the same way that transvestic homosexuals presently work as depilated prostitutes in most cities in Brazil or on Hotel Street in Honolulu. The reputation of the Greeks probably comes from the fact that bisexuals and heterosexuals used passive homosexuals and boys as secondary sexual outlet in much the way as is done in Mediterranean and Latin American countries today. The Northern Europeans, British, and Americans, who are most puzzled by the "Greek problem," are puzzled partly because homosexuals are not generally used by bisexuals and heterosexuals as secondary sexual outlet in the Northern European countries; yet these patterns are quite common, persisting in Southern Europe, the Arab world, and in many parts of Latin America and Asia (see, for example, Herdt 1981).

Gagnon and Simon have observed that the physical sexual activity of two men in ancient Greece or modern Western society may superficially be similar but that "the meanings attached to the behavior and its functions for society are so disparate in these cases that seeing them as aspects of the same phenomena except in the most superficial way is to vitiate all we know about social analysis" (Gagnon and Simon 1973, p. 6).

This view of Gagnon and Simon reflects the tendency of many observers to romanticize Greek homosexuality and give it a special place apart from the more mundane sexuality of the rest of the world. While it is difficult to know with certainty what psychological meanings the Greeks placed upon homosexuality, it is more reasonable to assume, unless there is clear evidence to the contrary, that the meaning of sexual activity between two homosexuals in ancient Greece does not differ significantly from the meaning of similar relations in modern Greece or in other countries of the world; nor is there any reason to believe that the meaning of similar activity between heterosexuals and homosexuals would vary significantly in ancient or modern times.

The interpretation of sexual behavior in historical or cross-cultural perspective should proceed upon the principle that human beings in other societies or in other historical epochs are similar to those in the contemporary world, unless strong evidence to the contrary exists, for it makes more sense to interpret human sexual behavior conservatively rather than exotically. For example, Ford and Beach (1951, p. 133) report that: "A few Crow men adopt women's dress and mannerisms, and live alone. Adolescent boys and occasionally older men visit these bate, as they are called. The bate stimulates the boy's genitals orally. One informant stated that there were four such men in his community and that seventeen of his adolescent friends visited them occasionally." The most reasonable interpretation of this report is that the bate are ordinary effeminate or transvestic homosexuals who are fellating adolescents and adult males, rather than exotic and unique individuals resulting from the social structure of Crow society.

The appearance of cross-dressing alone is strong but not positive evidence for the existence of homosexual orientation. It is possible that some instances of cross-dressing are associated with heterosexual cross-dressers. Heterosexual cross-dressers, however, generally do not assume women's work, do not associate with women in work roles or as a rule engage in sexual relations with other males. They tend instead to hold traditional male occupations. Reports of cross-dressing, the assuming of women's roles or women's work by males, of dancing and entertainment, in conjunction with sexual relations with other males, is very strong evidence of the existence of persons of homosexual orientation. Reports of transvestic homosexuals do not mean that only effeminate homosexuals exist, but that the effeminate homosexuals are the most obvious to the outside observer.

After the discovery and exploration of the new world, reports of the presence of homosexuals in the most unlikely places began to filter back to Europe through the observations of a wide variety of observers. It is important to note that it was the transvestic or cross-dressed homosexuals who received the most attention because they were the most visible, but it is also clear that masculine homosexuals were also found in the New World.

Edward Carpenter, the Victorian philosopher and pioneer in homosexual rights, reports a fascinating incident, which bears repeating in detail:

> Catlin, in his North American Indians
> (vol. 1, pp. 112-114), describes how on one
> occasion he was in a large tent occupied in

painting portraits of some of the chiefs of the
tribe (the Mandans) among whom he was stay-
ing, when he noticed at the door of the tent,
but not venturing to come in, three or four
young men of handsome presence and rather
elegantly dressed, but not wearing the eagle's
feathers of warriors. He mentally decided to
paint the portrait of one of these also; and on
a later day when he had nearly done with the
chiefs, he invited one of these others to come
in and stand for him. The youth was overjoyed
at the compliment, and smiled all over his face.
He was clad from head to foot in the skin of
the mountain goat, which for softness and white-
ness is almost like Chinese crepe, embroidered
with ermine and porcupine quills; and with his
pipe and his whip in his hand, and his long
hair falling over neck and shoulders, made a
striking and handsome figure, which showed,
too, a certain grace and gentleness as of good
breeding. "There was nought about him of the
terrible," says Catlin, "and nought to shock the
finest, chastest intellect." But to Catlin's surprise, no sooner had he begun to sketch his
new subject, than the chiefs rose up, flung
their buffalo robes around them, and stalked
out of the tent.

Catlin's interpreter afterwards explained to
him the position of these men and the part they
played in the tribal life; and how the chiefs
were offended at the idea of their being placed
on an equality with themselves. But the offense,
it seemed, was not on any ground of immorality;
but--and this is corroborated by the customs
of scores of other tribes--arose from the fact
that the young men were associated with the
women, and shared their modes of life, and
were not worthy therefore to rank among the
warriors [1914, pp. 21-22].

This story suggests that Catlin had encountered a clique
of masculine homosexual Mandans. They were obviously not
dressed in women's attire, but had created a special costume
which is not unusual in the homosexual world. For example,
gay San Franciscans in the 1970s referred to the "uniform"
of the "Castro Cadets" of the predominantly gay Castro Street
district. The "uniform" consisted of short beard, moustache,
Levis, undershirt, and colored handkerchief. Catlin's homosexual Indians, though not effeminate, apparently were disinterested in the warrior aspects of tribal life in much the same

way that homosexual men in modern societies tend to be relatively disinterested in the military, police, athletics, hunting,
and fishing aspects of modern society.

Much has been written about the berdache, a European
term used to refer to several forms of sexual variance observed in native Americans, and a good deal of misunderstanding still surrounds this concept. The principle misunder-
standings are that the discovery of berdache signified a new
form of sexual variance; that with the berdache the American
Indians consciously and socially created sexual variance; and
that the berdache is a single behavioral entity.

The word berdache is French and came into the sex
literature through French anthropologists in the eighteenth
century. The different native American societies in which
the berdache were observed, of course, had words in their
own language to refer to the behavior known to Europeans as
berdache. If the various reports of actual behavior subsumed
under berdache are examined closely, one encounters no unusual or unique forms of sexuality, but rather very familiar
manifestations of sexual variance known to contemporary sex
researchers: hermaphrodites, transvestites, transvestic homosexuals, and transsexuals. There does seem to be, of course,
significant variation among native Americans in the way they
treated these forms of sexual variance, as in modern societies,
and it should be pointed out that not all the North American
tribes approved of variant sexuality. In short, the literature
on the berdache tells us that the North American tribes produced the same types of sexual variants as do contemporary
societies. Native American societies did not consciously create
homosexuality, transvestism, or transsexualism, as is sometimes suggested, but like modern societies, they responded
to its existence.

Jonathan Katz (1976) has reviewed and excerpted the
historical literature dealing with first-hand reports of homosexuals in native American societies. Table 1.3 summarizes
Katz's review, noting name of the observer, date of the
observation, and name of the tribe. This summary certainly
suggests that persons of homosexual orientation existed in
native American societies since the earliest contact with Europeans. Although most are reports of males, several reports
of lesbians are included。

In all of this material, homosexuals appear to be few in
number relative to the number of heterosexual persons in
each society noted. In no case was there any evidence of a
homosexual society in which this behavior was encouraged,
although in some societies homosexual behavior was tolerated
or even officially recognized, in the sense that homosexuals
were given special duties or rites of passage. There is nothing in these observations which suggests that homosexuality
either increased or decreased over the four and a half centu-

TABLE 1.3   Reports of Homosexual Persons in Native American Societies

Year of Report	Observer(s)	Society or Tribe(s)
1528-36	Alvar Núñez Cabeza de Vaca	Florida Indians
1540	Hernando De Alarcón	California Indians
1562-67	René Goulaine de Laudonnière	Florida Indians
1564	Jacque Le Moyne de Morgues	Florida Indians
1593-1613	Francisco de Parreja	Timucuan
1673-77	Jacques Marquette	Illinois, Nadouessi
1702	Pierre Liette	Miami
1711-17	Joseph François Lafitau	Illinois, Sioux
1721	Pierre François Xavier de Charlevoix	Iroquois, Illinois
1750	Georg Heinrich Loskiel	Indians of Pennsylvania, New York, and North Carolina
1751-62	Jean Bernard Bossu	Choctaw
1775-76	Pedro Font	Yuma
1777	Francisco Palóu	California Indians
1801	Alexander Henry and David Thompson	Saulteur
1804-10	Nicholas Biddle	Mandan, Minitaree
1811	Claude E. Schaeffer	Kutenai
1819-20	Edwin James and T. Say	Konza, Omaha
1826	Thomas A. McKenney	Chippewa
1828	Isaac McCoy	Osage
1830	John Tanner	Ojibwa
1832-39	George Catlin	Sioux, Sacs, Fox, Mandan
1841	Pierre-Jean de Smet	Crow
1846	Francis Parkman	Sioux
1855-56	Edwin T. Denig	Crow
1876	H. Clay Trumbull	Arapahoe
1889	A. B. Holder	Absaroke, Sioux, Gros Ventres, Flathead, Nez Perces, Shoshone
1896-97	Matilda Coxe Stevenson	Zuni

Table 1.3 (continued)

Year of Report	Observer(s)	Society or Tribe(s)
1901-02	William Jones	Fox
1902	S. C. Simms	Crow
1907-12	Robert Henry Lowie	Crow
1930	Leslie Spier	Klamath
1931	C. Daryll Forde	Yuma
1931	Edward Winslow Gifford	Kamia
1933	Edward Winslow Gifford	Cocopa
1937	George Devereux	Mohave
1947	Dorothea Leighton and Clyde Kluckhohn	Navaho
1964	J. J. Honigmann	Kaska
1964	Bob Waltrip	Mohave

Source: Based on: Jonathan Katz, Gay American History (New York: Thomas Y. Crowell, 1976), pp. 281-334.

ries covered, nor that the Europeans had any influence upon the emergence of homosexuals in these tribes. In some cases, because descriptions are fragmentary, it is difficult to know how these persons would be classified according to the terminology of contemporary sex researchers. In some cases persons observed may have been transsexuals or heterosexual transvestites; however, the most frequently mentioned cases appear to be homosexuals, especially transvestic male homosexuals. The latter are mentioned frequently, not necessarily because they were most numerous, but because they were most obvious to the observer.

Observations of homosexuals by travelers were not limited to the indigenous peoples of North America. For example, the phenomenon of the mahu, or transvestic homosexuals, is reported at least three times from the late eighteenth century until the mid-twentieth century in Polynesia, and continues to exist in contemporary Polynesia. There is nothing in these reports to suggest that the incidence of the mahu in Tahitian society, comprising a very small percentage of the population, changed greatly during this period of time.

James Morrison, left ashore on Tahiti after the mutiny on the Bounty in 1789, noted:

> They have a set of men called mahu. These men
> are in some respects like the Eunuchs in India
> but are not castrated. They never cohabit with
> women, but live as they do. They pick their
> beards out and dress as women, dance and sing
> with them and are as effeminate in their voice.
> They are generally excellent hands at making
> and painting of cloth, making mats, and every
> other woman's employment. They are esteemed
> valuable friends in that way and it is said,
> though I never saw an instance of it, that they
> converse with men as familiar as women do. This,
> however, I do not aver as a fact as I never found
> any who did not detest the thought [Morrison
> 1935 in Levy 1971, pp. 12-13].

A few years later, in 1804, another early visitor, John Turnbull, attested to the fact that the mahu "eagerly swallows [the semen] down as if it were the vigor and force of the other; thinking no doubt thus to restore to himself greater strength" (Bouge 1955, p. 147).

Robert I. Levy, an anthropologist, spent 26 months during 1961-64 in two Tahitian speaking communities in French Polynesia, and writes that the mahu as a social type still exist. Levy reports that in a village of 300, called Piri, he found one mahu, a 16-year-old boy, and two or three other men of probable variant sexuality. He also reports that most villages report that there is usually one mahu, sometimes for periods of time there is no mahu, and for other periods of time there are two mahu. Levy's interpretation of the mahu phenomenon is that "persons were recruited for the role," as a conscious social product of Tahitian society, and further suggests that the function of the mahu is to more clearly define the masculine role for the heterosexual male (1971, pp. 20-21).

The various descriptions of mahu behavior are quite consistent with types of variant sexuality known to contemporary sex researchers. Mahu appear to have been and continue to be transvestic homosexuals. In Levy's explanation of the socially created mahu, their function of defining heterosexuality might be plausible except for the wide and probably universal appearance of people who strongly resemble mahu in other societies. The appearance of mahu-like persons in one society or even a few societies would constitute an anomaly necessitating explanation in terms of the social structure. On the other hand, the appearance of mahu-like persons in all societies, in all historical epochs, as is the more likely case, raises serious questions about the efficacy of social-structural explanations, especially explanations which depend upon conditions unique to a particular society.

THE CONTEMPORARY SOCIAL
CONSTRUCTIONIST VIEW

In the past few years there have appeared several works, mainly by British or Australian observers, which argue that homosexual orientation and identity are relatively recent developments of British or Western European origin. For example, Bray (1982) rejects the idea that homosexual individuals existed in the Renaissance period in England. He writes: "To talk of an individual in this period as being or not being 'a homosexual' is an anachronism and ruinously misleading" (p. 16), or again: "To the late twentieth century observer accustomed to the idea of a distinctive homosexual subculture amounting to a minority community it is a striking absence" (p. 56). Yet as he describes homosexual life in this period it becomes clear not only that homosexual persons existed, but that important elements of a homosexual subculture were already in place by that time.

Bray describes the phenomenon of the male brothel which existed in London as early as 1598. He suggests that these brothels likely consisted of taverns where young male prostitutes were able to entertain their clients. The existence of such taverns, about which we have only fragmentary knowledge, suggests that both a homosexual subculture and homosexuals existed. These taverns are forerunners of modern gay bars which are quite common in the English-speaking world. They more closely resemble "houses with boys," which are a combination bar and rooms for male prostitution. Such houses exist today in many countries of the world: the Netherlands, Germany, Brazil, Thailand, and the Philippines. Homosexual men universally form the vast bulk of their clientele, although the male prostitutes may be homosexual, bisexual, or primarily heterosexual youth.

The term sodomite appears to have been used in this period to refer to homosexual individuals. Bray (1982, pp. 54-55) writes that another form of prostitution existed in connection with the London playhouses and that: "Elizabethan and Jacobean theatre acquired a reputation for homosexuality, as Philip Stubbes graphically claimed. It was also a claim made by Edward Guilpin in similar terms in his Skialetheia, which describes a sodomite as someone 'who is at every play and every night sups with his ingles'; and it is repeated in Michael Brayton's The Noone-Calfe, where the theatres are denounced as one of the haunts of sodomite." These descriptions are consistent with contemporary observations of the theater in such large cities as San Francisco and New York, where homosexual men themselves joke about the large numbers of homosexuals both in the audience and professionally connected with the theater, dance, and opera companies.

Transvestic homosexuals were also part of the homosexual world of the late sixteenth century. These transvestites, like those in many parts of the world today, were to be found largely on the streets. According to Bray, transvestic homosexuality is extensively documented by a contemporary observer, Thomas Middleton, in his book Micro-Cynicon published in 1599.

As we move closer to the twentieth century, more historical materials are available to us. The notion that homosexual identity or homosexual individuals emerged only in the eighteenth century, as Bray contends, or in the nineteenth century as others contend (Adam 1978; Altman 1982; Weeks 1977) is largely a function of the greater availability of materials related to homosexual life, the closer we draw to our own times. However, by the early eighteenth century we have available from court records and other sources a fairly detailed picture of the homosexual subculture of London of that era.

It is clear from the description of the "molly house" and related activities pieced together by Bray from contemporary court records and popular journalism that a complex homosexual subculture existed in England in the early eighteenth century. This subculture in many respects bears remarkable similarity to the contemporary American or British homosexual subculture. The central focus of homosexual life seems to have been the molly house, which was either a private house or rooms over taverns in which homosexuals could congregate for social and sexual purposes. According to Bray these houses were scattered "across the whole of the built-up area north of the Thames, which by the early eighteenth century stretched without interruption from the slums of Wapping through the city and the environs of Smithfield Market to the wealthy western suburbs before the countryside began again beyond Westminster" (1982, p. 84). This suggests that the homosexual subculture was not an isolated, limited phenomenon but that it was relatively extensive as might be found today in large American or British cities. In the molly houses the homosexuals (then called "mollies" or "sodomites") entertained themselves in ways very similar to the ways in which some homosexuals entertain themselves in contemporary societies. Apart from specifically sexual activities, the customers were observed sitting in one another's laps, kissing, dancing, curtsying, and mimicking the voices of women--what today would be called "camping." The clientele of the molly houses did not follow social class lines, but as is often the case today, tended to cut across all social class lines. Some of the activities in the molly houses consisted of "drag" where transvestic homosexuals cross-dressed and imitated women. Bray reports on the contemporary description of an elaborate drag ball which bears remarkable similarity to a drag ball that might be found today in any large American city at Halloween. Transvestic homosexuals, then as now, were a common part of the homosexual world.

An organization which can be regarded as the forerunner of vice squads or the Moral Majority had made its appearance by this time. The Societies for the Reformation of Manners sponsored undercover agents to infiltrate the molly houses and to bring information to magistrates for prosecution (Bray 1982). According to Altman (1982), although homosexual behavior among men is very prevalent among various cultures, it is only in relatively modern Western societies that exclusive homosexuals are present in significant numbers. Altman also echoes the mistaken notion that homosexual subcultures and a sense of homosexual identity in Latin countries have been thwarted by a combination of Catholic teachings, political repression, and the Iberian macho tradition. He states further that the term "homosexual" has no meaning outside developed regions such as North America, Western Europe, Australia, and Japan.

These ideas are oddly ethnocentric and are primarily a result of that fact that English-speaking writers often rely exclusively upon materials available in English. For example, all of the Latin American countries have homosexual subcultures which probably have long histories. Luiz Mott (1984a), a Brazilian anthropologist, has recently examined the 30,000 documents pertaining to the Portuguese inquisitions that persisted from 1536 to 1821, and which included Brazil. The period for which most information is available is the seventeenth century. It is clear from these records that both homosexual persons and a homosexual subculture existed in Brazil in this period. Mott (1984a, p. 6) reports that the "records are remarkably detailed--real forerunners of the Kinsey interviews--with precise information on the sodomites (character, residence, locale, travels, education, religious knowledge, often ·description of physical appearance, and careful notation of the nature and frequence of sexual practices)." According to Mott (1984b), transvestic homosexuals as early as the late sixteenth century are reported living in Salvador, Bahia, in Rua Da Ajuda, a street where transvestites still live. Thus this element of a homosexual subculture has existed continuously in the same place in Salvador for 400 years.

With respect to the homosexual subculture of Lisbon, Mott (1984a) writes: "Seventeenth-century Lisbon struck me as more gay and worldly than that of 1983. There were inns openly patronized by sodomites, balls where transvestites danced and played instruments, much street prostitution, and men who served as go-betweens for male sexual encounters. I have many instances of both white and black transvestites."

It is true that political consciousness on the part of homosexuals did not emerge until nineteenth century England and Germany, but the emergence of political consciousness should not be confused with the emergence of homosexual identity and homosexual orientation. It is not surprising that such political consciousness emerged in England and Germany in the nineteenth century, since it was in these countries that homosexual relations remained criminalized long after decriminalization had taken place in the Latin world in the early nineteenth century.

Homosexual people in all parts of the world and all historical periods appear to have been capable of conceptualizing their homosexual identity, recognizing their sexual orientation, and organizing a life-style around this orientation. The extent to which this life-style has been organized has depended upon many elements, including size of society and societal attitudes; yet it is clear that homosexuals emerged in many parts of the world and in many historical epochs and did not depend upon the late nineteenth century British for instruction.

Similar evidence of the existence of homosexuals, male prostitution, transvestism, and homosexual links with the theater in Japan as early as the seventeenth century are documented by Collins (1983). The existence of homosexual characters in literary works suggests that such persons existed in Japanese society of that day. Referring to novels written in the late seventeenth century, Collins writes "Homosexual characters are liberally scattered throughout Ihara's other works which focus on the chonin class rather than the samurai" (1983, p. 11).

A situation somewhat similar to the English Elizabethan and Jacobean theater appears to have emerged in the seventeenth century in the Kabuki theater. Collins (1983, pp. 14-15), citing Evans and Evans (1975), writes:

> Wherever theaters flourished, so did male prostitution, for the most part homosexual. Published critiques (hyobanki) of young male actors, of their abilities outside rather than inside the theater, were first produced in Kyoto in the 1650s and soon spread to Osaka and Edo. (Evans, 1975, p. 27) In 1699 Kiseki produced The Actor's Vocal Samisen in three volumes, one for each of the main cities, which provided a guide to the most attractive male actors [Evans 1975, p. 31].

Collins (1983, pp. 12-13) further observes:

> Homosexuality also affected the development of Kabuki. The original purpose of the Kabuki in the early seventeenth century had been to advertise the charms of female prostitutes by lewd songs and explicit dances, but the disturbances caused by these displays threatened to destroy the social code. The samurai found the actresses irresistible and, in the government's eyes, were

wasting time and money in their pursuit. (Evans, 1975, p. 32) In 1629 the government banned these bawdy performances, but the decision backfired; it only rechanneled the popularity of "women's kabuki" toward "young men's kabuki." Male prostitutes had taken the women's places. They assumed the female roles and with their flat white masks of dramatic make-up, willowy figures, and seductive ways of walking, soon outshone their former colleagues. The uproar these youths caused seems to have been even worse. Jealous patrons or would-be patrons caused brawls in the audience. The shogunate officials could not ban these performances, however, because the Shogun Iemitsu enjoyed the company of the young actors. Iemitsu died in 1651, and the young men's kabuki was banned in 1652 [Childs 1977, p. 43].

THE STABILITY OF THE INCIDENCE OF HOMOSEXUALITY OVER TIME

It is of course difficult to prove that the rates of homosexuality (and heterosexuality) have remained stable over long periods of time. Heterosexuality seems to be the dominant sexual orientation everywhere, while homosexuality appears as a minor orientation. It is difficult to estimate rates of homosexuality before the emergence of modern social scientific research on sexuality, though there have been some attempts to do so. For example, Bloch (1942, p. 792) found reason to believe that the percentage of homosexuals in Cologne in the fifteenth century was nearly as high as estimates by Hirschfeld at the beginning of the nineteenth century. While many social scientists assume that Kinsey's data produced the first scientifically respectable, if imperfect, estimates of the incidence of sexual orientation in the general population, the first such estimates were actually produced by von Romer and Hirschfeld. Hirschfeld's achievements in research on variant sexuality (1980c), though widely ignored and sometimes discredited because he himself was a homosexual, surpass those of Kinsey in some respects. Hirschfeld's investigations were conducted in 1901 after Dr. A. von Romer studied the sexual orientation of a sample of Dutch university students in Amsterdam, and concluded that 1.9 percent were homosexual. Hirschfeld, desiring a larger sample, sent a letter enclosing an anonymous postcard-questionnaire with the question: "Is your sex instinct directed to women (W), men (M), or women and men (WM)?" The students were instructed to underline the appropriate response. There were 1,756 responses, nearly 60 percent, a rather remarkable response rate given the novelty of the undertaking. The results showed 94 percent heterosexual, 1.5 percent homosexual, and 4.5 percent bisexual. In 1904, the same kind of letter was sent to 5,721 Berlin metalworkers, with the addition of an instruction in the case of bisexuality to indicate which urge was stronger, toward men or toward women. The return rate was 41.6 percent, with the following results:

94.25 percent heterosexual

1.15 percent homosexual

.73 percent W and M

1.88 percent W̲ plus M

.58 percent W plus M̲

1.41 percent questionable*

Thus, three investigations in the early part of the country produced similar results: in both Amsterdam and Berlin, the rate of exclusive or near-exclusive male homosexuality was about 2 percent. The Berlin studies utilized a working-class and a middle-class sample and in both groups the rate is the same.

In reviewing the literature on the incidence of homosexuality, and in reassessing Kinsey's data, Gebhard (1972, pp. 22-29) estimates that about 4 percent of white, college-educated, adult American males are predominantly homosexual. He further concludes that this "crude estimate coincides rather well with some European calculations and with Havelock Ellis's guess." Ellis, in Sexual Inversion, first published in 1896, wrote: "Among the professional and most cultured element of the middle class in England, there must be a distinct percentage of inverts which may sometimes be as much as 5 percent, though estimates must always be hazardous" (1942, p. 64).

There has been virtually no work done on the incidence of homosexual orientation in non-Western societies. In 1983, Whitam administered a brief, Thai-translated questionnaire dealing with sexual orientation to a group of Thai students in Business Administration, Sociology, and Anthropology at a university in Bangkok, Thailand. The responses of 178 male students are shown in Table 1.4. If Kinsey ratings 4-6 are considered predominantly homosexual, then the 4.5 percent figure shown in Table 1.4 is quite consistent with Gebhard's estimate of 4 percent for the United States.

---

*For an excellent summary of Hirschfeld's investigations, see Leser (1961).

TABLE 1.4   Self-Reported Kinsey Ratings of 173 Male Thai Students

Kinsey Classification	Male	Percent
0	148	83.1
1	13	7.3
2	6	3.4
3	3	1.7
4	5	2.8
5	2	1.1
6	1	0.6

Source: Compiled by the authors.

N = 178 (100 percent).

In a review of historical and contemporary Japanese sources, Collins concludes that:

Japan has a long and consistent tradition of male homosexuality which is attested to in history and literature from the ninth century to the present. Though data on homosexuals is relatively recent, there is no reason to suspect that the incidence of males of homosexual orientation exceeds 5 percent of the population or that it has not remained stable over time. In this regard, Asayama's data is consistent with Kinsey's data, and even with Hirschfeld's and Ellis's conclusions [1983, p. 110].

Thus, for Japan as well as for some European and North American societies, the incidence of homosexuality appears to have been similar and appears to have remained stable over time. Karlen notes that the stable incidence of homosexuality has "provoked odd silence rather than more research" (1978, p. 227). Of course the implication of the finding that the incidence of homosexuality is similar in all societies and that it remains stable over time is of immense theoretical importance. We are clearly led away from pathological views and away from interpretations in terms of social structure and toward the view that homosexuality is, for whatever reasons, a permanent and predictable element in the spectrum of human sexuality with a biological basis.

Most analyses of cross-cultural aspects of human sexuality emphasize the infinite variability of human sexuality. Gagnon and Simon have written that sexuality "is subject to the socio-cultural moulding to a degree surpassed by few other forms of behavior" (1973, p. 261). A major study of homosexuality by the Institute for Sex Research by Bell and Weinberg emphasizes the diversity of homosexuals. They write: "A primary focus of this investigation is upon diversity--the way in which homosexual persons differ from each other" (1978, p. 24). While there are important cultural influences and considerable individual variation in the expression of human sexuality, an equally important but neglected problem in the social science of sex is the delineation of those aspects of human sexuality which are universal in human societies. As we have seen, homosexuality as a sexual orientation emerges regardless of social conditions. Such a finding, if true, is relevant not only for an adequate understanding of homosexuality, but for heterosexuality as well. In short, it means that heterosexual orientation is similarly stable in societies over time and place. While the specific incidence of heterosexual and homosexual acts may be subject to cultural and situational variations, heterosexual orientation seems to be the dominant form of sexual orientation everywhere. It is widely held in some quarters, especially in the Anglo-Saxon world, that sexual orientation is a capricious, delicately balanced matter, subject to infinite cultural variability. However, the view which emerges from cross-cultural research is that sexual orientation is not highly subject to redefinition by any particular social-structural arrangement. Just as small groups of homosexual persons inevitably and predictably emerge in all societies, heterosexuality remains a permanent, immutable, and dominant feature in all human societies.

2

PSYCHOSEXUAL DEVELOPMENT
OF HOMOSEXUALS

If it is true that homosexual persons emerge in all societies at the same rate, we might then ask whether the
psychosexual development of homosexuals is different from
society to society, or whether it proceeds along the same
lines cross-culturally. Are we considering behavior that is
developmentally similar or behavior that is different from
society to society? Do particular familial patterns common to
different societies create homosexuals? The social science of
human sexuality is dominated by the idea that sexual development is culturally variable. For example, Gagnon and Simon
(1973, pp. 17-18) write:

> Psychosexual development, while a universal
> component in the human experience, certainly
> does not occur with universal modalities. Even
> ignoring the striking forms of cross-cultural
> variability, we can observe striking differences
> within our own population, differences that
> appear to require not a unitary description of
> psychosexual development but descriptions of
> different developmental processes characterizing
> different segments of the population.

While there is widespread agreement that human sexuality is
a lifelong process, disagreement emerges when we begin to
delineate the specific dimensions of this generalization.
    Homosexuality as an orientation is characterized by sex-
ual behavior and gender behavior. Sexual behavior refers to
behavior which is specifically sexual in nature: sexual attraction, orgasm, potency of sex drive, object of sexual attraction, etc. Gender behavior refers to behavior which is not
specifically sexual, but which nevertheless seems to be linked

32

to sexual orientation. For example, gender behavior includes interest in athletics and levels of aggression. While it is widely assumed in the social sciences that both gender behavior and sexual behavior are highly malleable and subject to infinite cultural variability, cross-cultural examination of these aspects of the development of homosexuality does not entirely support this prevailing point of view.

CHILDHOOD ASPECTS OF GENDER BEHAVIOR

An important finding that has emerged in recent years is that adult sexual orientation, especially in males, can be predicted with considerable accuracy from the examination of early childhood behavior. Most of the research bearing on this finding is derived from the study of atypical sexual orientations--homosexual, transvestic homosexual, and transsexual. Most research on atypical sexual orientation has been done with males and has been focussed upon childhood cross-gender behavior. Playing with girls' toys, cross-dressing, preference for girls' games and activities, preference for the company of adults of the opposite sex, and being regarded as a sissy by others are strong indicators of later atypical sexual orientation. Marked preferences for other boys in childhood sex play often accompanies these cross-gender patterns of behavior and may also be considered predictive of later homosexual orientation (Whitam 1977, 1980). These behaviorial patterns have consistently been found to be linked with atypical sexual orientation in adulthood by researchers from different professional backgrounds using different research mothods.

At a very early age, both rudimentary sexual behavior and elements of gender behavior begin to emerge. For example, in a study of 110 effeminate boys, Green (1976) reported that 75 percent had cross-dressed before the age of four, and 97 percent before the age of six. Zuger (1970) found that 23 of the 25 effeminate boys in his study cross-dressed before the age of six and most before the age of three. Although it is true, of course, that many children exhibit occasional cross-gender behavior, marked and persistent cross-gender behavior seems to be strongly related to atypical adult sexual orientation.

Evidence on early cross-gender behavior has come from four main types of research: longitudinal, retrospective, observational, and parental reports. Research indicates that typical gender identity may appear as early as two years of age (Money and Tucker 1975; Kleeman 1971; Paluszny et al. 1973; Thompson 1975). Similarly, elements of atypical gender identity seem to appear very early. Almost uniformly the subjects of longitudinal studies have been boys whose effeminate behavior brought them to the attention of clinicians or researchers. This usually occurred early in life, and subjects were interviewed some time after puberty to ascertain their later sexual orientation. In his study of ten effeminate boys, Zuger (1966) found that seven were homosexual in adulthood. In a follow-up study of 15 effeminate boys, Lebovitz (1972) found what appeared to be eight homosexuals, three transsexuals, and four boys of indeterminate sexual orientation. In another follow-up study, Zuger (1978) reported that of the 16 boys in the study, eight were homosexual, two probably homosexual, one was transvestic, and one transsexual. In a follow-up study of feminine boys, Green (1979) reported two-thirds were homosexual or bisexual. Money and Russo (1979) re-interviewed a group of effeminate boys with whom Green had originally worked, and reported all five of them to be homosexual.

Retrospective studies also confirm the relationship between early cross-gender behavior and later sexual orientation. When adult homosexuals are asked about their childhood behavior, patterns similar to those found in the longitudinal studies emerge. Bieber et al. (1962) and Stoller (1968) found early cross-gender behavior to be associated with later sexual orientation. The evidence appears to be consistent regardless of the theoretical orientation of the researcher or method of data collection. For example, Evans (1969), with minor modifications to Bieber's questionnaire, obtained strikingly similar results. More importantly, Evans studied homosexuals who had never sought psychotherapy, whereas Bieber's data were based on psychoanalysts' reports about their patients. Saghir and Robins (1973) reported that 67 percent of the 89 homosexuals studied, versus 3 percent of the heterosexuals, recalled effeminate behavior in childhood. In administering questionnaires to 206 male homosexuals and 78 male heterosexuals in nonclinical situations, Whitam (1977) found that 44 percent of the homosexuals liked to cross-dress as children, in contrast to only 1 percent of the heterosexuals.

Another type of evidence on early cross-gender behavior comes from observational studies. In a laboratory study, Rekers and Yates (1976) reported that boys exhibiting cross-gender behavior played with female toys significantly longer than other boys and about as long as girls. Similar findings have been reported by Zucker et al. (1979b), who found that feminine boys played with opposite-sex toys longer than other boys. In observing the play of masculine and feminine boys, Green et al. (1972) found feminine boys played significantly longer with feminine toys. Interestingly, the introduction of parents into the play setting had little effect on the child's choice of masculine or feminine toys. Similarly, Green and Fuller (1973) found that feminine boys tended to spend significantly longer time holding dolls than did masculine boys.

Several studies utilizing parental reports of children's behavior suggest similar conclusions. Using maternal reports, Zuger and Taylor (1969) found cross-gender behavior reported more frequently for effeminate boys than for other boys. Bates and Bentler (1973) also used maternal reports and found that feminine boys played fewer masculine games and more feminine games than did other boys. Extending the questionnaire to include a broader range of cross-gender behavior than toy and play preference, Bates, Bentler, and Thompson (1973) found that feminine behavior was more frequently associated with feminine boys than with other boys.

Until recently, there has been an absence of normative data on early cross gender behavior. Bates et al. (1973) surveyed parents of children never referred for gender-related behavior and concluded that marked and persistent early cross-gendering is atypical. Zucker et al. (1979a) conducted a similar study to determine the prevalence of cross-gendering in very young boys, age 20 months to five years, and reported that extreme and frequent cross-gender behavior is atypical in the general population. In this study, masculinity and femininity factors derived from a 166-item questionnaire were also found to successfully discriminate a group of cross-gendered children from their siblings.

Most research on this topic has been limited to American society. If similar patterns of early cross-gender behavior appear in all societies and are linked to adult homosexual orientation cross-culturally, then the psychosexual development of homosexuals would appear to be similar in different societies.

Examination of Tables 2.1 through 2.5 reveals the same general pattern of cross-gender behavior obtained with respect to four different societies. The childhood behavior of homosexuals in Guatemala, Brazil, and the Philippines seems to be very similar to that in the United States. Moreover, it appears that homosexuals in the four societies report the various types of cross-gender behavior with about the same degree of frequency. For example, percentages of behavior related to doll-play and cross-dressing (Tables 2.1 and 2.2) range from 38 to 80 percent for homosexuals and from zero to 17 percent for heterosexuals. Homosexuals discuss their childhood behavior in much the same way in the four societies. Although the specific content of the behavior may be altered by culture, equivalent behavior is acted out in varying cultural settings. For example, an American child reported that at the age of nine he bought a cake mix at a convenience market. When his parents returned from work, he was baking the cake, attired in his mother's housecoat, a dish cloth tied around his head bandana-style, and his mouth covered with lipstick. A Guatemalan respondent reared in a traditional Indian society liked making tortillas and was skillful at bal-

TABLE 2.1 As a Child Were You Interested in Dolls, Paper Dolls, Sewing, Cooking, Etc.?

	Brazil				Guatemala				Philippines				United States			
	Heterosexual		Homosexual		Heterosexual		Homosexual		Heterosexual		Homosexual		Heterosexual		Homosexual	
	N	%	N	%	N	%	N	%	N	%	N	%	N	%	N	%
Yes	2	12	15	65	1	2	38	61	1	3	23	77	17	29	21	58
No	14	88	8	35	39	98	24	39	33	97	7	23	41	71	15	42
Totals	16	100	23	100	40	100	62	100	34	100	30	100	58	100	36	100

Brazil: $X^2 = 10.66469$ $\underline{p} = 0.0011$

Guatemala: $X^2 = 35.58432$ $\underline{p} = 0.0000$

Philippines: $X^2 = 36.96104$ $\underline{p} = 0.0000$

United States: $X^2 = 7.76911$ $\underline{p} = 0.0050$

TABLE 2.2 As a Child Did You Like To Dress in Womens' Clothes, Shoes, Jewelry, Purses, Etc.?

	Brazil				Guatemala				Philippines				United States			
	Heterosexual		Homosexual		Heterosexual		Homosexual		Heterosexual		Homosexual		Heterosexual		Homosexual	
	N	%	N	%	N	%	N	%	N	%	N	%	N	%	N	%
Yes	0	-	10	38	1	2	38	61	1	3	24	80	4	7	20	56
No	16	100	16	62	39	98	24	39	33	97	6	20	54	93	16	44
Totals	16	100	26	100	40	100	62	100	34	100	30	100	58	100	36	100

Brazil: $X^2_C = 6.09587*$ $\underline{p} = 0.0135$

Guatemala: $X^2 = 35.58432$ $\underline{p} = 0.0000$

Philippines: $X^2 = 39.75761$ $\underline{p} = 0.0000$

United States: $X^2 = 27.66148$ $\underline{p} = 0.0000$

*Yates' correction for continuity has been used for all chi square calculations reflecting at least one cell with an expected frequency value of 5 or less.

TABLE 2.3 As a Child Did You Prefer Play and Activities of Boys or Girls?

	Brazil				Guatemala				Philippines				United States			
	Heterosexual		Homosexual		Heterosexual		Homosexual		Heterosexual		Homosexual		Heterosexual		Homosexual	
	N	%	N	%	N	%	N	%	N	%	N	%	N	%	N	%
Girls	1	6	13	56	4	10	38	61	1	3	20	67	3	5	7	19
Boys	10	63	5	22	14	35	8	13	11	32	1	3	35	60	8	22
Liked both equally[a]	5	31	5	22	22	55	16	26	22	65	9	30	20	34	21	58
Totals[b]	16	100	23	100	40	100	62	100	34	100	30	100	58	99	36	99
2 by 2:	$X^2 = 10.89767$ $\underline{p} = 0.0010$				$X^2 = 20.91306$ $\underline{p} = 0.0000$				$X^2_c = 21.30899$ $\underline{p} = 0.0000$				$X^2_c = 7.58832$ $\underline{p} = 0.0059$			
3 by 2:	$X^2 = 11.05202$ $\underline{p} = 0.0040$				$X^2 = 26.59988$ $\underline{p} = 0.0000$				$X^2 = 30.84591$ $\underline{p} = 0.0000$				$X^2 = 14.20715$ $\underline{p} = 0.0008$			

[a]The bottom category has been excluded from computation of "2 by 2" calculations and included in "3 by 2" calculations in all tables reflecting both "2 by 2" and "3 by 2" chi square analyses.

[b]Percentage totals different from 100% due to rounding to nearest whole number in all tables reflecting chi square analyses.

37

TABLE 2.4 As a Child Did You Prefer the Company of Adult Males or Females?

	Brazil				Guatemala				Philippines				United States			
	Heterosexual		Homosexual		Heterosexual		Homosexual		Heterosexual		Homosexual		Heterosexual		Homosexual	
	N	%	N	%	N	%	N	%	N	%	N	%	N	%	N	%
Female	3	19	18	78	13	32	47	76	7	20	25	83	5	9	19	53
Male	3	19	2	9	15	38	8	13	8	24	1	3	20	34	2	6
Liked both equally	10	62	3	13	23	30	7	11	19	56	4	13	33	57	15	42
Totals	16	100	23	100	40	100	62	100	34	100	30	99	58	100	36	101
2 by 2:	X^2 = 2.52778 p = 0.1119				X^2 = 14.10675 p = 0.0002				X^2_c = 10.86188 p = 0.0010				X^2 = 22.71789 p = 0.0000			
3 by 2:	X^2 = 13.87406 p = 0.0010				X^2 = 18.84444 p = 0.0001				X^2 = 25.20049 p = 0.0000				X^2 = 25.91448 p = 0.0000			

38

TABLE 2.5 As a Child Were You Regarded as a Sissy?

	Brazil				Guatemala				Philippines				United States			
	Heterosexual		Homosexual		Heterosexual		Homosexual		Heterosexual		Homosexual		Heterosexual		Homosexual	
	N	%	N	%	N	%	N	%	N	%	N	%	N	%	N	%
Yes	13	81	16	70	3	8	52	84	2	6	29	97	7	12	30	83
No	3	19	7	30	37	92	10	16	31	94	1	3	51	88	6	17
Totals	16	100	23	99	40	99	62	100	33	100	30	100	58	100	36	100

Brazil: $X^2 = 0.20182$, $p = 0.6533$

Guatemala: $X^2 = 57.07524$, $p = 0.0000$

Philippines: $X^2 = 51.61530$, $p = 0.0000$

United States: $X^2 = 47.26355$, $p = 0.0000$

Note: "Yes" category includes "Not sissy exactly, but felt different from other boys."

39

ancing large baskets of fruit and vegetables on his head, as
is customary with the women in that society. The details of
early cross-gender behavior vary from society to society,
depending upon cultural definitions of sex-appropriate behavior, yet the behavior is functionally equivalent. While cross-
cultural analyses of homosexuality tend to emphasize the cultural variability of homosexuality, data in Tables 2.1 through
2.5 suggest that even such details of homosexuality as its
childhood forms may well be universal.

ADULT GENDER IDENTITY

Three broad groupings of adult homosexuals can be dis-
tinguished with respect to early cross-gender behavior. The
first consists of a small group, perhaps 10 percent, of homosexuals who manifested no early cross-gender behavior and
as adults are quite masculine in overt appearance and usually
have very traditional masculine occupations such as engineer
or electrician. One such clique of homosexuals was observed
and interviewed in Phoenix. This clique consists of eight
men, none of whom manifested early cross-gender behavior,
as children were indistinguishable from preheterosexual children, and as adults hold traditionally masculine occupations.
While all members of this friendship network are fully aware
of gay bars and the homosexual subculture and sometimes go
to gay bars, they are put off by the cross-gender aspects
of gay life such as "camping" and female impersonation.
Their social life tends to take place in their homes or in
outdoor activities. All members of this clique live with lovers
and are Kinsey fives or sixes. Thus, early cross-gender behavior is usually but not invariably linked with sexual orientation.
A second group, about 65 percent, forms the largest segment of the homosexual community and consists of persons
who were, as children, cross-gendered to varying degrees,
but as adults are overtly masculine. At puberty this group
experiences considerable masculinization and most cross-
gender behavior diminishes or disappears after puberty.*
This group manifests a wide range of occupational interests,
including very traditional masculine occupations, such as
physician or stock broker, but they also may be involved in
occupations related to the arts or even "gay" occupations
such as interior design.

---

*This observation has been tested and verified on a much
larger sample of 1556 homosexual men in the Chicago area.
See Harry (1983).

João is typical of homosexuals in this group. Growing up in a small town in the interior of Brazil, he exhibited extensive early cross-gender behavior; as a child he was called João-Mulher (Johnny-girl) because of his "sissy" behavior. He was sent to a Catholic boarding school in another town at the age of ten and just before puberty he became avidly interested in soccer, becoming an excellent soccer player during his school years. Even as an adult he played soccer for a team sponsored by the bank where he worked. At puberty his cross-gender behavior disappeared, but strong genital homosexual interests remained. He is a Kinsey six. This second group forms an important segment of what is known in the United States as the gay community.

A third group, about 25 percent of adult homosexuals, exhibited extensive early cross-gender behavior as children, and as adults remain more or less effeminate in their overt behavior, continuing to manifest some cross-gender behavior. This group is more likely than the other two groups to have "gay" occupations such as interior designer, florist, or hairdresser. This seems to be true in all societies studied. Nonetheless, homosexuals in this group manifest a relatively wide range of occupational interests. The adult cross-gendering process manifests itself in a wide variety of ways, ranging from occasional cross-dressing to almost full-time cross-dressing, or professional female impersonation. It is within this group that we find persons who in this work are called transvestic homosexuals. This term refers to overtly effeminate homosexuals who cross-dress frequently, or who do female impersonations informally or in clubs. Transvestic homosexuals often take on female names and use female terms of address among themselves. This seems to be true in the four societies studied. Transvestic homosexuals are discussed in detail in Chapter 3.

There appears to be a linkage between three elements: overt masculinity-feminity, Kinsey ratings, and the incidence of childhood indicators reported. As may be observed in Table 2.6, in a group of 132 Guatemalan heterosexuals, bisexuals, and homosexuals, the greatest number of childhood indicators is reported by Kinsey sixes (persons who are exclusively homosexual). The number of childhood indicators reported decreases proportionately across the Kinsey scale, with Kinsey zeros (exclusive heterosexuals) reporting the smallest incidence of childhood indicators. Similarly, the incidence of reported childhood indicators is greatest for homosexuals judged by the interviewer to be overtly feminine on a four-point scale (see Table 2.7). The incidence of childhood indicators decreases proportionately with movement toward the masculine end of the scale. Adult homosexuals who are overtly masculine report fewer childhood indicators than homosexuals who are overtly feminine. The more overtly effeminate the individual is judged to be, the higher the Kinsey

TABLE 2.6 Kinsey Rating and Number of Childhood Indicators for Guatemalan Heterosexual, Bisexual, and Homosexual Respondents

Number of Childhood Indicators[a]	0		1		2		3		4		5		6	
	N	%	N	%	N	%	N	%	N	%	N	%	N	%
0	18	53	2	33	3	37.5	3	20	2	29	0	--	1	2
1	13	38	2	33	1	12.5	7	47	1	14	1	6	3	7
2	3	9	0	--	1	12.5	3	20	0	--	1	6	5	11
3	0	--	2	33	2	25.0	1	7	2	29	4	22	3	7
4	0	--	0	--	0	--	1	7	1	14	5	28	6	14
5	0	--	0	--	0	--	0	--	1	14	5	28	15	34
6	0	--	0	--	1	12.5	0	--	0	--	2	11	11	25
Totals[b]	34	100	6	99	8	100	15	101	7	100	18	101	44	100

Note: Gamma = 0.71170; Pearson's r = .73279; p = 0.0000.

[a]Childhood Indicators refer to doll-play, cross-dressing, preference for girls' games, preference for company of older women, being regarded as a sissy, and preference for childhood sex play with boys.

[b]Percentages differ from 100% due to rounding to nearest whole number.

TABLE 2.7 Assessment of Overt Masculinity-Femininity and Number of Childhood Indicators for Guatemalan Heterosexual, Bisexual, and
Homosexual Respondents

Number of Childhood Indicators[a]	Overt Masculinity Rating							
	Very Masculine		Average Masculinity		Slightly Feminine		Very Feminine	
	N	%	N	%	N	%	N	%
0	9	43	19	28	1	3	0	--
1	5	24	20	29	3	10	0	--
2	2	10	7	10	4	13	0	--
3	4	19	7	10	3	10	0	--
4	1	5	5	7	5	17	2	17
5	0	--	7	10	9	30	5	42
6	0	--	4	6	5	17	5	42
Totals[b]	21	101	69	100	30	100	12	101

Note: Gamma = 0.61480; Pearson's R = 0.57297; p = 0.0000; N = 132.

[a]Childhood Indicators refer to doll-play, cross-dressing, preference for
girls' games, preference for company of older women, being regarded as a
sissy, and preference for childhood sex play with boys.

[b]Percentages differ from 100% due to rounding to nearest whole number.

TABLE 2.8 Kinsey Rating and Observer Assessment of Overt Masculinity-
Femininity for Guatemalan Heterosexual, Bisexual, and Homosexual
Respondents

Assessment of Overt Masculinity Femininity	Kinsey Rating													
	0		1		2		3		4		5		6	
	N	%	N	%	N	%	N	%	N	%	N	%	N	%
Very masculine	7	21	1	17	4	50	4	27	2	29	1	6	2	5
Average masculine	27	79	5	83	2	25	10	67	4	57	7	39	14	32
Slightly feminine	0	--	0	--	2	25	1	7	1	14	8	44	18	41
Very feminine	0	--	0	--	0	--	0	--	0	--	2	11	10	23
Totals*	34	100	6	100	8	100	15	101	7	100	18	100	44	101

Note: Gamma = 0.61522; N = 132.

*Percentages differ from 100% due to rounding to nearest whole numbers.

43

rating (see Table 2.8). Guatemalan responses were used in
Tables 2.6, 2.7, and 2.8 because this is the only group of
respondents for whom an objective observer assessment of
masculinity-femininity is available.

The discussion of early cross-gender behavior is controversial for various reasons. Some feminists reject the concept
of gender altogether, and some sex educators feel that calling
attention to the relationship between early cross-gender
behavior and adult sexuality will induce parents to punish
prehomosexual children. Nonetheless, the appearance of this
behavior and its relationship with later adult sexual orientation seem to be a permanent feature of homosexuality. More
importantly, early cross-gender behavior seems to be closely
connected with the origins of those elements of homosexuality
which are socially useful and constitute the unique contributions of the homosexual subculture to the larger social world.
Cross-gender behavior after puberty is often expressed by
participation in entertainment, dance, and other performing
arts. For example, one respondent reported strong cross-
dressing interests at age six and put on shows, while cross-
dressed, for the family on a farm in Southern Indiana. He
eventually became an actor. Not all children who exhibit
cross-gender behavior become professional entertainers, for
there are far more such individuals than available roles;
nonetheless, there is a close connection between early cross-
gender behavior and later adult activities connected with
entertainment. This connection is explored in detail in Chapter 4. It should be emphasized that cross-gender behavior,
which is often viewed with great consternation by parents
and viewed as pathological in the DSM-III, the official handbook of the American Psychiatric Association, is actually the
source of a major contribution which homosexuals make to the
society at large.

SEXUAL DEVELOPMENT

Early cross-gender behavior is a nonsexual manifestation
of emerging sexual orientation. Although we generally cannot
observe childhood sexuality directly, we can observe the
gender behavior which is closely related to the emerging
sexual orientation. Because of its usually secretive nature,
the puzzle of childhood sexual behavior is somewhat more
difficult to piece together than gender behavior, but it is
clear that sexual orientation is a lifelong process. While there
is considerable individual variation in sexual expression, the
sexual development of homosexual males closely parallels that
of heterosexual males.

It is widely assumed by some sex educators that childhood
sex play is of little significance for adult sexuality. For

example, Katchadourian and Lunde, authors of a widely used text on human sexuality, write:

> Much prepubescent sex play is motivated by curiosity and is influenced by the availability and sex of companions. To the extent that a child's companions are of the same sex, his sex play will likely be "homosexual." And, when a boy lies on top of a girl, it is often viewed as coital play. As children are often quite unaware of the significance of such acts, we should refrain from ascribing adult sexual motives to them. These activities are largely experimental, imitative, exploratory play, sexual only in a general sense. . . . It is particularly important not to label the sex play of children as deviant or perverse, no matter what it entails [1972, pp. 176-77].

While it is certainly not possible to precisely extrapolate adult sexuality and sexual orientation from childhood play, childhood sexual experiences cannot be dismissed as meaningless for adult sexual orientation. Most males, both heterosexual and homosexual, have some form of childhood sex play, and in this sex play emerging sexual orientation begins to manifest itself. Childhood sex play is not diffuse and vague with respect to sexual orientation. Some two-thirds to three-fourths of homosexuals in all four societies report that they were more excited by other little boys than little girls in childhood sex play (see Table 2.9). Similarly, heterosexuals report that sexual excitement in childhood was directed toward little girls. Moreover, the first sexual contacts of respondents in all societies tend to be closely related to adult sexual orientation. Some 75 to 90 percent of the homosexual respondents report that their first sexual contact was with males (see Table 2.10). Similarly, heterosexuals tend to report that their first sexual contact was with females. The age of first sexual contact varies considerably. In some cases first sexual contact occurs before puberty, and in some cases at puberty or in early adolescence. Regardless of whether contact occurs before or after puberty, there is general correspondence between the sex of the first sexual contact and the adult sexual orientation of respondents. By the age of 17, practically all respondents have had some sexual contact, as defined by "touching genitalia" (see Table 2.11). Regardless of age of first contact, sex of first contact is predictive of later sexual orientation.

Apart from actual sexual play or contact, feelings of attraction and fantasy are, of course, important elements in sexual development. Respondents were asked, "At what age

TABLE 2.9 In Childhood Sex Play Were You More Excited by Girls or Boys?

| | Brazil | | | | Guatemala | | | | Philippines | | | | United States | | | |
| | Heterosexual | | Homosexual | | Heterosexual | | Homosexual | | Heterosexual | | Homosexual | | Heterosexual | | Homosexual | |
	N	%	N	%	N	%	N	%	N	%	N	%	N	%	N	%
Boys	2	12	15	65	5	12	46	74	2	6	19	63	7	12	26	72
Girls	10	62	1	4	34	85	5	8	19	56	3	10	39	67	7	19
Both equally	0	--	0	--	0	--	0	--	2	6	1	3	1	2	3	8
Did not have sex play, can't remember, etc.	4	25	7	30	1	2	11	18	12	32	7	23	11	19	0	--
Totals	16	99	23	99	40	99	62	100	35	100	30	99	58	100	36	99

X² = 17.42803	X² = 60.94842	X² = 26.47390	X² = 42.37231
p = 0.0002	p = 0.0000	p = 0.0000	p = 0.0000

Note: Categories in which both heterosexual and homosexual frequencies are zero have been omitted in the calculation of chi square values.

46

TABLE 2.10 What Was the Gender of Your First Sexual Contact?

	Brazil				Guatemala				Philippines				United States			
	Heterosexual		Homosexual		Heterosexual		Homosexual		Heterosexual		Homosexual		Heterosexual		Homosexual	
	N	%	N	%	N	%	N	%	N	%	N	%	N	%	N	%
Male	0	--	18	78	3	8	47	76	3	9	27	90	3	5	27	75
Female	15	94	4	17	33	82	10	16	29	85	2	7	53	91	7	19
Mixed Group	1	6	1	4	4	10	5	8	2	6	1	3	2	3	2	6
Totals	16	100	23	99	40	100	62	100	34	100	30	100	58	99	36	100
2 by 2:	X^2 = 23.89952				X^2 = 48.76691				X^2 = 42.67182				X^2 = 52.20849			
	p = 0.0000				p = 0.0000				p = 0.0000				p = 0.0000			
3 by 2:	X^2 = 23.88136				X^2 = 48.65166				X^2 = 42.96730				X^2 = 52.17569			
	p = 0.0000				p = 0.0000				p = 0.0000				p = 0.0000			

TABLE 2.11 At What Age Did You First Have Sexual Contact, Touch Genitalia?

Stage (years old)	Brazil				Guatemala				Philippines				United States			
	Heterosexual		Homosexual		Heterosexual		Homosexual		Heterosexual		Homosexual		Heterosexual		Homosexual	
	N	%	N	%	N	%	N	%	N	%	N	%	N	%	N	%
6 and below	1	6	4	17	8	20	23	37	2	6	2	7	14	24	7	19
7 - 13	11	69	10	44	23	58	27	43	7	21	14	48	31	53	19	53
14 - 17	4	25	4	17	9	22	10	16	19	58	13	45	11	19	9	25
18 - 25	0	--	5	22	0	--	2	3	5	15	0	0	2	3	1	3
Totals	16	100	23	100	40	100	62	99	33	100	29	100	58	99	36	100

Brazil: $X^2 = 5.77733$, $p = 0.1230$

Guatemala: $X^2 = 5.12397$, $p = 0.1629$

Philippines: $X^2 = 8.23454$, $p = 0.0414$

United States: $X^2 = 0.63237$, $p = 0.8890$

were you first aware of attraction to males?" and "At what age were you first aware of attraction to females?" (see Table 2.12). By the onset of puberty, from 75 to 90 percent of the homosexual respondents were aware of their attractions for other males (see Table 2.12). Similarly, by the time of puberty most heterosexual respondents were aware of their attractions for females. These feelings of attractions generally precede the conceptualizing of sexual orientation as homosexual, which tends to come after puberty (see Table 2.13), although about 20 percent of the respondents in three of the societies were able to link their prepubescent sexual attractions with the concept homosexual, realizing by the time of puberty that they would be homosexuals as adults. Heterosexuals were more likely than homosexuals to become aware of their emerging sexual orientation prior to puberty.

While there is wide individual variability with respect to the awareness of homosexual interest on the part of homosexuals in childhood, the emerging sexuality of homosexuals tends to parallel that of heterosexuals, sometimes appearing as early as three or four years of age. Homosexual respondents frequently recall vivid details of their childhood sexual activity and attractions at very young ages. Homosexuals sometimes report rather elaborate homosexual fantasies which may precede any actual sexual experiences. One American respondent reported that between the ages of four and six he experienced a recurring dream-fantasy in which he descended into a cavern filled with muscular nude males who allowed him to touch and feel their bodies. During this period he conjured the fantasy when unhappy or when going to sleep. Another respondent at about the same age repeatedly dreamed about a muscular nude giant who periodically carried him off to sleep with him. A third respondent, who grew up in Washington, D.C., recalls the following incident which occurred before any overt sexual contact:

> I was riding in the car with my family at about
> the age of ten or eleven. It was a warm summer
> day and we stopped in Georgetown, near what
> I now know was a gay bar. The place was packed
> with guys standing around in front with their
> shirts off. I became very excited and though I
> didn't really know what the bar was all about, I
> told my parents that I wanted to get out of the
> car and go with those men. I became almost
> hysterical. I cried and begged my mother to let
> me go and live with them.

While it is widely accepted that children are sexual beings, the details of their sexuality have not always been adequately appreciated. In prehomosexual boys, overt sexual contact

TABLE 2.12 At What Age Were You First Aware of Attraction to Females (Heterosexuals) or Males (Homosexuals)?

Age	Brazil Heterosexual N	%	Homosexual N	%	Guatemala Heterosexual N	%	Homosexual N	%	Philippines Heterosexual N	%	Homosexual N	%	United States Heterosexual N	%	Homosexual N	%
6 and below	1	6	6	26	12	30	27	44	2	6	3	10	14	24	7	19
7 - 13	11	69	11	48	24	60	27	44	24	70	19	63	31	53	19	53
14 - 17	4	25	4	17	4	10	7	11	7	20	8	27	11	19	9	25
18 - 25	0	--	2	9	0	--	1	2	1	3	0	--	2	3	1	3
Totals	16	100	23	100	40	100	62	101	34	99	30	100	58	99	36	100

Brazil: X² = 4.45866 p = 0.2160

Guatemala: X² = 3.16608 p = 0.3667

Philippines: X² = 1.60433 p = 0.6584

United States: X² = 0.63237 p = 0.8890

TABLE 2.13 At What Age Did You Realize You Were Heterosexual/Homosexual?

Age	Brazil Heterosexual N	%	Brazil Homosexual N	%	Guatemala Heterosexual N	%	Guatemala Homosexual N	%	Philippines Heterosexual N	%	Philippines Homosexual N	%	United States Heterosexual N	%	United States Homosexual N	%
6 and below	1	100	0	--	0	--	0	--	4	12	3	10	7	12	1	3
7 - 13	7	41	0	--	11	28	12	19	13	38	5	17	26	45	6	17
14 - 17	9	53	9	39	22	55	35	56	16	47	16	53	21	36	9	25
18 - 25	0	--	13	56	7	18	13	21	1	3	6	20	4	7	17	47
26 - 35	0	--	1	4	0	--	2	3	0	--	0	--	0	--	3	8
Totals	17	100	23	99	40	101	62	99	34	100	30	100	58	100	36	100

Brazil: $X^2 = 21.58567$ $\underline{p} = 0.0002$

Guatemala: $X^2 = 2.16396$ $\underline{p} = 0.5391$

Philippines: $X^2 = 7.04737$ $\underline{p} = 0.0704$

United States: $X^2 = 29.30383$ $\underline{p} = 1.149$

(usually with other male children) and sexual attraction for male children or adult males, are relatively well-defined before puberty in the four societies studied. It should be emphasized that both early cross-gender behavior and sexual development in homosexuals occurs in the absence of socialization into these patterns. Boys in all societies are socialized into male gender behavior and girls into female gender behavior. There is no society (including American society) which socializes children into homosexual roles. Parents, after years of careful socialization into heterosexual roles, are usually shocked and disappointed when they discover they have reared a homosexual child.

There are a few societies, such as the traditional Mohave, which give official recognition to the existence of homosexuals through ritual, but it is clear from anthropological reports (Devereux 1963) that the Mohave society did not socialize children into homosexual patterns. Mohave families which had homosexual children were not particularly pleased, and the ritual is one in which homosexuality is recognized as inevitable though not desirable, through which the homosexual adolescent is given a legitimate place in society, and in which the parents are relieved of guilt for having produced a homosexual child.

Except for the Filipino sample, where toleration and amusement are common responses to doll-playing and cross-dressing, most parents are disapproving or indifferent to early cross-gender behavior. Indeed, even in the Filipino group there is little encouragement of such behavior (see Tables 2.14 and 2.15).

FAMILIAL FACTORS

Despite the widespread and influential view that homosexuality as a sexual orientation is socially determined, virtually no cross-cultural assessment of this belief has been undertaken. If familial factors are important determinants of homosexual orientation, these familial arrangements presumably operate similarly in all societies. Numerous studies, primarily American, have dealt with the question of familial factors; yet the results are inconclusive.

One of the earliest studies was that of Jonas (1944), who interviewed 60 homosexual patients and compared them to a group of heterosexual patients. Homosexuals expressed a strong preference for their mothers over their fathers. Miller (1958) studied a group of extremely effeminate federal prisoners and reported a pattern of overprotective mother and hostile or absent father. West (1959) compared homosexuals to neurotics and concluded that homosexuals had unsatisfactory relationships with their fathers and were overly close to their mothers.

TABLE 2.14 Attitude of Parents Toward Behavior of Prehomosexual Children Who Doll-Played

	Brazil		Guatemala		Philippine		United States	
	N	%	N	%	N	%	N	%
Strong disapproval, severe punishment	0	--	5	13	4	17	0	--
Disapproval, no punishment	4	25	7	18	4	17	7	33
Indifference	10	63	9	24	4	17	11	52
Toleration and amusement	0	--	5	13	9	38	2	10
Encouragement	1	6	0	--	1	4	1	5
They did not know about it	1	6	12	32	2	8	0	--
Totals	16	100	38	100	24	101	21	100

Note: X^2 = 40.16053; d.f. = 15; $\underline{p}$ = 0.0004.

TABLE 2.15 Attitude of Parents Toward Behavior of Prehomosexual Children Who Cross-Dressed

	Brazil		Guatemala		Philippines		United States	
	N	%	N	%	N	%	N	%
Strong disapproval, severe punishment	0	--	5	13	5	21	1	5
Disapproval, no punishment	4	40	7	18	3	13	6	30
Indifference	4	40	9	24	3	13	4	20
Toleration and amusement	0	--	5	13	10	42	5	25
Encouragement	0	--	0	--	1	4	0	--
They did not know about it	2	20	12	32	2	8	4	20
Totals	10	100	38	100	24	101	20	100

Note: X^2 = 23.99409; d.f. = 15; $\underline{p}$ = 0.0652.

Probably the best-known and most controversial research is that of Bieber et al. (1962), who found significant differences in parental relationships between homosexuals and heterosexuals. Homosexuals were characterized by either absent fathers or those fathers who spent very little time with their children. Typically, the fathers of homosexuals were hostile or distant, and the mothers were dominant and close-binding. O'Connor (1964) concluded that a poor relationship with a father or an absent father were etiological factors in homosexuality. Homosexuals were also found to be more attached to their mothers than to their fathers. O'Connor considered but rejected an alternative explanation of the data, that poor relationships with the father were a result rather than a cause of homosexuality. Brown (1963) reported that homosexuals were overly close to their mothers and lacked warm attachments to their fathers. Evans (1969) surveyed groups of nonpatient homosexuals and heterosexuals to determine if the differences noted earlier by Bieber appeared in groups who had never sought psychotherapy. The results were quite similar to Bieber's in that the configuration of the close mother and detached father again emerged. Thompson et al. (1973), in a sample controlled for race, age, sex, education, and religion, found parent-child relationships similar to those noted earlier by Bieber and others. Male homosexuals were characterized by close attachments to the mother and were more hostile toward the father. Stephan (1973) studied a group of 88 homosexuals active in the gay movement and compared them to a group of heterosexuals similar in terms of age and occupation. Again homosexuals viewed their mothers as dominant and more affectionate than their fathers. Another study published the same year by Saghir and Robins (1973) showed comparable results. Of the male homosexuals, 84 percent considered their father indifferent or uninvolved during childhood, as compared to 18 percent of the heterosexual subjects.

While a number of studies have found the warm-dominant mother, distant-hostile father pattern in the background of homosexuals, numerous studies report contrary findings. Bene's (1965) finding failed to support earlier work, concluding that the mothers of homosexuals do not tend to be overly attached, protective, and indulgent. Greenblatt (1966) found no differences between homosexuals and heterosexuals with respect to parental attitudes. Apperson and McAdoo (1968) found impaired father-child relationships, but also found impaired mother-child relationships. In a study of neurotic homosexuals and neurotic heterosexuals, Robertson (1972) found that homosexuals had the poorest relationship with their mothers, not their fathers. The findings of Buhrich and McConaghy (1978) do not support the idea that parental relationships are an important factor in homosexuality. Some studies are explicit in their rejection of familial factors. In comparing effeminate and noneffeminate boys referred for psychiatric treatment, Zuger (1970) found no evidence for the warm mother/hostile father configuration. Zuger concluded that effeminate behavior was inherent in the boys and was not the result of familial factors. Perhaps the most serious challenge to earlier findings comes from Siegelman (1974), who in a sample of 307 nonpatient male homosexuals and 138 hetero-sexual students, reported that mothers of homosexuals were less loving and more rejecting than those of heterosexuals. Siegelman (p. 16) notes: "The present findings, in fact, seriously question the existence of any association between family relations and homosexuality vs. heterosexuality." Using a large San Francisco sample (575 white homosexual males, 284 white heterosexual males, 229 white homosexual females, and 101 white heterosexual females), while not outright reject-ing the idea that familial factors are unrelated to the develop-ment of homosexual orientation, Bell, Weinberg, and Hammer-smith (1981, pp. 183-84) conclude: "contrary to widely accept-ed psychodynamic theories that have generally considered homosexuality to be the outcome of certain types of parental relationships or traits, we find the role of parents in the development of their sons' homosexuality to be grossly exag-gerated."

Tables 2.16 through 2.24 show responses to a series of questions commonly regarded in the psychoanalytic literature as causative of homosexuality. In most cases the questions are more or less comparable to several earlier studies, but are most directly comparable to the items used by Bieber and Evans. The following questions on familiar factors were used: father's attitude toward sex; mother's attitude toward sex; seductive mother; emotionally detached, distant father; hostile father; strong mother; warm mother; normal family; absent father. These tables analyze questions for which responses from all four societies are available.

Tables 2.16 through 2.24 present responses to questions having to do with familial factors commonly assumed to cause homosexuality. With respect to three of the nine questions, there are no statistically significant differences at the .05 level between homosexuals and heterosexuals in any of the four coun-tries. These include mother's attitude toward sex, seductive mother, and warm mother (Tables 2.17, 2.18, and 2.22).

For three of the questions (father's attitude toward sex, normal family, and both parents present) there are differences at the .05 level between heterosexuals and homosexuals in only one society (Tables 2.16, 2.23, and 2.24). For two ques-tions (hostile father, and strong mother) there are differences at the .05 level between heterosexuals and homosexuals in two of the four societies (Tables 2.20 and 2.21). For one question, detached-distant father, there are differences between hetero-

TABLE 2.16 What Was Your Father's Attitude Toward Sex?

Attitude	Brazil				Guatemala				Philippines				United States			
	Heterosexual		Homosexual		Heterosexual		Homosexual		Heterosexual		Homosexual		Heterosexual		Homosexual	
	N	%	N	%	N	%	N	%	N	%	N	%	N	%	N	%
Open and frank	0	--	1	4	8	20	5	8	8	24	4	13	6	10	2	6
Somewhat open	3	19	1	4	6	15	11	18	13	38	4	13	24	41	13	36
Quite puritanical	13	81	21	91	25	62	44	71	11	32	17	57	26	45	21	58
Father absent	0	--	0	--	1	2	2	3	2	6	5	17	2	3	0	--
Totals	16	100	23	99	40	99	62	100	34	100	30	100	58	99	36	100

Brazil: X^2 = 2.71336, $\underline{p}$ = 0.2575

Guatemala: X^2 = 3.12856, $\underline{p}$ = 0.3722

Philippines: X^2 = 8.45248, $\underline{p}$ = 0.0375

United States: X^2 = 2.80701, $\underline{p}$ = 0.4223

TABLE 2.17 What Was Your Mother's Attitude Toward Sex?

Attitude	Brazil				Guatemala				Philippines				United States			
	Heterosexual		Homosexual		Heterosexual		Homosexual		Heterosexual		Homosexual		Heterosexual		Homosexual	
	N	%	N	%	N	%	N	%	N	%	N	%	N	%	N	%
Open and frank	0	--	0	--	8	20	5	8	5	15	4	13	1	2	2	6
Somewhat open	4	25	1	4	6	15	11	18	11	33	3	10	22	38	13	36
Quite puritanical	12	75	21	91	25	62	44	71	16	48	22	73	35	60	21	58
Mother absent	0	--	1	4	1	2	2	3	1	3	1	3	0	--	0	--
Totals	16	100	23	99	40	99	62	100	33	99	30	99	58	100	36	100
	X² = 4.13122				X² = 3.12856				X² = 5.49952				X² = 1.05656			
	p = 0.1267				p = 0.3722				p = 0.1387				p = 0.5896			

58

TABLE 2.18 Was Your Mother Ever Seductive With You?

	Brazil				Guatemala				Phillipines				United States			
	Heterosexual		Homosexual		Heterosexual		Homosexual		Heterosexual		Homosexual		Heterosexual		Homosexual	
	N	%	N	%	N	%	N	%	N	%	N	%	N	%	N	%
Yes	0	--	0	--	1	2	6	10	2	6	3	10	1	2	2	6
No	16	100	23	100	38	95	54	87	31	91	26	87	57	98	34	94
Mother absent	0	--	0	--	1	2	2	3	1	3	1	3	0	--	0	--
Totals	16	100	23	100	40	99	62	100	34	100	30	100	58	100	36	100
2 by 2:					$X_C^2 = 1.01829$ $\underline{p} = 0.3129$				$X_C^2 = 0.02273$ $\underline{p} = 0.8802$				$X_C^2 = 0.17958$ $\underline{p} = 0.6717$			
3 by 2:					$X^2 = 2.03703$ $\underline{p} = 0.3611$				$X^2 = 0.39012$ $\underline{p} = 0.8228$							

TABLE 2.19 Was Your Father Emotionally Detached and Distant When You Were Growing Up?

	Brazil				Guatemala				Philippines				United States			
	Heterosexual		Homosexual		Heterosexual		Homosexual		Heterosexual		Homosexual		Heterosexual		Homosexual	
	N	%	N	%	N	%	N	%	N	%	N	%	N	%	N	%
Yes	5	31	13	56	17	42	27	44	7	20	13	43	9	16	22	61
No	11	69	7	30	19	48	29	47	24	70	12	40	47	81	14	39
Other	0	--	3	13	4	10	6	10	3	9	5	17	2	3	0	--
Totals	16	100	23	99	40	100	62	101	34	99	30	100	58	100	36	99
2 by 2:	X^2 = 4.05000				X^2 = 0.00864				X^2 = 5.21703				X^2 = 19.89652			
	$\underline{p}$ = 0.0442				$\underline{p}$ = 0.9259				$\underline{p}$ = 0.0224				$\underline{p}$ = 0.0000			
3 by 2:	X^2 = 6.39402				X^2 = 0.01150				X^2 = 6.07372				X^2 = 21.32312			
	$\underline{p}$ = 0.0409				$\underline{p}$ = 0.9943				$\underline{p}$ = 0.0480				$\underline{p}$ = 0.0000			

TABLE 2.20 Was Your Father Hostile Toward You When You Were Growing Up?

	Brazil				Guatemala				Philippines				United States			
	Heterosexual		Homosexual		Heterosexual		Homosexual		Heterosexual		Homosexual		Heterosexual		Homosexual	
	N	%	N	%	N	%	N	%	N	%	N	%	N	%	N	%
Yes	4	25	12	52	14	35	19	31	13	38	9	30	1	2	9	25
No	12	75	8	35	22	55	36	58	19	56	16	53	56	96	27	75
Other	0	--	3	13	4	10	7	11	2	6	5	17	1	2	0	--
Totals	16	100	23	100	40	100	62	100	34	100	30	100	58	100	36	100

2 by 2:

Brazil: $X^2 = 4.41000$ $\underline{p} = 0.0357$

Guatemala: $X^2 = 0.17760$ $\underline{p} = 0.6734$

Philippines: $X^2 = 0.12668$ $\underline{p} = 0.7219$

United States: $X^2_c = 10.11984$ $\underline{p} = 0.0015$

3 by 2:

Brazil: $X^2 = 6.76141$ $\underline{p} = 0.0340$

Guatemala: $X^2 = 0.22021$ $\underline{p} = 0.8957$

Philippines: $X^2 = 2.02805$ $\underline{p} = 0.3628$

United States: $X^2 = 13.10123$ $\underline{p} = 0.0014$

61

TABLE 2.21 Which Parent Was the Strongest When You Were Growing Up?

| | Brazil | | | | Guatemala | | | | Philippines | | | | United States | | | |
| | Heterosexual | | Homosexual | | Heterosexual | | Homosexual | | Heterosexual | | Homosexual | | Heterosexual | | Homosexual | |
	N	%	N	%	N	%	N	%	N	%	N	%	N	%	N	%
Mother	7	44	15	65	31	78	44	71	4	12	14	47	22	38	22	61
Father	9	56	8	35	2	5	10	16	26	76	11	37	36	62	12	33
Other	0	--	0	--	7	18	8	13	4	12	5	17	0	--	2	6
Totals	16	100	23	100	40	101	62	100	34	100	30	101	58	100	36	100

2 by 2:

Brazil: $X^2 = 1.76848$, $p = 0.1836$

Guatemala: $X^2_c = 1.72840$, $p = 0.1886$

Philippines: $X^2 = 11.27527$, $p = 0.0008$

United States: $X^2 = 6.15821$, $p = 0.0131$

3 by 2:

Guatemala: $X^2 = 3.05013$, $p = 0.2176$

Philippines: $X^2 = 11.54284$, $p = 0.0031$

United States: $X^2 = 9.36397$, $p = 0.0093$

TABLE 2.22 Which Parent Was the Warmest When You Were Growing Up?

| | Brazil | | | | Guatemala | | | | Philippines | | | | United States | | | |
| | Heterosexual | | Homosexual | | Heterosexual | | Homosexual | | Heterosexual | | Homosexual | | Heterosexual | | Homosexual | |
	N	%	N	%	N	%	N	%	N	%	N	%	N	%	N	%
Mother	15	94	19	83	31	78	44	71	18	53	24	80	51	88	33	92
Father	1	6	3	13	2	5	10	16	7	20	2	7	7	12	1	3
Other	0	--	1	4	7	18	8	13	9	26	4	13	0	--	2	6
Totals	16	100	23	100	40	101	62	100	34	99	30	100	58	100	36	101

	Brazil	Guatemala	Philippines	United States
2 by 2:	X^2_C = 0.03890 p = 0.8437	X^2_C = 1.72840 p = 0.1886	X^2_C = 2.35431 p = 0.1249	X^2_C = 1.24658 p = 0.2642
3 by 2:	X^2 = 1.25459 p = 0.5340	X^2 = 3.05013 p = 0.2176	X^2 = 5.32881 p = 0.0696	X^2 = 5.51002 p = 0.0636

TABLE 2.23 Was Your Family "Normal" or in Some Way Unusual?

	Brazil				Guatemala				Philippines				United States			
	Heterosexual		Homosexual		Heterosexual		Homosexual		Heterosexual		Homosexual		Heterosexual		Homosexual	
	N	%	N	%	N	%	N	%	N	%	N	%	N	%	N	%
Normal	13	81	11	48	27	68	34	55	29	85	25	83	41	71	24	67
Unusual in a negative way	3	19	12	52	7	18	22	35	4	12	3	10	8	14	8	22
Unusual in a positive way	0	--	0	--	6	15	6	10	1	3	2	7	9	16	4	11
Totals	16	100	23	100	40	101	62	100	34	100	30	100	58	101	36	100
2 by 2:	$X^2 = 4.45374$ $\underline{p} = 0.0348$				$X^2_c = 3.38648$ $\underline{p} = 0.0657$				$X^2 = 0.0$ $\underline{p} = 1.0000$				$X^2 = 0.91872$ $\underline{p} = 0.3378$			
3 by 2:					$X^2 = 4.00303$ $\underline{p} = 0.1351$				$X^2 = 0.52454$ $\underline{p} = 0.7693$				$X^2 = 1.29101$ $\underline{p} = 0.5244$			

TABLE 2.24 Were Both Parents Present in the Home While You Were Growing Up?

	Brazil				Guatemala				Philippines				United States			
	Heterosexual		Homosexual		Heterosexual		Homosexual		Heterosexual		Homosexual		Heterosexual		Homosexual	
	N	%	N	%	N	%	N	%	N	%	N	%	N	%	N	%
Both parents present	14	88	19	83	29	72	43	69	31	97	22	76	46	79	30	86
Father absent	2	12	4	17	10	25	17	27	1	3	7	24	11	19	4	11
Mother absent	0	--	0	--	1	2	2	3	0	--	0	--	1	2	1	3
Totals	16	100	23	100	40	99	62	99	32	100	29	100	58	100	35	100
2 by 2:	$X_c^2 = 0.0$ $p = 1.0000$				$X^2 = 0.08638$ $p = 0.7688$				$X^2 = 4.19515$ $p = 0.0405$				$X^2 = 0.87799$ $p = 0.3488$			
3 by 2:					$X^2 = 0.13138$ $p = 0.9364$								$X^2 = 1.00861$ $p = 0.6039$			

sexuals and homosexuals in three of the four societies (see Table 2.19).

Filipinos show differences at the .05 level with respect to puritanical father (Table 2.16), absent father (Table 2.24), detached-distant father (Table 2.19), and strong mother (Table 2.21). Americans show differences at the .05 level with respect to detached-distant father (Table 2.19), strong mother (Table 2.21), and hostile father (Table 2.20). Brazilians show differences with respect to detached-distant father (Table 2.19) and normal family (Table 2.23). Guatemalans do not report significant differences on any of the nine items. The hostile father is found only in the American homosexual sample. Thus, closest approximation to the classic configuration appears in the American data, where we find the strong mother, detached-distant father, and hostile father.

The emergence of early cross-gender behavior sets the stage for the potential of hostility and detachment. Presumably, heterosexual fathers in any society are unlikely to react favorably to early cross-gender behavior in their sons. The most marked pattern of hostility and detachment, especially hostility, is found in American society. Of the four societies studied, American society is both the most negative toward homosexuality and the society where most research on familial factors has been done.

These cross-cultural data on early cross-gender behavior are quite consistent with earlier research and suggest that findings on early cross-gender behavior easily lend themselves to generalization beyond American society. Early cross-gender behavior appears to be an intrinsic feature of male homosexuality, wherever it may be found. On the other hand, our data do not consistently support earlier findings relating familial factors with homosexuality. On the contrary, they suggest that familial factors are spuriously related to homosexual orientation. The warm-dominant mother/distant-hostile father constellation does not create homosexuals, but occurs probably as a culturally variable reaction to the culturally invariable emergence of early cross-gender behavior in homosexual populations.

Societies very widely with respect to their attitudes toward homosexuality and consequently toward early cross-gender behavior. These differences tend to be related to the more general sexual culture or erotic tradition which characterizes a given society. No societies encourage homosexuality, but societies do differ in the strength and nature of their reaction to homosexuality and its emergent forms, such as early cross-gender behavior.

The four societies studied represent three very different erotic traditions: the Anglo-Saxon, Latin, and Southeast Asian. Each has different attitudes and normative-legal systems regulating sexuality in general, and homosexuality more specifically. The United States is part of the Anglo-Saxon tradition, which of the three erotic traditions is the most repressive and hostile toward homosexuality.

It is inevitable that individual attitudes, including those toward the sexual orientation of one's children, reflect and are intertwined with these more general societal attitudes. The Anglo-Saxon dreads and fears producing homosexual offspring and frequently goes to great lengths to prevent such behavior, carefully watching children for signs of homosexuality and punishing early cross-gender behavior. American parents are sometimes so deeply disturbed at the discovery of a homosexual child that this becomes a major traumatic event. Parents may seek help for the homosexual child, including visits with a psychiatrist or psychologist, and may even go so far as to disown him or her. Latin American parents are not pleased to discover that their children are homosexual, yet the Latin American family is considerably more accommodating to homosexual children than the North American family. Latin families tend to adjust to the homosexual offspring as a fact of life and incorporate the child into the family, rather than casting him or her out. For example, as mentioned in Chapter 1, well-to-do Guatemalan families sometimes provide homosexual sons with private quarters inside the family compound. Filipinos, unlike Anglo-Saxons, view homosexuality as natural and inevitable in certain individuals and something about which little can or should be done. Such tolerant attitudes may be related to large families. In a family of eight or ten children it is not so important if one is homosexual, since it is probable the others will be heterosexual. Whatever the reasons, patterns of hostility toward homosexual children are clearly more marked in the Anglo-Saxon world than in either the Latin or Filipino.

In summary, then, the present study finds strong evidence that early cross-gender behavior appears in all societies and that it is consistently associated with later adult sexual orientation. Homosexual orientation tends to parallel the development of heterosexual orientation, with important dimensions appearing even before puberty. However, familial factors, which have often been regarded as causative, are probably not causative at all. They are instead culturally variable reactions to emerging childhood homosexuality. Early cross-gender behavior, even in societies that are tolerant of homosexuality, is likely to set the stage for withdrawal from the child by the heterosexual father. The pattern of the distant and hostile father, frequently noted in the psychoanalytic literature, is probably the result of the father's withdrawal from a child exhibiting cross-gender behavior, not the cause of his homosexuality.

3

THE TRANSVESTIC HOMOSEXUAL

Childhood cross-gender behavior, as we have seen, is a universal and inevitable aspect of homosexual orientation, emerging wherever homosexuals are to be found. Rather than being derived from particular social or familial factors, cross-gender behavior is a predictable aspect of childhood behavior of a significant number of homosexuals in all societies. Cross-gender behavior manifests itself in similar ways in different societies, although, as we will see, it is acted out in culturally different settings with societies reacting quite differently to its emergence.

All homosexual communities appear to produce a similar range of homosexual persons whose behavior ranges from very masculine to very feminine. The appearance in the homosexual world of a group of overtly cross-gendered adult men or transvestic homosexuals is one of the major features of the homosexual world which sets it apart from the heterosexual world. While most homosexuals, like heterosexuals, are rather ordinary in appearance and behavior, a group of highly cross-gendered, effeminate homosexuals emerges in all homosexual communities in sufficient numbers to give the homosexual world a somewhat different hue than that of the heterosexual world. All homosexual communities distinguish between masculine and feminine members, though this distinction may be culturally managed in different ways. This distinction remains an important fact of life for all homosexual communities, having far-reaching implications for the structure of those communities.

In reviewing estimates of percentages of effeminate homosexuals derived from various studies, Bancroft (1972, pp. 63-64) reports that Westwood (1952) found 19 percent of his sample to be either marked or slightly effeminate, Bieber et al. (1962) found some 27 percent of his sample to be either marked or slightly effeminate, and Schofield (1965) found 14 percent to be effeminate. In a more recent study using a larger sample, Bell, Weinberg, and Hammersmith (1981, p. 198) found 44 percent of their white male homosexuals to be "relatively effeminate" and 56 percent to be "relatively non-effeminate."

As we have seen, the cross-gender phenomenon which emerges in childhood is not a passing phase, but represents a rather permanent manifestation of homosexual orientation which has implictions for adult behavior as well. Some effeminate, cross-gendered homosexuals--called transvestic homosexuals--cross-dress frequently in informal situations or in clubs, shows, and other public situations as female impersonators. In the United States, terms such as queen, drag queen, transvestite, and female impersonator are used to designate finer distinctions within the cross-gendered spectrum. Societies cannot and do not create transvestic homosexuals, any more than they create masculine homosexuals or heterosexuals. Were transvestic behavior a social creation, it undoubtedly would not exist, since many societies disapprove of both homosexuality and cross-gender behavior.

All societies must come to terms with transvestic homosexuality, and they may do so in a variety of ways. Indeed the treatment of transvestic homosexuals is a major test of the tolerance for homosexuals in a particular society. Transvestic homosexuals are often outrageous and exotic in comparison to conventional heterosexual standards, and societies which can tolerate transvestic homosexuals seem to have little difficulty tolerating conventionally masculine homosexuals. The dichotomy between masculine and feminine homosexuals is not entirely a creation of the homosexual subculture. Rather, manifestations of cross-gender behavior appear early in homosexuals in all societies, and these persons usually enter the homosexual subculture with cross-gender patterns already evident, giving that subculture its cross-gendered dimension. While the subculture may organize adult cross-gender behavior in culturally variable ways, cross-gender patterns of adult behavior are a result of a fusion of already present inate cross-gender patterns with the adult homosexual subculture. Homosexual subcultures do not ex nihilo invent and organize cross-gender behavior.

The existence of masculine and feminine homosexuals in the same subculture is one of the fundamental facts of life of that subculture, and is explicitly or implicitly recognized by the subcultures through such terminology as butch and nellie, macho and loca. Although the ways in which these two elements interact are culturally variable, the fact of the existence of the two elements is culturally invariable.

TRANSVESTIC HOMOSEXUALS
IN THE UNITED STATES

Katz extracts an unsympathetic description of black transvestic homosexuals in Washington, D.C. written by Dr. Charles H. Hughes in 1893:

> I am credibly informed that there is, in the
> city of Washington, D.C., a convocation of
> negro men called the drag dance, which is an
> orgie of lascivious debauchery beyond pen
> power of description. I am likewise informed
> that a similar organization was lately suppressed
> by the police of New York City.
> In this sable performance of sexual perversion
> all of these men are lasciviously dressed in wom-
> anly attire, short sleeves, low-necked dresses
> and the usual ballroom decorations and orna-
> ments of women, feathered and ribboned head-
> dresses, garter grills, flowers, ruffles, etc. and
> deport themselves as women. Standing or seated
> on a pedestal, but accessible to all the rest, is
> the naked queen (a male), whose phallic member,
> decorated with a ribbon, is subject to the gaze
> and osculations in turn of all the members of
> this lecherous gang of sexual perverts and phal-
> lic fornicators.
> Among those who annually assemble in this
> strange libidinous display are cooks, barbers,
> waiters and other employees of Washington
> families, some even higher in the social scale--
> some being employed as subordinates in the
> Government departments [1976, pp. 42-43].

This passage is interesting in what it reveals of the
American attitude toward transvestic homosexuality. Moral
repugnance, if not exclusively American, seems to be a relatively permanent aspect of the Anglo-Saxon attitude toward
transvestic homosexuals. In the United States they are
generally a despised group subjected to considerable violence
by the general public, and treated by police as a dangerous
and criminal class. This account also suggests that drag
activities were not limited to whites, but cut across racial
and social class lines much as they do today. Transvestic
homosexuals appear to come from a wide variety of family
structures, racial and ethnic backgrounds, and social classes. Despite the disapproval of some gay rights groups and
intermittent police harassment, drag balls still take place in
most large American cities. Newton writes:

> There are many opportunities for the male
> homosexual who is so inclined to "get into drag"
> in a social context. The most formal of these
> is the annual Halloween "drag ball," which is
> traditional in most large cities. Since the central
> event of most of these balls is a beauty contest,
> most of the participants make a serious attempt
> at impersonation through the use of "high drag,"
> that is, very formal female attire and all that
> goes with it--high heels, elaborate hair-do (usu-
> ally a wig), feminine make-up, and formal acces-
> sories, and if possible, a male escort in formal
> men's evening wear. The Halloween balls are,
> moreover, not the only formal events that pro-
> vide opportunities for drag. For instance, the
> homosexual community of Fire Island, New York,
> sponsors a drag ball and contest during the
> summer; some cities have New Year's balls as
> well [1972, p. 34].

American attitudes are closely related to British attitudes,
which despite the good press enjoyed by Great Britain, are
actually quite repressive of homosexuality. Quentin Crisp's
autobiography (1968) attests to lifelong harassment by police
and the public despite the fact he never completely cross-
dressed. His manner and dress were quite effeminate, though
falling short of drag.

The transvestic homosexuals tend to be a source of em-
barrassment and controversy to the American gay rights
movement. For different reasons, both gay men and lesbians
are embarrassed by them. When the organizers of the gay
march on Washington for July 4, 1979, met in Houston to plan
the event, there was discussion of dress-codes for the march,
whether cross-gender clothing would be prohibited, and even
whether highly cross-gendered persons--transvestic homosexuals and transsexuals--should participate in the march at all.
Some more masculine leaders in the American gay movement
prefer to draw a distinction between themselves and the more
highly cross-gendered persons; some even go so far as to say
that transvestic homosexuals are not really homosexual.

Some American lesbian feminists have long objected to
drag queens and female impersonators on the grounds that
they perpetuate traditional stereotypes of women or are otherwise demeaning to women. For example, at a program designed
to observe the seventy-fourth anniversary of the San Francisco earthquake, in April 1980, at the Castro Theatre, the
San Francisco Lesbian Chorus walked out of the theater to
protest male actress Charles Pierce's female impersonation act
(The Voice 1980).

The official line of some American gay rights organizations is to deny any relationship between sexual orientation and behavior, thus obviating the need to deal politically or scientifically with the cross-gender phenomenon. For example, the position of the Gay Activist Alliance is:

> The common heterosexual notion that homosexuals are all alike is without foundation, and so is the old homosexual saw that "it takes one to know one." No one can tell who is or isn't homosexual by appearance or outward behavior alone. There are Hollywood sex goddesses who are lesbians. There are professional football players who are homosexuals. There are weak, limp-wristed heterosexual men and tough, swaggering heterosexual women. There are children who seem to fit the homosexual stereotypes and may develop a homosexual orientation because they're expected to. And there are homosexuals who adopted the stereotypes in adolescence, either as a symbol of revolt or because we were brainwashed into believing that that's the way we were "supposed" to act [Free Spirit Newsletter 1978].

Such statements ostensibly have been regarded as liberal views frequently shared by the social-scientific community and are incorporated into text books on deviant behavior and human sexuality. The failure on the part of American gay rights organizations--dominated by masculine homosexuals and lesbian feminists--to recognize, deal with, and thus protect the rights of transvestic homosexuals reflects the hostile attitude of a homophobic society. For example, some American gay rights organizations prefer to dismiss the infamous effeminate hairdresser as nonexistent or as a stereotype of the heterosexual world, rather than to recognize the hairdresser's right to exist and to regard his work as a legitimate and useful occupation. While the transvestic homosexual hairdresser in the United States is widely regarded as repulsive and undesirable, in the Philippines he is regarded as endowed with a special gift, or at the very least, as someone who is doing his best to earn an honest living. Transvestic homosexuals in the American subculture are frequently discriminated against by more masculine homosexuals. Macy Williams, a local-born Hawaiian female impersonator reported that he was called upon by a macho gay bar in Waikiki to bring his troupe of female impersonators to the bar for a special show designed to earn money for the gay rights movement. Some weeks after the fundraising event, when Macy returned to the bar dressed in a unisex outfit and light makeup, he was turned away and told that drag queens were not allowed.

Drag queens are not infrequently refused service in macho western and leather bars. GiGi, a Filipino transvestic homosexual from a well-to-do film family in Manila, was ejected from a bathhouse in San Francisco because he had breast development from taking hormones.

While the gay subculture reflects the more general social class lines in the society, the cross-gender phenomenon creates the potential within the homosexual community for still another form of stratification based on the masculine-feminine continuum. The American homosexual subculture, particularly, stratifies on the basis of masculinity-femininity. While transvestic homosexuals come from all social class levels, classlike or even castelike lines are frequently drawn against them. Some masculine homosexuals frequently express disdain for drag queens and often do not want to be in the same bar with them. In the United States, it is the more masculine homosexuals who tend to control the homosexual subculture. They own or operate most of the gay bars, bathhouses, clubs, and control the gay political organizations. While drag shows have a following among some masculine homosexuals and among some lesbians, hostility toward drag queens is pervasive in the American homosexual community.

TRANSVESTIC HOMOSEXUALS IN LATIN AMERICA

In Latin America there is considerably more tolerance for transvestic homosexuals than in the United States. Attitudes toward the transvestic homosexual in Latin America resemble those toward the prostitute and the fate of these two erotic minorities is frequently linked legally and politically. If prostitutes and transvestic homosexuals are not treated with reverence in Latin America, it must also be said they are not despised. Rather than being regarded with shock and moral repugnance, they are treated as part of ordinary social reality. Neither prostitutes nor transvestic homosexuals in Latin America (except special cases such as Cuba and Argentina) are subjected to systematic police surveillance and harassment, as in the United States.

The prostitute and the transvestic homosexual in Guatemala often linger together at the same street corners, talking or waiting for customers. In Brazil, transvestic homosexuals are sometimes to be found in houses of prostitution even in small towns. Police in Guatemala are said to occasionally pick up the locas (effeminate homosexuals) for anal intercourse. Whether this is literally true is not as important as what it says about the relationship between police in Latin America and the locas. The police do not see the locas as threatening, but as harmless and perhaps ridiculous or as secondary sex-

ual objects to be used at will. The sexual use of the queen
enhances rather than threatens the Latin male's masculinity.
The more sexual objects over which the Latin male holds
sway, the more macho he is considered.

In the larger cities of Latin America, cross-dressed locas
frequently work as prostitutes or otherwise solicit in the
streets or in public parks. Sometimes heterosexual men have
sexual relations with the locas in dark areas of a park or
inside cars. Latin men, upon discovery of the real sex of the
loca, are likely to either go through with the sexual act or
quietly abandon the situation, but they rarely engage in violence. In contrast, the transvestic homosexual prostitutes of
Hotel Street in Honolulu report that upon discovery of their
real sex they are frequently beaten by naive haole service-
men. Heterosexual or bisexual men sometimes frequent homosexual bars in Latin America to pick up locas, perhaps for
money or as ancillary sexual entertainment. It is not regarded
as demeaning for heterosexual men to be seen in the traditional Latin homosexual bar. The locas may flirt with the
tipsy machos who are sometimes induced to dance with them.
In the famous bar "El Faro" in San Salvador, El Salvador on
Saturday nights heterosexual males dance openly with the
locas. In a well-known bar in a lower-class neighborhood in
Santiago, Chile, there are large open-air dance halls where
both heterosexuals and homosexuals mix freely and drink
Chilean wines. Macho-loca couples may be seen dancing side
by side with heterosexual couples.

A bar just outside Guatemala City is run by several
transvestic homosexuals. At least half the customers are
machos who drink there either for entertainment or to be
picked up by locas. In the smaller Latin American countries
and cities such as Guatemala, the social life of the locas
takes place in cantinas, on the streets, or in parks. In
Guatemala City, locas do imaginary strips to imaginary music
while standing on park benches.

The life of the São Paulo louca is much more sophisticated
than that of the loca of Guatemala City. Some of the transvestic homosexuals perform in shows in the expensive, chic
clubs of São Paulo.

The life of the Brazilian travesti is described as follows
(Whitam 1979, p. 16):

> The 'shows' constitute an entertainment genre
> unique to Brazil, which reflect the country's
> rich musical tradition. The 'show,' a form of
> cabaret theatre rarely seen nowadays in the U.S.,
> consists of elaborate dance routines, singing,
> miming, drag acts, samba, and above all, beauti-
> ful and costly costumes derived from the 'fantas-
> ias' (costumes) of Carnaval, often designed by

Sao Paulo's leading dress designers. The shows
are taken quite seriously by the audience and
the casts of 15 to 20 people, who rehearse ardu-
ously for as long as two months and receive only
a small wage for their performances. The results
are frequently charming. The setting for the
two-hour show is formal--waiters in white jackets,
reservations necessary, sometimes obtainable
only by the layout of an extra 20 cruzeiros, all
in all, producing a splendid cabaret scene, sen-
suous and decadent.

Night life in the clubs peaks during Carnaval,
when everyone goes to the bars. Even those who
never have enough money other times of the year
manage the jacked-up prices. During Carnaval
the music is exclusively samba--samba, samba,
samba. For the Paulista, as for all Brazil, during
those four days all the ordinary sounds of the
world stop and only the samba can be heard. The
homosexual clubs are crowded and especially conspicuous are the 'travestis' (drag queens) in
their incredible Carnaval 'fantasias.' Plans for
these elaborate costumes often begin immediately
after the preceding Carnaval and may cost hundreds or even thousands of dollars. The 'travesti' in Brazil occupies an important position in
the homosexual life in São Paulo. On the whole,
there are perhaps no more 'travestis' in São
Paulo than in any North American city of similar
size. However, the 'travesti', especially if
elegant and beautiful, is treated with a degree
of respect unknown in the U.S. The most desirable of the 'travestis' move in upper-class circles, where it is regarded by straight men as
very chic to be seen with Rogeria, Valeria, or
Samantha, the most beautiful of São Paulo's
'travestis.' Some 'travestis' perform sexual
acts for money, sometimes with married men or
business executives, receiving as much as 2,000
cruzeiros ($140) a night.

In 1984 the most celebrated media event in Brazil was the
appearance of Roberta Close, a beautiful travesti with breast
development from hormones and penis intact. Roberta Close
appeared on the covers of the Brazilian edition of Playboy and
Manchete, Brazil's most popular magazine for a general audience, and on the covers of other magazines and front pages
of numerous newspapers. "She" appeared on major television
programs and in Brazil's most famous nightclubs. Roberta
Close's prominence was received by the general public with

great interest. Many heterosexual men regarded her as sexually attractive and publicly admitted they wanted to have sexual realtions with her.

In São Paulo, where urbanization has given the Paulista more freedom from families than in most other places in Latin America, the relations between masculine and transvestic homosexuals tend to be quite harmonious. Masculine homosexuals take an interest in the activities of the more famous transvestic entertainers, and their antics are followed and discussed good-naturedly. During Carnaval many of the most elaborate costumes are worn by well-known travestis, whose photos appear in the Manchete and other of Brazil's most popular magazines, along with other prize winning costumes. During Carnaval some of the well-to-do travestis order expensive gowns from Paris, New York, or Rome and promenade around the Hilton, one of São Paulo's most fashionable areas. Generally, the travestis are not harassed as long as they have their documents in order, as with other Brazilian citizens.

In a number of buildings in downtown São Paulo, as many as half the apartments are known to be occupied by homosexual tenants. The sight of lovers or friends living together in downtown buildings is treated with indifference. Living arrangements are characterized by considerable personal freedom, and even the travesti is tolerated in a laissez-faire atmosphere.

Right-wing military dictatorships do not automatically translate into repression of transvestic homosexuals and other sexual minorities. All governments are selective in the groups which they repress. Despite the Latin tradition of military dictatorships, except under special circumstances, homosexuals have not generally been included among those elements in society regarded as subversive or dangerous to the government. Conversely, the so-called Anglo-Saxon democracies have traditionally regarded homosexuals as sufficiently dangerous as to require police surveillance. It is somewhat ironic that at the time this research was being conducted in Brazil, the American government was harshly criticizing the Brazilian government for its treatment of political prisoners. At the same time, American homosexuals were far more susceptible to police harassment and prosecution than Brazilian homosexuals, who probably enjoy more personal freedom than homosexuals in any other country in the Western hemisphere, including the United States and Canada.

TRANSVESTIC HOMOSEXUALS IN THE PHILIPPINES

The case of the Philippines illustrates even more clearly the lack of relationship between the type of government and the treatment of transvestic homosexuals. The Marcos regime, in much the same way as the Brazilian government, has been subjected to considerable criticism by liberal elements in the United States. These criticisms are no doubt justifiable in some respects. However, it should again be pointed out that the jailing of political dissidents or leftists does not necessarily mean that homosexuals or other sexual minorities are also prosecuted. Societies differ widely in defining homosexuals as politically dangerous, and to a large extent, such definitions depend upon the erotic traditions or sexual cultures of particular societies.

Because of tolerant Southeast Asian cultural traditions, transvestic homosexuals in the Philippines enjoy even more personal freedom than in either North or South America. While Filipinos, like other peoples, are not delighted by the appearance of early cross-gender behavior, they (especially Filipino mothers) appear to be considerably more tolerant of this behavior than in other societies studied. (Refer to Tables 2.14 and 2.15 in Chapter 2.) They regard such behavior as inevitable in certain cases, and tend to regard it as part of the natural order of family life that one's child may be bayot.

Transvestic homosexuals in the Philippines probably enjoy more personal freedom and prestige than in any other major contemporary society. While in the United States the masculine homosexuals control the social organization of the homosexual world, the reverse can be said to be true in the Philippines. Insofar as homosexual social organization exists--and it is limited compared to the complex organization of the United States--it is the transvestic homosexuals who control that organization. Masculine homosexuals do not participate extensively in the social-organizational aspects of the life of the bayot of Cebu. The term sward is a term used by the homosexuals in Cebu to designate both social class--middle- or upper-class background--and degree of cultural refinement. Thus, swards are middle class homosexuals who are educated and knowledgeable about the arts and culture. Bayot is a more general term for homosexuals which may be used in a descriptive way to refer to all homosexuals or may imply transvestic homosexuality. Swards themselves sometimes use the term bayot to refer to homosexuals of lower socio-economic status.

This distinction between sward and bayot is illustrated in the following description taken from research field notes. The respondent is James, an intelligent, well-educated sward who sometimes crosses the line between sward and bayot:

> Recently a boyot was hit and killed by a jeepney, while he was crossing the street-- drunk. He was quite poor--one of the 'barefoot set.' His friends took up a collection for his funeral. While as a sward I was not actu-

ally a close friend, I felt I was needed in the
situation, and helped some with the funeral,
which was held 27 kilometers outside of Cebu
City. His friends could not refrain from camping at the funeral. They would say 'poor
Emiliano, or should we say Emily?' Everyone
would giggle and then for a while would be
serious and cry. They would open the casket
and put makeup on his face and say things
like 'Emily would have liked a little more pow-
der on her cheeks.' It was funny and sad at
the same time.

Although the swards in Cebu are not all transvestic,
many are. There are masculine swards, but the masculine
swards who participate openly in this dominant homosexual
group in Cebu tend to work in fashion design or related
occupations. Fashion and grooming are an important part
of the social life of the swards, which tends to take place
in and around the beauty and fashion shops. Most swards
live with their families, and there are few private apartments where social life may take place. There is, therefore
a good bit of running back and forth among the various
hair and fashion salons.

Several of the swards of Cebu are well-known in the
fashion world of the Philippines, and they are serious prac-
titioners of the design and making of both male and female
clothing. They are highly regarded by the heterosexual community, and their patrons include Cebu's leading citizens.
For example, an annual fashion show is organized by one of
Cebu's leading sward fashion designers, presented at one of
the city's principal hotels and attended by many leading
citizens. It should be emphasized that the general public in
Cebu is aware of the sexual orientation of their hairdressers
and clothing designers, but this is in no way detrimental to
their success. It is considered as perfectly natural that hair
and clothing designers should be homosexuals.

Cross-dressing manifests itself at the parties of the
swards in the form of elaborate costumes designed especially
for the frequent sward parties on birthdays or holidays,
usually held in the "Satellite Disco" at the top of a downtown
hotel. Cross-dressed swards walk openly in the main streets
and hotel lobby in their costumes and are regarded with
great interest and amusement by bystanders.

On Sundays, there is usually a group of swards at the
swimming pool of the first class Hotel Magellan, where, for
an entrance fee, nonguests may swim and drink. There are
usually a couple of tables of swards who camp, gossip, and
put makeup on in full public view. GiGi, a highly cross-
gendered transvestic homosexual, uses the ladies' dressing

room to change, without comment, though her sexual orientation and sexual identity are public knowledge.

Perhaps the most popular activity of the transvestic homosexuals in Cebu and other parts of the Philippines is the "fashion show," which is really a drag beauty contest. Such shows have evolved in recent years as a popular entertainment form for the general public. In contrast to drag shows in the Anglo-Saxon world, which are usually performed for primarily homosexual clientele in often "disreputable" locations, the Filipino fashion show is regarded as good, clean, family entertainment. Children comprise a substantial part of the audience and are among the most ardent fans of the contestants. The Filipino fashion shows have become popular all over the country with the sophisticated and unsophisticated alike, but they are especially popular in smaller cities and towns. They are often sponsored by the Kiwanis or other civic clubs or performed as part of the annual town fiesta. Hart (personal communication 1979) reports on a bayot fashion show which was sponsored by the Rotary Club in the town of Compostela in the province of Cebu. Another fashion show in Cebu was sponsored by the local Commander of the Philippine Constabulary and was presented for the enjoyment of the neighborhood near the base. Preparation for the pageant began late in the afternoon in one of the downtown beauty shops, where the 20 or so contestants arranged their hairdos and previously selected costumes. For this pageant, the class distinction between sward and bayot was relaxed for the sake of beauty and the two groups mixed freely. An older bayot served as director or impresario, controlling the financial and organizational aspects of the affair. After considerable attention to hair styles, makeup, and costumes, the contestants were transported to the scene of the function in pre-arranged jeepneys. An outdoor stage and 100 or so small wooden chairs had been arranged by the host neighborhood, which consisted of children, housewives, husbands, and some constabulary personnel, who had paid a peso to attend. Final makeup and costumes were applied in an improvised backstage. There was the usual three categories of beauty: native costume (Miss Maylasia, Miss Argentina, etc.), bathing suit, and ball gown. Perhaps the most interesting aspect of the show was the audience and the relationship of the audience to the participants. The audience was extremely sympathetic and receptive. The children then screamed with delight at each new costume. The whole event, carried off without the slightest hint of hostility, took on the character of an innocent neighborhood theatrical event. There were crowd favorites, of course, and the five judges chosen from the neighborhood carefully and seriously tabulated their choices. The prizes, consisting of money and trophies, were paid for by the commander of the constabulary and presented by leading citizens of the neighborhood.

In Bacolod, also in the Visayas, transvestic homosexuals occupy a conspicuous place in the annual Christmas festivities, the most important social event of the year in this sugarcane capital of some 300,000 persons. Nearly all of the traditional folk-dancing is done by homosexuals, with transvestic homosexuals taking female roles and masculine homosexuals the male roles. In the Christmas festivities of 1979, the queen of the festivities was a transvestic homosexual, crowned by the leading matrons of Bacolod in the lobby of the principal hotel with townspeople as the audience. The sexual orientation of the homosexuals was public knowledge, and their participation in these activities was regarded as routine.

THE "REAL" TRANSVESTITE

Despite the fact that all homosexual communities are characterized by rather conspicuous cross-dressing, many students and the general public are under the impression that "most transvestites are heterosexual." For example, Daniel G. Brown (1961, p. 1017) in the Encyclopedia of Sexual Behavior writes, "Research and clinical studies indicate that the majority of male transvestites are predominantly or exclusively heterosexual throughout their lives." Pomeroy (1968, p. 378) similarly leads one to believe that most transvestites are heterosexual when he writes that "Males who cross-dress are usually heterosexual; in fact, transvestites, as a group, are more heterosexual than the general population." In writing that transvestites are heterosexuals, sex researchers have given the general public, even the educated public, the impression that anyone who cross-dresses or otherwise exhibits cross-gender behavior is heterosexual.

Perhaps confusion on this point derives from the fact that the behavior itself is confusing. There are actually two important manifestations of transvestism, homosexual and heterosexual, which are quite distinct phenomena. Some sex researchers have limited the use of the term transvestism to heterosexual transvestism, on the erroneous assumption that homosexual transvestism is just "playing at cross-dressing." Some heterosexual transvestites, not wanting to be identified as being homosexual, have insisted that they are the "true transvestites" and take a demeaning attitude toward drag queens and female impersonators.

Of course, if transvestism is by definition limited to heterosexual transvestites, then all transvestites are heterosexual. This view, which has grown in popularity in recent years, is helpful in that it calls attention to the existence of heterosexual transvestites, but it adds confusion to the issue by excluding transvestic homosexuals, whose patterns of transvestic behavior are different from, although not less psychologically or socially important than, those of heterosexual transvestites. A more appropriate view is that heterosexual and homosexual transvestism are two distinct phenomena, both of which may have important implications for our understanding of the origins and nature of sexual orientation and gender identity. Heterosexual transvestites generally have traditionally masculine occupational interests and behaviors. They do not seem to manifest facile abilities in makeup and grooming as do the homosexual transvestites. Homosexual transvestites, unlike heterosexual transvestites, not only are given to dressing and grooming themselves, creating elaborate hair styles, sewing gowns and special effects, but in the work-a-day world often perform similar services, working as beauticians or dress designers.

Transvestic and effeminate homosexuals everywhere seem to be very much involved in "homosexual" occupations, such as fashion design, hairdressing, or interior design. Some 90 percent of the hairdressers and dressmakers in Cebu are homosexual, and these occupations are regarded by the general public and homosexuals themselves as bayot occupations. Philippine President and Mrs. Marcos appear at homosexual organizations to make awards to hairdressers and fashion designers for their contributions to the Philippine economy. Homosexuals in all societies occupy a wide range of occupations, yet the tendency of American social scientists to dismiss any connection between sexual orientation and occupational interests as stereotypic obscures social reality and denies homosexuals credit for the functions they perform in society as a result of their sexual orientation.

It would be difficult to argue that the behavior of homosexual transvestites is less psychologically meaningful or more superficial than that of heterosexual transvestites. Most transvestic homosexuals were highly cross-gendered as children, and their transvestic behavior appears to be a relatively permanent and important dimension of their lives.

The use of the term transvestite to refer exclusively to heterosexual transvestites seems unjustified. As Katz points out, both types of transvestism were recognized by the early twentieth century sexologists, including Hirschfeld, who invented the term "transvestite." Katz (1976, p. 210) writes: "German sexologists Magnus Hirschfeld published a book, Die Transvestiten, in 1910, and English homosexual emancipation theorist Edward Carpenter, writing in an American journal, used the term cross-dressing in 1911. In 1913 and 1920, the terms, D'Eonism, aesthetic, and sexo-aesthetic inversion were used by Havelock Ellis to categorize the same phenomena, but were either too clumsy or esoteric to become popular." The most accurate evaluation of the sexual orientation of transvestites comes from Hirschfeld who probably saw more transvestites professionally than any modern sex researcher. Hirsch-

feld originally used the term to refer to both heterosexual
and homosexual transvestites (1944, p. 197).

While contemporary sex researchers and texts have led
us to believe that "most transvestites are heterosexual,"
transvestism and the broader cross-gender phenomenon
affects the homosexual world in ways in which the heterosexual world is not affected. Cross-gender behavior is
manifested in many different ways in the homosexual world
and is one of the elements which gives the homosexual
world its distinctive qualities. Homosexuals and heterosexuals all live in the same world and share much in common,
but the homosexual world has distinctive qualities which are
not a part of the everyday heterosexual world. For example,
consider the cross-gendering of pronouns and the use of
female names. While all homosexuals do not engage in such
behavior, enough homosexuals do so--usually in fun--as to
give many conversations among homosexuals a cross-gendered
twist which heterosexual conversations do not have. In all
four societies studied, the sex reversal of pronouns occurred.
American homosexuals sometimes substitute she for he; in
Spanish, ella is frequently used instead of el; and in Portuguese, ela is often used instead of ele. In Cebuano, the
feminine term of address da is often substituted for the masculine ba.

American scholars often assume that transvestic homosexuality is uniquely American. For example, the American anthropologist Newton (1972, p. 113) suggests that transvestic
homosexuality is somehow American in origin, writing that:
"drag, like violence, is as American as apple pie. Like violence, it is not an accident or mistake nor is it caused by a
few people's weak character. It is an organic part of American culture--exactly the 'flip side' of many precious ideals.
Many, if not most (white) female impersonators are from
small towns in middle and southern America; they are home
grown." Transvestic homosexuality, like violence, is American,
but it is also Guatemalan, Brazilian, Filipino, and quite probably universal. Neither drag nor violence are American inven-
tions, and although it is outside the province of this report
to speculate on the origins of violence, it is patently clear
that drag, like other manifestations of cross-gender behavior,
is an intrinsic aspect of homosexuality wherever it may be
found.

4

THE HOMOSEXUAL SUBCULTURE

Homosexuality subcultures appear in all societies, given that sufficient aggregates of people exist. In small, isolated, traditional societies it is difficult for homosexual subcultures to emerge, although individuals of homosexual orientation do exist in such societies. These individuals may live out their entire lives in isolation, never realizing there are other homosexuals in the world. Such persons were observed in traditional societies of Guatemala. One such individual lived in San Juan Chamelco, a Kechki-speaking town in the Guatemalan highlands. The following is excerpted from the field notes of a student:

> Ishquicuink in Kechki language signified a man who sometimes acts like a man, sometimes like a woman. Such a man was pointed out to me by various persons in the village as being Ishquicuink. He was a man of about 40 years of age, whose job was assistant to a curandera or folk-healer. He invited me to visit his house. He lives with his mother, a sister, and a niece. Upon arriving at his house, he offered us a glass of lemonade that he himself made. As we arrived at lunchtime he set the table, served the food, cleaned off the table, and washed the dishes. I asked him if he was married or had been. To both questions his answer was no. He also added that he did not want to marry because women are such a problem [Mejia de Rodas 1976].

Where there are sufficient aggregates of people, even in traditional societies, the rudimentary forms of the homosexual subculture become apparent. For example, in the Guatemalan

Indian town of Chimaltenango, two men lived together as lovers, wearing typical Indian clothing in an outwardly traditional Indian adobe house. The house, however, was decorated in a manner strikingly different from the other Indians. It was meticulously and elaborately decorated, a characteristic frequently found in homosexual subcultures. Warren (1974) has documented this in her study of the American homosexual subculture. The occupation of the lovers was that of stringing pine needles in decorative strands, traditionally used in Guatemala for holidays and other festive occasions, and supplying flowers for weddings. In essence these two men were florists, involved in the arts of embellishment, which in larger societies are universally linked with homosexual subcultures.

A male homosexual from the Havasupai tribe of about 300 persons living at the bottom of the Grand Canyon in Arizona, reported three males of homosexual orientation and another six who are either bisexual or willing to participate in homosexual activity. One of the homosexuals is highly transvestic, cross-dresses, and has a reputation for weaving the best baskets in the village. Another is an effeminate homosexual, whose duties include annually organizing, supervising, and designing clothes for "Miss Havasupai," who competes with other Indian tribes in an annual beauty pageant. Again, transvestic homosexuals in many societies are engaged in giving shows, pageants, and related activities.

Even in traditional, rural societies themes common to all homosexual subcultures are seen to emerge in at least a rudimentary way. Larger populations include larger numbers of homosexuals, and with the larger numbers of homosexuals, a more complex homosexual social organization becomes possible. Although urbanization obviously plays an important role in the social organization of homosexuals, it should be emphasized that urbanization does not create homosexuality. Rather, it is through the larger numbers of homosexuals brought together through urbanization that fully elaborated homosexual subcultures emerge.

One of the remarkable aspects of homosexual subcultures is the extent to which they resemble each other. While the subcultures in the United States, Guatemala, Brazil, and the Philippines emerge within the broader social and cultural contexts, which influence them in important ways, there are other important aspects in which the subcultures are strikingly similar, despite the differing social and cultural contexts.

CROSS-CULTURAL SIMILARITY OF
OCCUPATIONAL INTERESTS

The range of occupational interests among homosexuals is similar in the four societies studied. Social scientists have

often assumed, presumably out of egalitarian motivation, that
the occupational interests of homosexuals are identical to those
of heterosexuals, but in so doing they have ignored sexual
orientation as a sociological variable of considerable importance
in human behavior, inadvertently deterring the exploration of
the unique contributions which homosexuals make to the larger
society. For example, Gore Vidal echoes the popular belief
that homosexual orientation has no bearing on other nonsexual
dimensions of an individual's behavior. Vidal states that "homosexual' is just an adjective that describes a sexual act between
two members of the same sex . . . nothing more" (Altman
1978, p. 4). More importantly, Kinsey held a similar point of
view:

> It would encourage clearer thinking on these
> matters if persons were not characterized as
> heterosexual or homosexual, but as individuals
> who have had certain amounts of heterosexual
> experience and certain amounts of homosexual
> experience. Instead of using these terms as
> substantives which stand for persons, or even
> as adjectives to describe persons, they may
> better be used to describe the nature of the
> overt sexual relations, or of the stimuli to
> which an individual erotically responds [Kin-
> sey, Pomeroy, and Martin 1948, p. 617].

Akers (1977) suggests that homosexuality is simply same-
sex contact without implications for nonsexual behavior. C.A.
Tripp (1975) concludes that homosexuals and heterosexuals are
different only with respect to the nature of their erotic interests. Thus, many writers deny a direct relationship between
sexual orientation and nonsexual aspects of behavior.
Despite such views, it is widely assumed by homosexuals
themselves that there is a connection between sexual orientation and other aspects of their lives. There is an implicit
assumption in the homosexual world that the occupational structure of the homosexual world is different from that of the
heterosexual world. For example, a homosexual attending a
homosexual party would reasonably expect to find in attend-
ance persons of a relatively wide variety of occupations; yet
there are limits to these expectations. Of course it is not
expected, except in special circumstances, that a large portion
of persons will be hairdressers or interior designers, yet
these and similar professions appear with predictable frequency
in homosexual gatherings. While such occupations are frequently dismissed by social scientists as stereotypes, it is
assumed in homosexual circles that hairdressers and interior
decorators are a legitimate part of the homosexual world. The
presence of hairdressers and interior decorators at homosexual

functions emphatically does not violate the assumptions of homosexuals about the occupational structure of the homosexual world. Although social scientists often deny that homosexual hairdressers and decorators exist in greater frequency within the homosexual subculture than within the heterosexual society, homosexuals are themselves accustomed to the over-representation of certain professions in the homosexual world. Hart (1968) has reported rather remarkable patterns of occupational interests in the rural Philippines (see Table 4.1).

While relatively few homosexuals in absolute numbers are hairdressers and decorators, the occupational structure in the homosexual world nevertheless tends to be different from that in the heterosexual world. While it is well known in the homosexual world that homosexuals may and do occupy the full range of occupations, including airplane pilot, automobile mechanic, and professional athlete, a preponderance of pilots, mechanics, and athletes at a homosexual function would violate the assumptions that many homosexuals hold about their world. The following lists of occupations of guests at middle-class homosexual gatherings, as recorded in field notes, are characteristic of masculine middle-class cliques:

Honolulu, July 4, 1979:

Two advertising executives, one English professor, one owner of an art gallery, one landscaper-gardener, one commercial artist, one produce manager in a supermarket, two physicians, one interior designer, two graphics designers.

San Francisco, April 1980:

One disc jockey, one high school Spanish teacher, one mover and hauler, one physician, one psychiatrist, one student of Italian, three artists (painters), one accountant, one linguist-interpreter, one trader in jewels and precious stones, two musicians (choral music), one teacher of art for preschool children, one architect.

Phoenix, February, 1980:

One architecture student, one landscape architect, one architect, two accounting students, one carpenter, two printers, one engineering student, one graphics designer, one student of drama, one teacher of Spanish, one art teacher, one music student.

Such configurations are probably typical for gatherings of middle-class masculine homosexuals. Of course, occupational

Table 4.1 Occupation of <u>Bayot</u> (Male Homosexuals) and <u>Lakin-on</u> (Female Homosexuals) in Dumaguete City, Negros Oriental, 1967

Occupations	Bayot	Lakin-on	Total
Dressmaker*	18	--	18
Beautician*	13	--	13
Manicurist*	7	--	7
Clerk (commercial store)	4	9	13
Policewoman	--	1	1
Clerk (government)	1	5	6
Teacher	3	11	14
Cook*	6	1	7
Housekeeper*	5	6	11
Maid*	1	5	6
Babysitter (yaya)*	2	--	2
Laborer	--	9	9
<u>Labandera</u> (washwoman)*	3	--	3
<u>Tuba</u> gatherer	--	1	1
<u>Tuba</u>/vegetable vendor*	2	--	2
Bartender	2	--	2
Interior decorator*	2	--	2
Musician	--	2	2
Bus driver	--	5	5
Artificial paper flower maker*	1	--	1
Student	--	3	3
Totals	70	58	128

*Regarded as women's work.

<u>Sources</u>: Adapted from Donn V. Hart, "Homosexuality and Transvestism in
the Philippines," <u>Behavior Science Notes</u> 3 (1968):227. Reprinted with per-
mission.

structures of homosexuals depend to some extent upon the
larger structural arrangements in the society at large. Affluent societies with a large middle-class enable more persons,
including homosexuals, to achieve their vocational aspirations.
For example, in the United States there are more opportuni-
ties for persons to achieve certain occupational goals than in
a small society such as Guatemala. It is interesting and sometimes sad to note that lower-class homosexuals in Guatemala
and the Philippines often harbor ambitions similar to the occupations actually achieved in more prosperous countries such
as Brazil or the United States. Some ambitions, given the
nature of the economic, educational, and stratification structures of these countries, are unlikely to be fulfilled. As an
example, a thirty-two-year-old Guatemalan respondent with a
ninth grade education, from a poor family, earnestly desired
to be a linguist and professor of literature and languages.
Over a period of several years, with what little money he had
saved, he had studied both English and French. At the time
of our conversation he was attempting to finish high school
by attending school at night, carrying around and reading
books about Spanish literature whenever time permitted.

While it is true that male homosexuals may occupy any
occupational category, there are certain tasks toward which
they seem consistently drawn and in which they appear to be
over-represented relative to their presence in the population
at large. There are other occupations which homosexuals
seem to consistently avoid, and these are under-represented
relative to their presence in the population.

Several major themes pervade the occupational structure
of homosexual world: house and home, embellishment, language, helping professions, grooming, entertainment, and the
arts are among the most distinctive. When asked the question:
"If you could choose any occupation, regardless of your
present occupation, education, or qualifications, what would
you like to do or be?" between 40 percent and 50 percent of
the male homosexuals in the United States, Brazil, and the
Philippines (Guatemalan responses on this item are not available) selected an occupation related to the arts and entertainment, while between 5 percent and 10 percent of the heterosexual males in these societies selected the arts and entertainment. Homosexuals tend to avoid occupations having to do
with manipulation of heavy machinery, law enforcement, military, and related occupations involving physical aggression.
Moreover, such occupational interests and patterns of avoid-
ance appear cross-culturally in homosexual communities.

The house and home theme goes far beyond the well-
known example of the interior decorator. The homosexual subculture is characterized by a pervasive interest in houses,
which appear quite early. Many homosexuals report liking to
draw pictures of and plans for houses when they were very

young children. Charles, a 21-year-old masculine homosexual
studying business administration, began advising his affluent
parents at age thirteen on designs for a new house which was
being planned. At first his parents dismissed his advice as
childish prattle, but soon became aware that his suggestions
were quite sound. In his early teens he continued advising
his parents not only on the design of the house but upon the
interior as well. By the age of 15 his parents were seriously
relying upon him to decorate their new and expensive home.
While architecture cannot be considered a homosexual profession, there is a strong homosexual presence within it. Homosexuals are not so much interested in the construction, plumbing, and heating, as they are in the designing of the house
itself--both outside and inside. Ray, an architecture student,
reports he is bored by his architectural courses having to do
with structural aspects, but excited by the design courses.
He reports the heterosexual students sense his lack of interest. In a recent group project, Ray was chosen by the other
architecture students in the group to be in charge of design
and color, whereas the heterosexual students took charge of
construction, heating, and plumbing. In addition to the house
itself, the grounds are of considerable interest to homosexu-
als--landscaping, gardening, trees, lawns, flowers, plants--
and accordingly there is a homosexual preference for such
occupations. Homosexuals are interested in houses and buildings of historical interest and are often quite active in the
preservation of such structures. Well-to-do homosexuals are
frequently active in the remodeling of older houses and in the
renovation of older neighborhoods. It is the homosexuals in
many of the larger cities of the United States who have been
active in the renewal of decaying neighborhoods. The most
conspicuous example is that of San Francisco, where homosexuals have been largely responsible for much of the preservation and renovation of deteriorating neighborhoods.

THE ARTS OF EMBELLISHMENT

The embellishment theme is particularly interesting and
important in the homosexual world. The tendency to embellish
refers not so much to creating tangible objects as to making
aesthetically pleasing those objects which already exist. With
respect to magazines, for example, homosexuals are not so likely
to be involved in the manufacture of paper or the machines
which put the pages together as in the writing, illustration,
and design of the magazine. The American gay press is largely male, and in the past few years it has produced numerous
publications of high-quality writing and design. There is a
strong homosexual presence in all occupations which involve
embellishment: graphic design, advertising, illustration. A

respondent in San Francisco, a graphic designer, reported he had a difficult time finding work, in his words "because there were so many gay people in San Francisco." The connection between design and homosexuality is frequently assumed by homosexuals themselves.

While languages are not ordinarily regarded as being associated with homosexuality, there is some evidence to suggest this connection. For example, there is a strong homosexual presence in the teaching of languages, which includes the teaching of foreign languages at the secondary and university levels, as well as the teaching of English to foreign students. Homosexuals sometimes manifest an interest in languages which seems incongruous with the level of their education and the requirements of their work. A 30-year-old Hawaiian respondent, three-fourths Japanese and one-fourth Irish, works as an accountant and does not use foreign languages in his work. Because of his own interest in languages, he has become fluent in Russian, French, and Spanish, in addition to fluency in English and Japanese acquired in the home. Barry, a 21-year-old language student, is already fluent in Russian, Italian, French, and Spanish. Adam is a 22-year-old linguist and poet-translator who speaks and works in six languages, including the difficult art of translating Japanese poetry into English.

Travel, perhaps related to the language theme, is a prominent topic of homosexual conversation and interests. There are many homosexuals involved in the travel and hotel industries. Homosexual oriented travel magazines and other more general homosexual periodicals frequently feature articles on travel and foreign countries. While this is in part a function of affluence in American society, homosexuals in less affluent countries spend a good bit of time thinking and dreaming about travel in foreign countries. One occupation which is especially popular among homosexuals in all societies studied is that of flight attendant for the airlines. Jobs with international carriers are valued highly. An article in Christopher Street openly discusses the high incidence of homosexuals among flight attendants (Hughes 1978, p. 30). One respondent, an airline pilot, reports he is attracted to male flight attendants, but feels he must restrain his sexual interests because everyone who works for the airlines knows that many attendants are homosexual, and he does not want to be known as homosexual for fear of losing his job. Pilots are predominantly heterosexuals. Still another respondent, himself homosexual, was in charge of a training program for a major airline and had processed 500 male flight attendants. He estimated 75 percent of the 500 were homosexual.

As has been noted, many homosexuals are found in traditional occupations and professions such as doctor, lawyer, teacher, and businessman. Yet even in such occupations sex-

ual orientation seems to give a predictable twist to the arrangement within these businesses and professions. For example, in
the medical profession homosexuals are more likely to be pedia-
tricians, psychiatrists, and dermatologists than surgeons.
Homosexual lawyers are more likely to be real estate lawyers
than criminal lawyers. Homosexual professors are more likely
to be found in helping professions such as social work or
counseling than in physics or chemistry. Homosexual business-
men are more likely to be in real estate, restaurants, gift
shops, and bookstores than heavy appliance stores, automobile
dealerships, or manufacturing. In Laguna Beach, California,
where one-third of the population is homosexual, most of the
gift shops, bookstores, restaurants, record stores, and antique
shops are owned or operated by homosexuals, while service
stations, automobile dealerships, and supermarkets generally
are owned by heterosexuals. The division of labor in the homosexual summer communities of Cherry Grove and the Pines on
Fire Island is even more striking. About 90 percent of the
residents of these two communities are male homosexuals, about
5 percent lesbians, and about 5 percent heterosexual families.
Fire Island is a narrow island off the southern coast of Long
Island, some 30 miles long and a quarter of a mile wide. There
are no automobiles and few commercial establishments. In the
homosexual communities of the Pines and Cherry Grove there
are no more than 25 commercial establishments. The restaurants,
gift shop, flower shop, ice cream shop, discos, and bars are
owned or operated by homosexuals, while heterosexuals control
the supermarkets, liquor stores, and appliance stores. Large
appliances, such as stoves and refrigerators, are sold and
installed by heterosexuals. Plumbing and heavy carpentry are
generally done by heterosexuals. The ferry boats which connect Fire Island and Long Island are maintained and operated
by heterosexuals. The taxi boats which connect the several
communities on Fire Island with each other are also operated
by heterosexuals. In São Paulo, where many homosexuals work
in a large Ford plant, there is a standing joke among homosexuals themselves about the large number of homosexuals who
work with the interior and upholstery of automobiles rather
than with the mechanical aspects.

ENTERTAINMENT AND THE ARTS

Observation of homosexual subcultures in all four societies
confirms a strong interest in entertainment and the arts and
such a connection is widely assumed in all four homosexual
subcultures. In the United States, for example, The Advocate,
probably the most widely read gay publication, devotes extensive coverage to the arts, movie reviews, interviews with gay
painters, writers, and actors. Nearly all gay publications such

as Blueboy, Christopher Street, and The Sentinel reflect very
strong interests in the theater and the arts. For example, the
San Francisco Sentinel is a general gay newspaper, well written and edited. The format usually consists of two sections,
of which the second half is devoted entirely to entertainment
and the arts. There is no sports section. Conversations in
the gay world frequently focus on the arts and entertainment.
When dance troupes perform in smaller cities, blanket invita-
tions to the entire company are sometimes issued by affluent
homosexuals with the expectation that most of the male dancers
will be homosexual. For example, in 1979 when the San Francisco Ballet visited and performed in Honolulu, a cocktail party
designed to raise funds for the arts was held at Hamburger
Mary's, the leading gay bar and restaurant in Waikiki. The
members of the dance troupe were guests of honor. While not
all attending were homosexual, the assumption here is that the
connection between the ballet and homosexuality is so close
that a gay bar-restaurant is a perfectly logical place to hold
such an event. In 1979, in connection with the filming of
Can't Stop the Music in the Galeria in San Francisco, extras
were solicited for an elaborate dance scene. So many homosexual men showed up that the scene could not be shot until
several days later when more women could be included. Cult
figures in the entertainment world such as Judy Garland,
Marlene Dietrich, and Bette Midler receive considerable attention in the homosexual press. One such cult figure, Mae West,
observes: "The entire Broadway theater (in the 1920s) was
filled with homosexuals in every creative field from costumes
to playwriting" (West 1959, p. 93). Catherine Deneuve, the
French actress, commenting on the homosexual presence in
movies a half-century later observes: "In France, most of the
actors are homosexual. In England, many are, and the same
in the States; but in most European countries it is a vast
majority" (Haddad 1978, p. 91).

In the Pines and Cherry Grove on Fire Island it is common practice for most of the summer homes to fly flags and
banners of various kinds, often state or national flags honor-
ing visiting guests from other states or countries. When Judy
Garland died, all the flags in Cherry Grove and Pines were
placed at half-mast.

Estimates of the percentages of male homosexuals in several professional dance companies in the United States, Mexico,
Brazil, the Philippines, and Venezuela range from 80 to 100
percent. These estimates refer to the dancers only, although
choreographers, who are usually former dancers, are often
homosexual. Female dancers tend to be heterosexual. In the
Philippines, in situations where traditional folk dances are
performed, both male and female parts are often danced by
male homosexuals, with males cross-dressed for the appropriate female parts. In the Senac restaurant and theater in the

Pelourinho district of Salvador, Bahia, the most famous locale in Brazil for the performance of Bahian folk dancing, all of the 15 male dancers are homosexual, while the female dancers are heterosexual.

Much the same can be said for certain other entertainment forms. The American musical theater, where acting, singing, and dancing are combined, is characterized by a pronounced homosexual presence. The more closely the activity is connected to performance activities--as well as the writing, composition, directing, set design, and costume design--the stronger the homosexual presence. In many respects, the American musical theater can be regarded as virtually a homosexual creation. While much of the American public remains ignorant of such connections, an examination of the sexual orientation of the major figures in the musical theater--actors, singers, dancers, and composers--would reveal far more homosexuals than one would expect by chance. Recent biographies of two of the most celebrated figures in musical theater, Cole Porter and Noel Coward, treat their homosexuality openly. In a large American city, a member of a critics' circle, an organization consisting of the major theater and movie critics, reported that 16 of 20 critics are homosexual. Not all persons in the theater are involved in acting, singing, dancing, and costuming, of course, and the further removed from these activities, the more heterosexual the occupations tend to be. For example, lighting, technical aspects of recording, and carpentry, tend to be heterosexual occupations.

In an analysis of the emergence of the gay theater, Don Shewey writes:

> Doric Wilson described to me the apprehension of gay actors about playing in gay roles and the irony of homophobia in the theater business. "Most of the Broadway is gay-produced, gay theatre. For instance, A Chorus Line is basically the work of a number of gay people. These same gay people, if you say 'gay theatre' to them, immediately think 'second-rate', because somehow gay is second-rate. . . ." [Shewey 1978b, p. 92].

Shewey also describes the birth of Off-Off Broadway theater (1978b, p. 63):

> The accidental birth of Off-Off Broadway is generally attributed to Joe Cino, whose Caffe Cino started out in 1958 as a Bohemian hangout . . . before long the Cino had become a real theatre . . . and from the beginning most--if not all--of the Cino were gay.

Regarding the presence of homosexual women in the theater, Shewey comments (1978a, p. 81):

> Also, I wish I could say that the use of the word 'gay' in this article refers to both men and women. Unfortunately, this is not the case. For reasons attributable partly to the society we live in and partly to the peculiar traditions of the theatre, there has been very little theatre written/created from a lesbian perspective. Gay theatre is as male-dominated as a straight theatre . . . although a great many women are employed in powerful (if unglamorous) technical and administrative theatre jobs, women playwrights are sadly scarce (Shewey 1978a, p. 81).

The entire issue of Christopher Street for June 1978 was given over to analysis of gay theater. This magazine reported that gay theater is developing so rapidly that a national organization has been established for gay theater groups to keep in touch. Helbing states, "At the rate gay theater groups are proliferating, they will need to keep in touch with one another to share ideas and experiences (1978, p. 8). Helging adds that since February 6, 1973 one gay Off-Broadway theater had produced over 20 plays as well as cabarets and lectures and that in San Francisco new companies seem to form almost every week.

There is a remarkable homosexual presence at every level from Broadway to small theatrical companies around the country. Homosexuals appear not only to be important in creating entertainment forms for the heterosexual world-at-large, but simultaneously produce entertainment forms specifically for homosexual audiences. This connection holds cross-culturally. For example, in Guatemala City 32 of 35 males in a semi-professional acting company are homosexual. Similarly, among Brazil's homosexuals there is a very strong interest in the arts and entertainment. The gay nightclubs of São Paulo have produced a unique entertainment genre, a musical revue, with singing, acting, dancing, and especially elaborate costumes. In 1976, the homosexual presence in the Brazilian television industry was so pervasive as to provoke a national cause célèbre, resulting in an order by the ministry of communications prohibiting the hiring of homosexuals. The Brazilian magazine Lampião is dominated by articles about the arts and entertainment.

Latin American homosexuals have their own collection of actress-cult figures, who in appearance and characterization resemble some of the American figures. Mercedes Carreño is a Mexican actress/sex symbol who performs in B-grade movies, where she is typically lost in the jungle and raped by escaped convicts. Isabel Sarli, an Argentine sex goddess, is also popular with Latin American homosexuals. A Guatemalan respondent offered, "If I were a woman I would like to be Mercedes Carreno or Isabel Sarli." Teri Velasquez and Fanny Cano, both popular with Latin American homosexuals, make films in which they portray prostitutes-with-hearts-of-gold or bad women who marry rich and respectable men. Sara Montiel was the Spanish sex symbol in the 1950s and early 1960s who typically played the poor but beautiful and talented singer, discovered in a tawdry nightclub, promoted to fame and riches by a love-stricken impresario.

The Latin Americans are of course familiar with European and American as well as Spanish and Latin American stars and movies. Liza Minelli in the 1970s was especially popular in Guatemala. A middle-class Guatemalan homosexual respondent described the opening of the movie <u>Cabaret</u>:

> On New Year's Day 'Cabaret' opened in Guatemala City. All the queens in Guatemala went. My best friend Rudy Ochoa bought the record, and learned all the words. There were 'Cabaret' parties where the music from 'Cabaret' was played and people were supposed to come dressed like characters in 'Cabaret.' Several people even went around town with hats and canes dressed like the master of ceremonies. One person I know from a wealthy family went to a tailor and had an entire cabaret outfit made.

That this interest in entertainment is not superficial is suggested by comments of Brazilian homosexuals in response to questions about occupational interests:

> My first association with the gay world was when I began to participate in an amateur theatrical group. There were many homosexuals in the group. One young man declared his love for me. I didn't accept it at first, but later did.
>
> I would like to be a model or actor as I have the height, posture, and I am thinking about trying to be a model but am not sure whether I will be successful.
>
> For two years I did try acting on television, but it didn't work out.
>
> When I go to the theatre, I always think that I would like to be up there acting.
>
> I was always interested in acting. When I was in my early teens, I wrote off to the United States for movie star photos, and pasted them all over my room.

> I have always wanted to be an actor; even
> now I would like to be an actor. I always
> thought about being on the stage. Even now
> I think about it.

Homosexuals figure prominently in the dances of the Brazilian
carnaval. The Baile de Enxutos in the Cine São José is exclusively homosexual, attended by some 5,000 costumed participants. Some are dressed as men but many as women in elegant, expensive fantasias. The homosexual presence is impres-
sive in all activities connected with carnaval--parades, dances,
and costume contests. According to a Brazilian respondent,
"carnaval is the time of year you see the most homosexuals.
The clubs are full of queens dressed in outrageous costumes.
You can do anything you want to during this time and nothing will happen to you."

The Filipino homosexuals similarly are widely involved in
entertainment. They follow closely both Filipino and American
films. The prolific Filipino film industry employs many homosexuals, including some of the country's leading actors, directors, and writers. Many Filipino movies feature homosexuals
in character roles, usually quite sympathetically. While many
of these roles are comic parts, homosexuals are shown in the
context of everyday life, as friends of (or even protected by)
the main characters, not as murderers and psychopaths as is
often the case in American films. The homosexual character
parts are very popular with the Philippine audiences, especially children, who are delighted by and applaud their appear-
ances.

In the late 1970s, in Manila, one of the most popular television programs was an amateur show open to the public in
which anyone might appear as a singer or miming popular
singers. So many male homosexuals appeared on the program
that the directors had to announce to the public that the
program was for everyone, not just homosexuals.

The Cebuano homosexuals are quite active in the dramatic
arts. A theatrical group was formed by the Cebuano bayot
several years ago. The Boys in the Band was translated into
Cebuano by them and was performed with great success. One
of the most interesting aspects of this production was that
Cebuanos were able to translate every nuance of American
homosexual conversation and argot into Cebuano. Because
most high schools in Cebu do not have full-time drama teachers or programs, part-time people are hired from outside the
school system to direct dramatic programs. These programs,
as well as neighborhood dramatic productions, are usually
directed by homosexuals, who write, direct, and costume the
plays. The transvestic homosexuals in the Philippines have
developed the female impersonation beauty contest as a form
of entertainment. These are performed all over the Philippines

and are especially popular in the working class neighborhoods and smaller cities and towns.

The connection between entertainment and homosexuals is not limited to the four societies studied. It is widely held among American homosexuals that the reason for the defection of Soviet dancers is because of their homosexuality and a desire for more personal as well as artistic freedom. That there is a strong homosexual presence in Soviet dance, in much the same way as in the West, is suggested by a Soviet homosexual who writes:

> The ballet world is especially vulnerable to the tactics of the K.G.B. There are so many gays with so much to lose. Everyone is forced to play-act, to get married, and to affirm their loyalty constantly because of their frequent trips abroad. Salaries are small and these trips mean a great deal. . . . In the Kirov company, to my knowledge, every fourth person is an informer. Some are gays who have been caught and are now trying to be loyal and redeem themselves; others are compensating for their fear that they will be caught. The result is a particularly thick poisonous atmosphere, but one which shrouds gay life throughout Russia [Schuvaloff 1976, p. 21].

The connection between homosexuality and the arts in the USSR is not new, as suggested by Lauritsen and Thorstad (1974, p. 68): "In January 1934, mass arrests of gays were carried out in Moscow, Leningrad, Kharkov and Odessa. Among those arrested were a great many actors, musicians, and other artists."

ENTERTAINMENT AND CROSS-GENDER
BEHAVIOR

A remarkable twist to the entertainment function of homosexuals is the role of transvestic homosexuality. Transvestism in the theater often has been mistakenly interpreted as incidental and inconsequential behavior. For example, Money and Tucker (1975, p. 122) write: "An expert actor can play opposite-sex roles. In traditional Japanese theater today men still play all the parts, but to make the performance convincing takes a lot of practice over a long period of time. Before women were allowed on the European stage, many male actors specialized in female roles and performed them well." The implication here is that cross-gender activity on the stage is merely an artifice of expert acting ability. A more plausible interpretation is that the taking of opposite sex roles resulted from the presence of homosexuals in the theater. Many of the Kabuki actors wear female attire off the stage in their daily lives, strongly suggesting a link between transvestic homosexuality and the Kabuki theater. Christopher Street reports that in recent years at least one American gay theater company produced ordinary plays with men taking women's roles (Helbing 1978, pp. 6-7).

Cross-gender roles in the theater appear in various historical epochs and societies. While this is often interpreted as culturally determined, it is important to note that the cross-gender role, in the context of the theater, almost always involves males taking female parts, not vice versa. In examining the attitudes toward homosexuality in seventeenth century England, Burg (1983) discusses the work of William Prynne entitled Historio-Mastix: The Players' Scourge. Published in London in 1633, "Prynne wrote at length of the pernicious influence of the stage and players on public morality." Burg writes:

> Among the many vices he cataloged was the acting of female parts by men and boys. Women were not permitted on the stage in the early decades of the seventeenth century, and this resulted in the encouragement of transvestism among players, both during and after performances. Prynne denounced the practice of males donning female garb for any purpose. He explained such activities were disgusting, revolting, and repugnant, counter to the judgments of both pagan and Christian scholars from earliest recorded history, and contrary to the revealed will of God. It was a wickedness, Prynne explained, of "which my Inke is not black enough to discypher." In addition, men donning the raiment of women encouraged the practice of sodomy he charged. Not only did "Players and Play-haunters in their secret conclaves play the Sodomites," but their effeminate manner and their example encouraged it among the general population. In proper Puritan fashion, Prynne did not ignore the opportunity to denounce sodomy in his excoriation of transvestism among players, and he left no doubt that he considered it lewd, unnatural, abominable, and worse than adultery [1983, pp. 18-19].

This passage suggests that homosexuals were quite active in the theater of the seventeenth century, that they might well have pushed women aside in their eagerness to perform, and that transvestic activity occurred outside the confines of the theater. The allegation that "men donning the raiment of women encouraged the practice of sodomy" probably correctly reflects the connection between cross-dressing and homosexuality, but incorrectly interprets the sequence. Rather than sodomy being caused by men donning the raiment of women, homosexuals, some of whom cross-dressed, whether on or off the stage (or both), practiced sodomy. Prynne's comment on their "effeminate manner" lends credence to this interpretation.

The entertainment complex appears to be connected, directly and indirectly, with homosexual occupations. The activities of costuming, makeup, and hair arrangement, which can be dismissed as part of show business, are in reality closely related to the real-life occupations of fashion design, interior design, and cosmetology. Moreover, interest in arranging hair seems to appear quite early in the childhood experiences of homosexuals; that is, before contact with the homosexual subculture (see Table 4.2). While not all fashion designers and hairdressers are transvestic homosexuals--some are quite masculine--there tends to be a general association between effeminate and transvestic homosexuals and these occupations. Moreover, when they come together in groups, transvestic homosexuals almost inevitably produce shows. While the content of these shows may vary from society to society, all highly transvestic homosexual groups produce an entertainment form as a prominent social activity. The local-born transvestic homosexuals of Honolulu produce a rather elaborate show on Hotel Street, which reflects island music and dance. The transvestic homosexuals of São Paulo produce a unique genre of musical review strongly influenced by the music and costumes of the carnaval. At present, the most popular nationally televised program in Brazil is a program featuring transvestic homosexuals shown at "prime time." The Filipinos have developed the beauty pageant as an entertainment form with its own rather elaborate social organization. It is not accidental that transvestic homosexuals produce entertainment forms. They do not ordinarily produce hospitals, athletic teams, or schools as social creations, but consistently and predictably produce entertainment forms which, in a sense, might be regarded as prototypic.

That the urge to entertain is highly developed in transvestic homosexuals is suggested by both Kando's study of homosexual transsexuals and Newton's observation of the world of female impersonation. Several of Kando's 17 male-to-female transsexual subjects wanted to be actresses. At the time of Kando's interviews, four of the 17 were working as dancers and two as actresses. Thus six out of a total of 17 were actually entertaining. Of the remainder, two were hairdressers, one a waitress, three were secretaries, and one was a research scientist (Kando 1973, p. 25).

In her work on female impersonators in the United States, Newton (1972, p. 7) recognizes the entertainment aspects of transvestic homosexuality when she writes, "Female impersonators form an illegitimate junction of the homosexual and show business subcultures: they can be considered as performing homosexuals or homosexual performers."

The various elements of the arts and entertainment are sometimes combined in unusual ways in the personality of individual homosexuals, creating what might be regarded as a unique combination and arrangement of elements which are probably found only, and then only rarely, in a single homosexual personality. The career of Darcy Penteado, one of Brazil's leading artists, openly homosexual, illustrates such genius. When a child, he created with his two younger brothers a theater that combined marionettes and clothes, and which developed into a popular traveling theater, giving performances in schools and homes. Later he produced these shows for children's television programs, with special performances at the Museum of Modern Art of São Paulo. At 16 he worked as an illustrator and copyist of parts in a stove factory. At the same time he tried his hand at designing women's clothes, without commercial success. At 18 he worked on a humor magazine, doing illustrations, designs, caricatures, and cartoons. At 19 he designed book covers and did illustrations for children's books. At 22 he held his first exposition of paintings. At 27 he achieved one of his ambitions and produced an avant-garde fashion show for an exclusive women's club. At 28 he wrote and illustrated a book for children about producing plays. At the same time he was writing popular articles about fashion in leading magazines in Brazil. In his mature years he designed innumerable sets and costumes for television and theater, won a prize for the design of an album cover, worked as a professional illustrator, painted and held national and international exhibitions, worked as a portraitist, wrote several novels and books of poetry, wrote for the women's and literary sections of São Paulo's leading newspapers, and wrote several plays which have been produced on stage (Penteado 1976, pp. 9-10).

While there are some views in American gay political circles and in social-scientific communities which deny the relationship between homosexuality and female impersonation, there is no doubt that such persons are usually homosexual in their sexual orientation and have long regarded themselves as part of the homosexual subculture. Newton (1972, p. 20) writes: "Female impersonators are an integral part of the homosexual subculture, and yet collectively they are a separate group within it. Many of these most distinctive characteristics and problems of female impersonators as a group spring from their membership in the homosexual subculture on the one hand, and their special relationship to it on the other."

TABLE 4.2 As a Child Did You Like to Comb or Arrange the Hair of Your Mother, Sister, or Female Friends?

| | Brazil | | | | Philippines | | | | United States | | | |
| | Heterosexual | | Homosexual | | Heterosexual | | Homosexual | | Heterosexual | | Homosexual | |
	N	%	N	%	N	%	N	%	N	%	N	%
Yes	2	13	14	61	1	3	24	80	3	5	8	22
No	14	87	9	39	33	97	6	20	55	95	28	78
Total	16	100	23	100	34	100	30	100	58	100	36	100

Brazil: $X^2 = 9.1245$, $p = 0.0023$

Philippines: $X^2 = 39.7576$, $p = 0.0000$

United States: $X^2_c = 4.7081$, $p = 0.0299$

TABLE 4.3 As a Child Did You Want to be a Movie Actor?

| | Brazil | | | | Philippines | | | | United States | | | |
| | Heterosexual | | Homosexual | | Heterosexual | | Homosexual | | Heterosexual | | Homosexual | |
	N	%	N	%	N	%	N	%	N	%	N	%
Yes	6	38	17	74	11	32	22	73	18	31	18	50
No	10	62	6	26	23	68	8	27	40	69	18	50
Total	16	100	23	100	34	100	30	100	58	100	36	100

Brazil: $X^2 = 5.1710$, $p = 0.0228$

Philippines: $X^2 = 10.7166$, $p = 0.0009$

United States: $X^2 = 3.3811$, $p = 0.0661$

Filipino homosexuals assume that the linkage between cross-dressing, female impersonation, and homosexual orientation is so close that they do not have a separate conceptual category for transvestite. It is assumed to be perfectly normal behavior for homosexuals, especially effeminate homosexuals, to cross-dress. The masculine Brazilian homosexuals tend to have cordial relations with the transvestic homosexuals and recognize them as an integral part of the Brazilian homosexual world. Recently, however, the Brazilian magazine Lampião has featured so much material having to do with travestis that the usually tolerant masculine homosexuals have begun to complain.

Table 4.3 summarizes responses to the questions: "As a child did you want to be a movie star or actor/actress or did you think that when you grew up you would be a movie star or actor/actress?" Data in this table suggest that interest in acting appears very early in childhood, long before there is any contact with the gay subculture. While the data reported here are retrospective, Green and Money (1966) have noted that effeminate boys have an extraordinary interest in acting. On the basis of observation of children who exhibit persistent cross-gender behavior, Green and Money (1966, p. 30) conclude that "their acting interest emerged prior to their awareness of the link between homosexuality and the theatre. . . . These findings suggest that the high incidence of homosexuality in the theater is not due solely to the theater offering them a social haven during adulthood but that play-acting may reflect basic personality traits present since boyhood."

Stoller (1968, p. 127-28) reports on the exceptional artistic and entertainment abilities of three highly feminine four- to five-year-old boys with whom he worked. He describes these boys as follows:

> The artistic ability (creativity) all three showed became apparent to their mothers by age three and was immediately discovered by their teachers as soon as they entered nursery school. The following are reported by these mothers (and confirmed by others).
> Heightened sensitivity to perception: Each boy has been entranced with sight (colors, patterns, painted pictures); hearing (music and other harmonious or rhythmical sounds); and touch (by the feeling of materials, especially cloth textures, but including other touching and handling of animate and inanimate objects). In addition, all are reported to respond intensely to sounds and smells that are not even noticed by others.
> Painting: All have shown precocious ability with paints and other coloring materials, not only

in the flamboyant use of colors but also in imaginative, well-formed objects expansively placed on the paper and telling an understandable story.

Dancing and mime: All improvise graceful dances to music, in one case performed before audiences; in addition, they enjoy making light, tender and feminine gestures during play to enhance the reality of the make-believe.

Creative writing: In the years before they have learned to write, these children are nonetheless telling original stories to audiences and creating plays, which they also produce and direct with siblings and friends before audiences.

Acting: This is not merely imitative (though imitation is keenly developed) but, like the dancing, skillfully and enthusiastically improvised.

'Designing' of clothes, jewelry, hair styles, makeup: While these talents are rudimentary, the ardor with which the children watch and critically evaluate related displays of their mothers' femininity have astonished (and, unfortunately, thrilled) all three mothers. The boys are constantly giving their mothers advice, and the mothers consider their sons' taste better than many adults', and comment on the originality of the boys' suggestions for modish style.

Stoller concludes: "The qualities these boys express, taken en masse, seem to be beyond the powers of most normal children."

Using rather large samples from the Chicago area (Chicago Gay Nonstudents N = 1453; Chicago Gay Students N = 87; DeKalb Gay Students N = 31; DeKalb Nongay Students N = 203), Harry (1982, p. 64) found "a sizable association between childhood cross-gendering and persistent acting interest." He reports:

Among those with no childhood cross-gendering 54 percent had no acting interests as compared with 24 percent among those highly cross-gendered during childhood. Hence, it would appear that the inclusion in our gay samples of persons who were not cross-gendered during childhood reduces or eliminates the gay-heterosexual differences. This is borne out by the fact that, if we exclude from the analysis those

> gay respondents who were not cross-gendered
> during childhood . . . a significant difference
> between the heterosexuals and the three gay
> groups combined appears. . . . There are no
> significant differences on this measure among
> the three gay groups.

Thus it appears likely that interest in acting is linked not merely to homosexual orientation, but more specifically to the cross-gendering process.

STEREOTYPES AND THE HOMOSEXUAL SUBCULTURE

Regularities which appear in the homosexual subculture are frequently seen by sociologists as the result of stereotyping by the heterosexual world. For example, Farrell and Nelson (1976, pp. 109-10) suggest: "If one perceives others identifying him as a homosexual and reacting to him in accordance with the popular stereotype, his self-definition may incorporate the stereotype. These responses and accompanied feelings of stigma are likely to be experienced with frustration, bitterness, withdrawal into a homosexual group, and enculturation to a deviant role may be the outcome."

Indeed the labeling perspective in sociology tends to view the homosexual subculture in its entirety as nothing more than the creation of the heterosexual world. One variation of such a view is examplified by Simmons' influential analysis of deviant subcultures. Simmons (1978, p. 280) writes, "In . . . indirect ways society's condemnation 'creates' the deviant subculture. When disapproval eases, the 'subculture' may attenuate or even disintegrate."

A still slightly different variation of this general idea is proposed by Kitsuse (1978, p. 17) who proceeds upon the principle that "it is only when individuals are defined and identified by others as homosexuals and accorded the treatment considered 'appropriate' for individuals so defined that a homosexual 'population' is produced for sociological investigation."

Of course, while it is true that the labeling process, especially in terms of laws and police enforcement, impinges on the lives of homosexuals, available evidence does not suggest that the homosexual subculture is a creation of the dominant society. The labeling perspective ignores a substantial body of material which has emerged in the past few years which suggests that the homosexual orientation and gender identity emerge quite early (Bieber et al. 1962; Zuger 1966; Zuger and Taylor 1969; Green 1974, Green 1976; Whitam 1977), long before the alleged labeling process takes place. Furthermore, this line of research has produced evidence which suggests the early emergence of sexual orientation is much the same from society to society (Whitam 1980b).

Thus, some of the behavior which gives the homosexual subculture its distinctive characteristics is already beginning to manifest itself in homosexual children and adolescents before contact with the homosexual subculture. Such evidence suggests that such social forms as entertainment have strong intrinsic links to sexual orientation and early cross-gender behavior. Homosexual orientation and cross-gender behavior, as we have seen, are closely linked. Both the genital and gender manifestation of homosexuality, which are frequently the object of negative sanctions by the larger society, are closely related to positive functions which homosexuals perform for the society at large. While it is not possible to say precisely what the shape of entertainment and the arts would be like without the homosexual presence, it is safe to say they would be greatly attenuated.

We have thus far seen that a small percentage of homosexual persons appear in all societies, and that sexual orientation, appearing very early, eventually produces homosexual subcultures which tend to have many of the same behavioral elements, regardless of the more general culture. Such behavioral elements as embellishment, entertainment, and the arts, are not merely stereotypes created by the larger society, but are socially useful activities which homosexuals provide for the larger society because of, not despite, their sexual orientation.

5

THE PUZZLE OF ATHLETICS

During the 1950s, the idea that homosexuals are different from other people only in their choice of sex object was popularized by the work of Kinsey and his associates (1948), who conceived of sexual orientation as nothing more than a point on a sexual continuum. According to this view people cannot be characterized as either homosexual or heterosexual, but as having sexual experiences which fall between the polar points of the continuum. This idea has become influential in the social sciences, and it has led to neglect in the exploration of sexual orientation as a sociological variable affecting human behavior. This chapter deals with the way in which sexual orientation shapes athletic interests, a topic frequently debated but insufficiently assessed scientifically.

In 1975, Lynn Rosellini, reporter for The Washington Star, wrote a series of articles claiming that several male professional athletes were either homosexual or bisexual (Garner and Smith 1977). This assertion evoked angry reactions from sports fans, which were intensified when David Kopay, an ex-running back for the San Francisco Forty-niners, Detroit Lions, Washington Redskins, New Orleans Saints, and Green Bay Packers, publicly revealed his homosexuality (Kopay and Young 1977). Such an admission contradicted the ideal of the virile athlete, especially that of the professional football idol.

One of the few empirical studies of the relationship between sexual orientation and athletic behavior is that of Garner and Smith (1977), who surveyed male university athletes in an unspecified sport in order to determine the extent of their homosexual activities. These researchers found higher than expected levels of homosexual experience among athletes in this varsity sport. Garner and Smith have never publicly revealed the particular sport studied and as we shall see, since the <u>type</u> of sport seems to be linked with sexual orientation, the implication of their findings cannot be accurately assessed without knowing which sport was studied.

ATHLETIC INTERESTS OF MALES

Saghir and Robins (1973) found distinct differences in the leisure interests of heterosexual and homosexual men. The majority of homosexual men were found to have no interest in participating in or viewing such national sports as football and baseball, and they were more interested in noncontact sports such as swimming, tennis, and skiing. Two-thirds of the heterosexual men were interested in team sports, while only 10 percent of their homosexual counterparts reported a similar interest. Homosexual men also reported more interest in artistic pursuits than did their heterosexual counterparts.

Bell, Weinberg, and Hammersmith (1981, pp. 12-13) report on a sample of 575 white homosexual men and a comparison group of 284 white heterosexual men in San Francisco. Oddly enough, these researchers throughout most of the analysis report on white heterosexual and homosexual males, for the most part ignoring sizable groups of black respondents. With regard to the white homosexual males (WHMs) and white heterosexual males (WHTMs) these researchers write:

> We found several differences between the white homosexual men (WHMs) and the white heterosexual men (WHTMs) in our study with respect to their childhood interests and activities.
>
> Far fewer homosexual than heterosexual men reported having enjoyed boys' activities (e.g. baseball, football) 'very much' (WHMs: 11%, WHTMs 70%).
>
> A minority of the respondents, homosexual or heterosexual, said they had enjoyed sterotypical girls' activities 'somewhat' or 'very much' (e.g. playing house, hop-scotch, jacks); these responses however, were given by more homosexual than heterosexual men (WHMs: 46%, WHTMs: 11%).
>
> The homosexual and the heterosexual men also differed in the extent to which they enjoyed activities less strongly associated with gender (e.g. drawing, music, reading). Twice as many homosexual as heterosexual men reported having enjoyed such solitary activities 'very much' (WHIMs: 68%, WHTMs: 34%) [1981, pp. 75-76].

Harry (1982) in a study done in Chicago, using an even larger sample of homosexual men than Bell, Weinberg, and Hammersmith, found similar differences between homosexual and heterosexual men with regard to athletic interests. Using three samples of homosexual men: a large group of 1,434 who responded to questionnaires left in gay bars and other places in Chicago, a group of 89 gay students in Chicago, and a group of 32 gay students in De Kalb, Illinois; and using a comparison group of 204 heterosexual male students from De Kalb, Harry reports, "There are no significant differences among the three gay groups . . . and the only notable difference is that between the three gay groups combined and the heterosexuals" (p. 116).

While many observers and researchers deny any connection between sexual orientation and athletics, homosexuals themselves often acknowledge that there are group differences between homosexuals and heterosexuals, at least with respect to certain behaviors: sports, leisure time activities, and occupational choice. Even some gay liberationists, who are critical of macho male activities and who probably correctly view sports as being tied into the repressive political and military aspects of male heterosexuality, observe that gay males are less athletic than heterosexual males. For example, John Mitzel (1973, p. 16) writes in Gay Sunshine: A Journal of Gay Liberation: "Opposite to the majority culture of repressed macho straights, gay males have virtually no interest in organized competitive sports. Of course there is a certain interest in superstar professional athletes themselves, partly as conversation items resulting from the massive publicity given them, partly because they are attractive, well-built men who are presented as symbols of sexual potency."

Male homosexual communities do not, as a rule, produce extensive athletic organizations. In large populations of homosexual males such as in San Francisco, athletic homosexuals exist in sufficient number to field a softball team or even to sponsor such events as the Gay Olympics in the summer of 1982. On the whole, however, male homosexual communities do not manifest a substantial interest in athletics or such traditionally masculine leisure-time activities as hunting and fishing. Perhaps the most common complaint gay men have about their childhoods is that of the conflict between fathers and sons because of the sons' lack of interest in athletics and other traditionally masculine pursuits. Examination of the homosexual press, which is largely male dominated, reveals enormous interest in entertainment and the arts and virtually no interest in athletics. As noted in the Chapter 4 discussion on homosexuals and the arts, the San Francisco Sentinel devotes half of each edition to entertainment and the arts and does not contain a sports section. While New Year's Day finds most males in the United States at television sets watching football bowl games, at a gay 1978 New Year's Day party in Los Angeles only six gay men out of some 200 were watching football. The remaining 194 were talking, partying, and drinking, with very little interest in the bowl games evident (field notes 1978).

Three anecdotes reveal the attitudes of (at least many) gay men toward athletics and other traditionally masculine behavior. Joe is tall and lanky, built along the lines of a "typical" basketball player. He has never been interested in basketball but is an excellent swimmer. He was asked to participate in a film being made for the general public by a gay-related group in San Francisco which was attempting to dispel the "stereotype" that homosexuals are not athletic. The filmmaker had gathered a group of some ten similarly built "basketball types." Joe reported that he thought the movie was somewhat deceptive since none of the men chosen were interested in basketball. Some of the gay men appearing in the film made disparaging remarks about it since they felt most gay men were not enthusiastically interested in basketball.

Jim was walking with two of his gay friends near a university when a female student with car trouble ran up and asked them to take a look at her engine because it wouldn't start. The three looked at each other and replied in unison, "We don't know anything about cars." Out of hearing distance, they laughed and agreed the female student had mistaken them for heterosexuals, implying that if she had known of their homosexual orientation she wouldn't have expected them to know anything about cars.

João, a Brazilian homosexual respondent who was very much interested in soccer and played every weekend for the team sponsored by the bank in which he worked, underwent considerable teasing and even ridicule by his turma, or clique of homosexual friends (few of whom were interested in sports) because of his athletic interests. They accused him of trying to be falsely macho to impress people.

When the questionnaire was first administered to the Filipino male homosexuals, they insisted that volleyball be inserted in the checklist on athletic interest, because this was the bayot (homosexual) sport in the Philippines. The Philippine homosexuals, especially the more effeminate bayot, have also developed a type of camp basketball which they play as an entertainment for the general public. They play it in effeminate clothes, makeup and use exaggerated feminine gestures in throwing the ball or running, eliciting audience laughter. It is played in a self-mocking manner, exaggerating their ineptitude in this sport.

ATHLETIC INTERESTS OF FEMALES

While social scientists often dismiss the strong athletic interests of lesbians as false stereotyping, lesbians themselves talk openly about them. For example, Gagnon and Simon (1973, p. 178) conclude that the "female homosexual follows conventional feminine patterns in developing her commitment to sexuality and in conducting not only her sexual career but her nonsexual career as well." Similarly, Rosen (1974, p. 65) contends that the "only difference between the lesbian and other women is the choice of love object." Saghir and Robins (1973, p. 312) found homosexual women very similar to homosexual men in their leisure interests. They write: "Homosexual women show no significant preference for team sports. . . . In their leisure interests, homosexual women, like homosexual men, prefer predominantly individual sports and artistically oriented hobbies."

Reporting on 229 white homosexual females (WHFs) and 101 white heterosexual females (WHTFs) in their San Francisco sample, Bell, Weinberg, and Hammersmith found homosexual females to have significantly higher levels of interest in athletics and traditional male activities than did heterosexual females. These researchers summarize their conclusions as follows:

> Fewer of the homosexual than of the heterosexual women said they enjoyed typical girls' activities (e.g., playing house, hopscotch, or jacks) very much more (WHFs: 13%, WHTFs: 55%).
> More of the homosexual respondents said they enjoyed typical boys' activities (e.g. baseball, football) very much (WHFs: 71%, WHTFs: 28%).
> About half the homosexual women, but very few of the heterosexual women, recalled having worn boys' clothes and pretended to be a boy, excluding such occasions as Halloween and school plays (WHFs: 49%, WHTFs: 7%).
> The homosexual and the heterosexual women did not differ with regard to their enjoyment of activities that are less strongly associated with gender (e.g. drawing, music, reading).
> These comparisons, then, corroborate the findings of other investigators that prehomosexual girls are much more likely than preheterosexual girls to display gender nonconformity in their play activities [1981, p. 147].

In Phoenix, according to estimates by lesbians themselves, some 50 percent of the members of the women's softball league are lesbians, and they traditionally gather in a favorite lesbian bar after the games. A lesbian professional golfer estimated that half of the professional women golfers in the United States are lesbians, and she discussed in some detail a schism which emerged between the lesbians and heterosexual women on professional golf circuits. One of the most common jokes among lesbians has to do with the large proportion of women's physical education teachers who are lesbian. Allusions to this fact are common, even trite, in lesbian conversations. One lesbian respondent, now a physical education teacher, won the women's amateur golf tournament at the age of 14 in a city of some 200,000. Such precocious athletic interests and achievements by lesbians are quite common. In interviewing a group of six professionally employed lesbians about their athletic interests, the conversation turned toward the topic of wrestling and a discussion of who could outwrestle whom. Lesbians seem to be prominent in the areas of police and military activity, which are related in complex ways to athletic activity. It is commonly acknowledged and widely discussed by lesbians who have been in the armed services that a large proportion of women in the military are lesbian. Pat Bond, a lesbian who became well-known as a result of her appearance in the gay-produced movie The Word is Out and subsequent nightclub acts, openly discusses the purge of large numbers of lesbians from the U.S. Army in Japan after World War II (Berube 1983). Six women were hired several years ago to serve on the police force of Boise, Idaho. All six were lesbians, and all six were fired when this fact became known through the tapping of telephones.

CROSS-CULTURAL ASPECTS OF
ATHLETIC INTERESTS

While the question of the relationship of sexual orientation to athletics is interesting in its own right, perhaps more important is examining its implications for our general understanding of gender identity. If significant patterns of cross-gender behavior occur in homosexual populations without socialization into these patterns, as seems to be the case, then we have some insight into the sources of gender-related behavior in heterosexual males and females. It is commonly assumed by social scientists that interest in either athletics or entertainment is purely social in nature and that any differences between males and females with respect to interests in these activities is entirely a result of socialization. However, the universal interest occurring cross-culturally manifested by heterosexual males as a group in aggressive, contact team sports seems to argue against the contention that the interest in athletics manifested by heterosexual males is purely social in nature. If similar patterns of cross-gender behavior occur among homosexuals in different societies, as is the case (Whitam 1980b and 1984), this too suggests something other than a purely socially derived basis for certain gender-related activities, the most conspicuous of which are athletics and entertainment. If lesbians in all societies manifest strong athletic interests and male homosexuals weak athletic interests, this would then represent evidence for a nonsocially derived basis for these differences. Since these interests seem to appear quite early, often before puberty, and since they appear in widely different societies, it would stretch beyond reason the contention that these patterns can only be socially derived and culturally transmitted. Moreover, the physiological basis of athletics and other aggressive activities are well established in the physical sciences, though many social scientists ignore these findings.

One of the gratifying aspects of interviewing in the third world is that respondents do not know the response that is ideologically correct in terms of contemporary western social scientific, gay liberationist, or feminist thought. Homosexuals in the provincial cities and rural areas of other countries have little idea what homosexuals in the United States are like and how they behave. For example, the bayot of Cebu were surprised to learn that American homosexuals have leather and western macho type bars and attire. Many Filipino lesbians do not realize there are lesbians in the United States.

In an attempt to clarify the relationship between athletic interests and sexual orientation, several items bearing on this topic are presented in Tables 5.1 through 5.8. In order to bring these data into clearer focus, lesbian materials have been introduced. These data are part of an on-going, cross-cultural parallel study of female homosexuality not yet completed. Only female data from the United States and the Philippines are available. Because controversy has frequently centered upon whether or not lesbians are athletic, preliminary findings are offered here. Findings from several groups are presented: American male and female heterosexuals and homosexuals, Brazilian male heterosexuals and homosexuals, Filipino male and female heterosexuals and homosexuals.

American lesbian respondents consisted of a largely middle-class professional group in Phoenix. The comparative sample of heterosexual females consisted of sociology students at Arizona State University. Lesbian responses in the Philippines were obtained in the summer of 1981 in Cebu City with the help of two female sociology-anthropology majors experienced in interviewing. These respondents were obtained from working-class and middle-class neighborhoods where the students had previously done survey research work. The comparative group of heterosexual females consisted of students at Teacher's College, University of San Carlos, in Cebu City. The responses analyzed here consist of those on the questionnaire directly or indirectly related to athletic activity. Responses shown in Tables 5.1 through 5.4 are directly related to athletic activity. Tables 5.1 and 5.2 summarize retrospectively reported "degree of participation in sports" as a child and "type of sports" in which respondents participated as a child or adolescent. Tables 5.3 and 5.4 are "forced-choice" items related to attitudes toward sports at the time of the interview. Table 5.3 summarizes responses to the question: "If you were forced to participate in one of the following sports, which would you choose: Football, Baseball, Basketball, Wrestling, Gymnastics, Swimming?" Table 5.4 summarizes responses to the question: "If you had an expense paid vacation with friends, where would you choose to go? Hunting, Fishing, Golfing, Beach, Skiing?" In the Philippine version of the questionnaire, water-skiing was substituted for skiing since snow-skiing is so remote from the experiences of the Filipinos. The advantage of the forced-choice type of item is that it enables us to hold constant such variables as social class and economic access and to measure personal desires without respect to whether the respondent has actually experienced an activity. It measures what the respondent would prefer doing if he or she had the opportunity. By forcing and limiting choices to the same several alternatives in various societies, the forced-choice item allows us to hold constant the variable of culture. Furthermore, this type of item may serve as a check on retrospectively recalled data.

Three tables (5.5, 5.6, and 5.7) reflect athletic interests more indirectly. Table 5.5 summarizes responses to the question: "As a child, were you regarded as a sissy or tomboy?" Tables 5.6 and 5.7 show responses to the questions, "As a child, were you afraid of being physically hurt as in rough and tumble sports, diving from high places, etc.?" and "As a child, did you like fighting (physically) with other children?" Table 5.8 summarizes responses to a forced-choice item on occupational preferences. Two of the occupations--clerk in a hardware store and service station attendant--are traditionally male occupations, while the other three are sex-neutral.

Several general conclusions are obvious from an examination of these tables. On nearly all items, lesbians indicate higher levels of athletic interests than do heterosexual females. Homosexual males indicate lower levels of athletic interest than heterosexual males on all items. In fact, the patterns of athletic interests of homosexual males seem to be generally similar to those of heterosexual females, and the patterns of athletic interest of lesbians resemble those of heterosexual males. Particularly important is the type of sport. Physically aggressive, contact team sports seem to be avoided by homosexual males and preferred by heterosexual males. Lesbians seem to indicate preference for physically aggressive, contact sports

TABLE 5.1   As a Child Did You Participate in Sports?

	Male				Female			
	Heterosexual		Homosexual		Heterosexual		Homosexual	
	N	%	N	%	N	%	N	%
Brazil								
Yes, very much	9	56	7	30				
Somewhat	7	44	6	26				
No	0	--	10	44				
Total	16	100	23	100				

$$X^2 = 9.37245$$
$$\underline{p} = 0.0092$$

	Male				Female			
Philippines								
Yes, very much	25	74	8	27	7	21	20	62
Somewhat	8	24	15	50	22	67	7	22
No	1	3	7	23	4	12	5	16
Total	34	101	30	100	33	100	32	100

$$X^2 = 15.19737 \qquad X^2 = 14.11694$$
$$\underline{p} = 0.0005 \qquad \underline{p} = 0.0009$$

	Male				Female			
United States								
Yes, very much	39	67	9	25	26	58	32	82
Somewhat	14	24	21	58	16	36	7	18
No	5	9	6	17	3	7	0	--
Total	58	100	36	100	45	101	39	100

$$X^2 = 15.96654 \qquad X^2 = 6.74829$$
$$\underline{p} = 0.0003 \qquad \underline{p} = 0.0342$$

TABLE 5.2 As a Child or Adolescent, in Which Sport Did You Actively
Participate, If Any?

| | Male | | | | Female | | | |
| | Heterosexual | | Homosexual | | Heterosexual | | Homosexual | |
	N	%	N	%	N	%	N	%
Brazil								
None	0	--	8	35				
Soft sports[a]	1	6	4	17				
Hard sports[b]	15	94	11	48				
Total	16	100	23	100				

$$X^2 = 9.46386$$
$$p = 0.0088$$

Philippines								
None	3	9	11	37	8	24	7	22
Soft sports	4	12	15	50	24	73	13	41
Hard sports	27	79	4	13	1	3	12	38
Total	34	100	30	100	33	100	32	101

$$X^2 = 27.86321 \qquad X^2 = 12.63223$$
$$p = 0.0000 \qquad p = 0.0018$$

United States								
None	4	7	7	19	3	7	1	3
Soft sports	6	10	24	67	13	29	14	36
Hard sports	48	83	5	14	29	64	24	62
Total	58	100	36	100	45	100	39	101

$$X^2 = 43.753 \qquad X^2 = 1.08570$$
$$p = 0.0000 \qquad p = 0.5811$$

[a] Soft sports = gymnastics, track, tennis, swimming.

[b] Hard sports = football, basketball, baseball, soccer.

115

TABLE 5.3 If You Were Forced to Participate in One of the Following Sports, Which Would You Choose?

| | Male | | | | Female | | | |
| | Heterosexual | | Homosexual | | Heterosexual | | Homosexual | |
	N	%	N	%	N	%	N	%
Brazil								
Football	7	44	6	26				
Baseball	1	6	0	--				
Basketball	1	6	2	9				
Wrestling	0	--	0	--				
Gymnastics	0	--	1	4				
Swimming	7	44	14	61				
Total	16	100	23	100				

$$X^2 = 3.60326$$
$$\underline{p} = 0.4624$$

| | Male | | | | Female | | | |
| | Heterosexual | | Homosexual | | Heterosexual | | Homosexual | |
	N	%	N	%	N	%	N	%
Philippines								
Football	3	9	3	10	2	6	2	6
Baseball	3	9	2	7	1	3	6	19
Basketball	24	71	4	13	1	3	15	48
Wrestling	0	--	0	--	0	--	1	3
Gymnastics	0	--	15	50	9	27	1	3
Swimming	4	12	6	20	20	61	6	19
Total	34	101	30	100	33	100	31	98

$$X^2 = 29.75193 \qquad X^2 = 30.72739$$
$$\underline{p} = 0.0000 \qquad \underline{p} = 0.0000$$

| | Male | | | | Female | | | |
| | Heterosexual | | Homosexual | | Heterosexual | | Homosexual | |
	N	%	N	%	N	%	N	%
United States								
Football	14	24	0	--	6	13	2	5
Baseball	14	24	3	8	8	18	17	44
Basketball	17	29	2	6	6	13	6	15
Wrestling	1	2	2	6	0	--	2	5
Gymnastics	6	10	12	33	10	22	2	5
Swimming	6	10	17	47	15	33	10	26
Total	58	99	36	100	45	99	39	100

$$X^2 = 37.45674 \qquad X^2 = 13.21216$$
$$\underline{p} = 0.0000 \qquad \underline{p} = 0.0215$$

TABLE 5.4 If You Had an Expense Paid Vacation with Friends, Where Would You Choose to Go?

| | Male | | | | Female | | | |
| | Heterosexual | | Homosexual | | Heterosexual | | Homosexual | |
	N	%	N	%	N	%	N	%
Brazil								
Hunting	0	--	0	--				
Fishing	3	19	1	4				
Golfing	1	6	1	4				
Beach	11	69	21	91				
Skiing	1	6	0	--				
Total	16	100	23	99				

X² = 3.99737
p = 0.2617

| | Male | | | | Female | | | |
| | Heterosexual | | Homosexual | | Heterosexual | | Homosexual | |
	N	%	N	%	N	%	N	%
Philippines								
Hunting	17	50	6	20	1	3	5	17
Fishing	2	6	0	--	1	3	6	20
Golfing	1	3	1	3	2	6	0	--
Beach	14	41	21	70	26	79	19	63
[Water] skiing	0	--	2	7	3	9	0	--
Total	34	100	30	100	33	100	30	100

X² = 10.45169   X² = 12.21181
p = 0.0335   p = 0.0158

| | Male | | | | Female | | | |
| | Heterosexual | | Homosexual | | Heterosexual | | Homosexual | |
	N	%	N	%	N	%	N	%
United States								
Hunting	4	7	0	--	2	4	1	3
Fishing	14	24	1	3	3	7	19	49
Golfing	1	2	0	--	0	--	1	3
Beach	24	41	27	75	31	69	10	26
Skiing	15	26	8	22	9	20	8	21
Total	58	100	36	100	45	100	39	102

X² = 14.20260   X² = 23.47582
p = 0.0067   p = 0.0001

TABLE 5.5 As a Child Were You Regarded as a Sissy (Male)/Tomboy (Female)?

| | Male | | | | Female | | | |
| | Heterosexual | | Homosexual | | Heterosexual | | Homosexual | |
	N	%	N	%	N	%	N	%
Brazil								
No, was a regular guy/girl	13	81	6	26				
Yes, or felt different from other guys/girls	3	19	17	74				
Total	16	100	23	100				
		$X^2 = 11.49278$						
		$\underline{p} = 0.0007$						
Philippines								
No, was a regular guy/girl	31	94	1	3	28	85	14	44
Yes, or felt different from other guys/girls	2	6	29	97	5	15	18	56
Total	33	100	30	100	33	100	32	100
		$X^2 = 51.61530$				$X^2 = 12.00194$		
		$\underline{p} = 0.0000$				$\underline{p} = 0.0005$		
United States								
No, was a regular guy/girl	51	88	6	17	18	40	3	8
Yes, or felt different from other guys/girls	7	12	30	83	27	60	36	92
Total	58	100	36	100	45	100	39	100
		$X^2 = 47.26355$				$X^2 = 11.63077$		
		$\underline{p} = 0.0000$				$\underline{p} = 0.0006$		

TABLE 5.6   As a Child Were You Afraid of Being Physically Hurt?

| | Male | | | | Female | | | |
| | Heterosexual | | Homosexual | | Heterosexual | | Homosexual | |
	N	%	N	%	N	%	N	%
Brazil								
Yes	9	56	15	65				
No	7	44	8	35				
Total	16	100	23	100				

$$X^2 = 0.32058$$
$$p = 0.5713$$

| | Male | | | | Female | | | |
| | Heterosexual | | Homosexual | | Heterosexual | | Homosexual | |
	N	%	N	%	N	%	N	%
Philippines								
Yes	9	26	21	70	25	76	15	47
No	25	74	9	30	8	24	17	53
Total	34	100	30	100	33	100	32	100

$$X^2 = 12.12678 \qquad X^2 = 5.72597$$
$$p = 0.0005 \qquad p = 0.0167$$

| | Male | | | | Female | | | |
| | Heterosexual | | Homosexual | | Heterosexual | | Homosexual | |
	N	%	N	%	N	%	N	%
United States								
Yes	19	33	23	64	23	51	6	15
No	39	67	13	36	22	49	33	85
Total	58	100	36	100	45	100	39	100

$$X^2 = 8.70907 \qquad X^2 = 11.79713$$
$$p = 0.0032 \qquad p = 0.0006$$

TABLE 5.7   As a Child, Did You Like Fighting (Physically) With Other
            Children?

	Male				Female			
	Heterosexual		Homosexual		Heterosexual		Homosexual	
	N	%	N	%	N	%	N	%

Brazil

Yes, or did not mind so much	12	75	10	43				
No	4	25	13	56				
Total	16	100	23	99				

$$X^2 = 3.81295$$
$$\underline{p} = 0.0509$$

Philippines

Yes, or did not mind so much	31	91	13	43	21	64	17	53
No	3	9	17	57	12	36	15	47
Total	34	100	30	100	33	100	32	100

$$X^2 = 16.97996 \qquad X^2 = 0.73918$$
$$\underline{p} = 0.0000 \qquad \underline{p} = 0.3899$$

United States

Yes, or did not mind so much	34	59	9	25	11	24	17	44
No	24	41	27	75	34	76	22	56
Total	58	100	36	100	45	100	39	100

$$X^2 = 10.11656 \qquad X^2 = 3.44615$$
$$\underline{p} = 0.0015 \qquad \underline{p} = 0.0634$$

TABLE 5.8   If You Were Forced to Choose One of the Following Jobs, Which
Would You choose?

	Male				Female			
	Heterosexual		Homosexual		Heterosexual		Homosexual	
	N	%	N	%	N	%	N	%
Brazil								
Clerk, hardware store	2	12	1	4				
Service station attendant	2	12	2	9				
Waiter/waitress	3	19	7	30				
Clerk, stationery store	2	12	5	22				
Clerk, drugstore	7	44	8	35				
Total	16	99	23	100				

$$X^2 = 2.09685$$
$$p = 0.7180$$

	Male				Female			
Philippines								
Clerk, hardware store	16	47	2	7	3	10	7	23
Service station attendant	8	24	2	7	1	3	9	29
Waiter/waitress	2	6	4	13	2	7	7	23
Clerk, stationery store	6	18	12	40	7	23	2	6
Clerk, drugstore	2	6	10	33	17	57	6	19
Total	34	101	30	100	30	100	31	100

$$X^2 = 22.32610 \qquad X^2 = 18.80508$$
$$p = 0.0002 \qquad p = 0.0009$$

	Male				Female			
United States								
Clerk, hardware store	19	33	6	17	5	11	13	33
Service station attendant	10	17	1	3	3	7	10	26
Waiter/waitress	16	28	18	50	14	31	5	13
Clerk, stationery store	2	3	5	14	10	22	4	10
Clerk, drugstore	11	19	6	17	13	29	7	18
Total	58	100	36	101	45	100	39	100

$$X^2 = 12.53527 \qquad X^2 = 15.61044$$
$$p = 0.0138 \qquad p = 0.0036$$

(Table 5.2). Filipino heterosexual females seem to prefer less physically aggressive sports, such as tennis and swimming, but there is no difference between American lesbians and heterosexual females. The forced choice item for sports (Table 5.3) is particularly interesting in that it allows respondents to choose sports regardless of availability, economic status, etc. Here these patterns are perhaps most distinct. Heterosexual males and lesbians prefer physically aggressive sports, football, baseball, and basketball, while homosexual males and heterosexual females prefer less physically aggressive sports, such as gymnastics and swimming. Culture, physical environment, and level of economic development impinge upon the way in which the sports institution emerges in a given society. Affluent, highly developed societies in temperate climates, with wide climatic variations and seasonal changes, such as the United States and Western Europe, are more likely to develop complex athletic organization than less developed, less affluent, tropical countries, such as the Philippines and Brazil.

For example, in the United States, football, baseball, and basketball are regarded as the three major sports, tend to be dominated by male heterosexuals, and are regarded as macho sports. These sports are preferred by both American heterosexual males and American lesbians. Football (which to the Brazilians means soccer) is the major sport in that country. In the Brazilian samples soccer is chosen most often by the heterosexual males, while swimming is chosen most often by the homosexual males.

Of these three societies, the Philippines has the least developed and least complex sports organization. The major sport as well as the macho sport is basketball, which is preferred by both heterosexual males and lesbians and avoided by homosexual males, who prefer gymnastics, and heterosexual females, who prefer swimming. Of course, specific sports are cultural creations, and by examining Table 5.3 it becomes clear that responses are being shaped by the particular athletic arrangements in each society. Underlying these specific conditions is the culturally invariable tendency for the emergence of similar patterns of athletics among heterosexual males. If these patterns are universal, they offer evidence suggesting that differences and similarities among the four sexual orientational groups are not purely social in nature.

While there is a wide individual variation within the four sexual orientational groups, group differences seem to emerge with respect to the way these groups manifest gross motor activity and the way this motor activity is transmuted into socially functional behavior. For example, gymnastics, which is popular with homosexual males and heterosexual females, bears considerable resemblance to dancing with respect to the way the body is moved and controlled. In gymnastics, then, athletics and entertainment are subtly merged. While athletics have long been recognized as having some intrinsic connection with masculinity, even biologically, it seems likely that entertainment, particularly its most physical form, dancing, is the intrinsically feminine counterpart to male athletics. Thus, the cross-gender process in homosexual males accounts for their unusually strong interest in entertainment, particularly dancing, and their relative indifference to rough, physically aggressive, team sports. The entertainment aspects of homosexual males are thus related to their low level of athletic interest. The material presented in the remaining tables tends to offer corroborating evidence for these general differences. For example, with respect to the forced-choice of a vacation (Table 5.4), somewhat different choices appear for the four groups. While the beach tends to be universally popular, fishing, traditionally a masculine sport, is preferred by American as well as Filipino lesbians. Very significant differences between homosexuals and heterosexuals appear with respect to childhood tomboyism and sissy behavior (Table 5.5), with very large percentages of homosexual males reporting they were sissies and very large percentages of lesbians reporting they were tomboys, regardless of the society in which they were raised. This suggests that athletic interests are formed quite early, long before contact with a homosexual subculture. Tables 5.6 and 5.7, having to do with childhood fears of physical injury and feelings about physical fighting, suggest rather consistent patterns cross-culturally: heterosexual males and lesbians were less fearful of physical injury and fighting than were homosexual males and heterosexual females. Finally, Table 5.8, while not directly reflecting athletic interests, suggests that cross-gendering, which is relevant for sports activities, may also have implications for more general occupational interests. Lesbians and homosexual males tend to choose traditional male occupations (clerk in hardware store and service station attendant) which entail more gross motor activity, such as lifting heavy objects, and more movement of the upper body than the more sex-neutral occupations (waiter/waitress, clerk in stationery store, clerk in drugstore) chosen by homosexual males and heterosexual females.

ATHLETIC INTERESTS AND STEREOTYPES

Some observers no doubt will object to the presentation of these materials on the grounds they contribute to "stereotypes" about homosexuals. Such social scientists may find themselves in the curious position of being the "last to know" what ordinary homosexuals take for granted. While many homosexuals themselves either discuss such differences openly or behave upon the assumption that the differences exist, most social scientists try to whitewash homosexuals by denying that there are behavioral differences of any kind between homosexuals and heterosexuals. Presumably, if such differences are denied, the general public will become more tolerant of homosexuals. However, it should be remembered that the concept of stereotypes emerged in connection with studies of race prejudice. The stereotypes to which social scientists most strongly objected had to do with allegedly negative traits of blacks-- low intelligence, biological inferiority, laziness, etc. Many social scientists are still locked into a logic derived from the struggle for racial equality in the 1940s through 1960s, which asserted that the goals of racial equality are furthered by a repudiation of stereotyping. While the repudiation of stereotyping may have been an effective tool in the achievement of civil rights for blacks and other racial minorities, it cannot be assumed that the same scientific material or the same political stance is efficacious for the achievement of equal rights for homosexuals.

It is not our assertion here that all homosexuals are alike with respect to athletic interest. There are wide variations in the behavior of homosexuals which are apparent to the most casual observer of the homosexual world. What is being presented are group differences, not individual differences, which appear to be linked to sexual orientation. If male homosexuals have relatively low levels of interest in athletics and strong interests in the arts and entertainment, as has been suggested here and which many homosexuals themselves acknowledge, this fact can hardly be construed as negative unless athletics are negatively valued. If lesbians are disproportionately involved in athletics, as has been suggested here and which many lesbians themselves acknowledge, this can hardly be construed as negative unless athletics are negatively valued. Rigid adherence to the notion that all generalizations about human behavior are to be eschewed as stereotypes is essentially anti-intellectual and certainly contrary to empirical social scientific inquiry. After all, the social sciences view generalizing about human behavior as a fundamental tenet of sociological inquire. Politically, the failure to explore and publish findings on these dimensions of human behavior supports the already current view in the Anglo-Saxon countries that the homosexual is someone to be tolerated (if one holds "liberal" views on the subject), but that lesbians and gay men make no particular contribution to society.

Although it is our assertion here that sexual orientation is an important variable in determining athletic interests, this does not mean that sexual orientation is the only determinant of the particular arrangement of athletic interests in a society. High levels of athletic interests occurring cross-culturally on the part of heterosexual males and lesbians, and low levels of athletic interests occurring cross-culturally on the part of heterosexual females and homosexual males, suggests that a biological component may underlie this behavior. This does not mean that all aspects of athletic interests are biologically

determined. Important cultural elements may occur simultaneously with biological elements. For example, the high presence
of blacks in such American sports as basketball and football
is probably related to cultural factors such as opportunity
and recruitment practices. Nonetheless, sexual orientation continues to operate with respect to the athletic behavior of black
heterosexuals and homosexuals. Black homosexuals resemble
white homosexuals in their patterns of cross-gender behavior
and athletic interests. For example, in black homosexual argot
in San Francisco black homosexuals widely refer to each other
jokingly as sissies. With regard to blacks, Bell, Weinberg, and
Hammersmith conclude that:

> In most respects the overall picture that
> emerges from the path analysis for the black
> males replicates what was found for the white
> males. Among the blacks as among the whites,
> for instance, Childhood Gender Nonconformity
> appears as an important predecessor of Adult
> Homosexuality. For black males, the Childhood
> Gender Nonconformity variable consisted of how
> feminine the respondent said he had been while
> he was growing up and how much he enjoyed
> or disliked typical boys' activities during the
> grade-school years. . . . Among blacks as
> well as whites, then, nonconforming gender
> identity and interests appear to have been con-
> nected to the development of a homosexual ori-
> entation [1981, p. 196].

While special talents in athletics and dancing have sometimes been attributed to blacks as biological characteristics,
particularly in racist folklore, no scientific evidence to support
these contentions has emerged. Unlike male homosexuals, who
are greatly over-represented in dance, entertainment, and
the arts, as has been suggested, it would be difficult to make
a case that blacks are similarly over-represented. It is very
doubtful that blacks are numerically represented in the arts
even in proportion to their 10 percent presence in the general
population in the United States. Nor do any such special connections between blacks and athletics or dance occur cross-
culturally.

The linkage between sexual orientation, athletic behavior
and biological components--particularly hormones--is well-
established in the physical sciences, though widely ignored
by most social scientists. Despite a rapid accumulation of evidence regarding this linkage, most social scientists still regard
all differences between homosexuals and heterosexuals (not to
mention differences between males and females) as entirely
social in nature.

HORMONAL DETERMINANTS OF
ATHLETIC INTERESTS

Diamond and Karlen summarize as follows some of the behavioral effects of androgens (male hormones) on the male body and behavior:

> Besides their sexual effects, androgens help maintain a male's muscle tone, hair patterns (on head, face, and body), voice tone, sperm production, and reproductive tract--in fact, almost every male physical and behavioral trait. They enhance general activity levels, aggressiveness, perseverance, territoriality, and dominance. In contrast, castration, loss of androgens with aging, and taking antiandrogens . . . all decrease these characteristics [1980, p. 87].

Maccoby and Jacklin (1974) in an extensive review of the research literature having to do with male-female differences conclude that the "sex difference in aggression has a biological foundation" (p. 242). These authors continue:

> Let us outline the reasons why biological sex differences appear to be involved in aggression: 1) Males are more aggressive than females in all human societies for which evidence is available. 2) The sex differences are found early in life, at a time when there is no evidence that differential socialization pressures have been brought to bear by adults to "shape" aggression differently in the two sexes. 3) Similar sex differences are found in man and subhuman primates. 4) Aggresion is related to levels of sex hormones, and can be changed by experimental administrations of these hormones [pp. 242-43].

In elaborating upon the last point, these authors "present here some of the well-established generalizations" as follows:

> 1. Male hormones (androgens) function during prenatal development to masculinize the growing individual. Genetic females exposed to abnormally high (for females) levels of androgens prenatally are masculinized both physically and behaviorally, including elevated levels of threat behavior and rough-and-tumble play. . . .
> 2. Male hormones increase aggressive behavior when they are administered postnatally, even without prenatal sensitization. . . .

3. More aggressive males tend to have higher
current levels of androgens [pp. 243-46].

Maccoby and Jacklin further conclude that "there is little doubt
that the human male is more interested in competitive sports
than the human female" (p. 247).

While the relationship between hormones and human behavior is far more complex than has been suggested here, it is
clear that hormones play a much more decisive role in certain
kinds of behavior--particularly aggression and its specific
manifestations such as athletics--than most social scientists are
willing to admit.

Numerous studies have attempted to assess differences in
hormonal levels between homosexuals and heterosexuals. Meyer-
Bahlburg (1977) has reviewed this body of data. Although with
regard to hormone levels many of these studies have found no
differences between homosexuals and heterosexuals, others
have found differences. Kolodny et al. (1971) in comparing a
group of 30 male homosexual students with 50 heterosexual
students, found a close correlation between levels of testosterone and Kinsey ratings; the more heterosexual the Kinsey
rating, the higher the level of testosterone measured. Lower
plasma testosterone levels were especially marked in Kinsey
fives and sixes. Margolese (1970) compared 15 healthy homosexual males with ten healthy heterosexuals and found that
homosexuals had consistently lowered ratios of androsterone to
etiocholanolone. Such lowered ratios are characteristic of women. Margolese and Janiger (1973) compared 24 healthy heterosexual males with 32 healthy homosexual males and successfully
replicated their earlier findings. Lowered androsterone to etiocholanolone ratios were especially marked in men who were
exclusively homosexual.

Among females, Gartrell et al. (1977) found a sample of
lesbians to have significantly higher levels of testosterone
than did a comparison group of heterosexual women. In reviewing the literature on sex hormones and female homosexuality,
Meyer-Bahlburg (1979, p. 101) concluded that "Sex hormone
levels were found to be normal in the majority of homosexual
women, but about a third of the subjects studied had elevated
androgen levels."

While most of the research on hormones and homosexuality
has been directed at finding a causative link between hormones
and sexual orientation, such a connection has not yet been
established. The links which do exist suggest that hormones
are even more indirectly related to sexual orientation through
levels of aggressive activity, especially athletic interests. The
linkage between athletic interests and sex (male and female)
has been well-established. The cross-cultural data presented
here having to do with elevated levels of athletic interests on
the part of lesbians and lowered levels of athletic interests by

homosexual males are consistent with hormonal data if the concept of cross-gendering is taken into account. Insofar as hormones are linked to sexual orientation they are likely to be linked to non-sexual behavior such as athletic interest rather than to sexual orientation per se. While no research has been done on the relationship between hormones and dance and entertainment, the finding that such interests appear consistently in groups of male homosexuals cross-culturally is suggestive of the possibility that activities related to dance and entertainment may be essentially feminine behavior appearing in male homosexuals through the cross-gendering process and that such activities may well have a hormonal basis.

6

EROTIC TRADITIONS

While societies do not create homosexuals, their universal emergence presents all societies with the common task of reacting to them. In some societies homosexuals have been regarded as having special powers as witches or healers, and they are approved of under these special circumstances. More commonly, some societies have accepted the inevitability of homosexuals and have made provision for their social acceptance once they appear. No societies unconditionally encourage homosexuals or foster their appearance. Most societies simply recognize their existence in the scheme of human sexuality and social life. Some societies have been repressive of homosexuals, even regarding their behavior as a capital offense. Under British law until 1861, homosexuals could be put to death. According to Hyde (1970), the Home Office reported in 1811 that four out of five convicted sodomists were executed, but only 63 out of 471 persons were executed for other capital offenses.

Table 6.1 is a rough classification of contemporary societies with respect to the legal status of homosexual persons, based upon legal codes and enforcement practices. Countries in the first group are those which are particularly repressive of homosexual persons and where homosexuals have been singled out for special abuse and containment, or even elimination, either through legislative action or through informal police procedures. In some of these countries, such as the Soviet Union, repression of homosexuals is in part based upon longstanding cultural traditions of intolerance for homosexuals, coupled with contemporary political aims. In other countries, such as Iran, which traditionally has been rather tolerant of homosexuality, repression of homosexuals seems to be a temporary result of chaos and revolution, social conditions which sometimes bring about repression of homosexual populations.

TABLE 6.1 Repression and Tolerance of Homosexuals in Countries of the World

Very Repressive	Somewhat Repressive		Somewhat Tolerant		Very Tolerant	
Argentina	Algeria	Saudi Arabia	Antigua	Mexico	Bahrain	South Korea
Cameroun	Angola	South Africa	Anguilla	Nepal	Brazil	Sweden
China	Austria	Sudan	Bahamas	Nicaragua	Bulgaria	Thailand
Cuba	Australia	Surinam	Barbados	Oman	Burundi	Western Samoa
Gibraltar	Bermuda	Syria	Belgium	Peru	Colombia	
Iran	Canada	Taiwan	Belize	Portugal	Comores Islands	
Libya	Chile	Togo	Benin	Qatar	Costa Rica	
Malawi	Czechoslovakia	Turkey	Burma	Reunion	Denmark	
Mauritania	Djibouti	United Kingdom	Cayman Islands	St. Kitts-Nevis	Dominican Republic	
Mozambique	Greece	United States	Ecuador	St. Lucia	Egypt	
Romania	Hong Kong	Uruguay	Eire	St. Vincent	Fiji Islands	
U.S.S.R.	Hungary	Yugoslavia	El Salvador	Seychelles	Ghana	
Yemen	India	Zaire	Ethiopia	Singapore	Guatemala	
	Jordan	Zambia	East Germany	Spain	Haiti	
	Kenya		Finland	Sri Lanka	Honduras	
	Kuwait		France	Switzerland	Ivory Coast	
	Morocco		Iceland	Tahiti	Malta	
	New Caledonia		Indonesia	Tanzania	Mauritius	
	New Guinea		Italy	Tonga Islands	Maylasia	
	New Zealand		Israel	Trinidad-Tobago	Micronesia	
	Niger		Jamaica	Tunisia	Monaco	
	Nigeria		Japan	United Arab Emirates	Netherlands	
	Pakistan		Luxembourg	Venezuela	Norway	
	Panama		Macau	Zimbabwe	Philippines	

Source: Compiled by the authors.

For the most part, the second category includes countries in which homosexuality is illegal and in which laws against homosexual conduct are actually enforced. Perhaps the most conspicuous countries in the category are the Anglo-Saxon countries, primarily the United States, Great Britain, Canada, Australia, and New Zealand. In most of the countries in this category, vice squads or similar special governmental agencies are active in the enforcement of laws against homosexuality, particularly in public or quasi-public places (Humphreys (1975). In a few cases there is governmental activity directed against homosexuals through informal police practices without legal codes. However, in most countries in this category, laws against homosexual activity provide the basis for enforcement practices.

The third category includes countries, such as most of Latin America, that have never criminalized homosexual conduct, or countries that have not adopted consenting adults laws, yet there is little or no enforcement of the codes which do exist despite the existence of laws proscribing homosexual behavior. Many of the former British colonies fall into the latter category. For example, laws against homosexuality resulted from British colonialization in the West Indies, but in practice most of these countries are tolerant of homosexuals by tradition and laws are generally not enforced. In countries of this category, vice squads or their equivalent are the exception rather than the rule. While it is possible to be prosecuted in some of these countries (and this sometimes happens) there is no systematic police attention directed toward homosexuals.

The last category includes those countries which are particularly tolerant of homosexuality. The legal codes of a few of these countries, such as the Philippines and Thailand, are silent on the subject of male homosexuality, with the exception of forcible sexual relations. Other countries, such as Brazil and Colombia, have long had consenting-adult laws. Homosexuals in this category of countries are not seen as a threatening group which requires surveillance. Some of these countries--Norway, Denmark, Sweden, and the Netherlands--represent the most progressive countries of Western Europe with respect to decriminalizing homosexuality, and were among the first in northern Europe to adopt consenting-adults statutes. Most countries in this category have longstanding traditions of toleration for homosexual persons.

Societal attitudes toward homosexuals, especially in complex Western societies, are themselves quite complex and are easily misunderstood. It is often assumed by North Americans that because Latin Americans are predominantly Catholic, machistic, and because many Latin American countries have military dictatorships, they are necessarily more repressive of homosexuality than North American societies. While it is

difficult to generalize about Latin America, societal attitudes
on the whole tend to be more tolerant than those in North
America. The differences in attitude between North Americans
and Latin Americans may be understood in the context of differences in what might be called "erotic traditions."
Perhaps the earliest attempt to delineate what are here
called "erotic traditions" was Sir Richard Burton's famous
essay, "The Sotadic Zone," first published in 1885-1886 as
part of the original edition of Arabian Nights but usually
deleted from subsequent versions (Burton, n.d.). While there
is some similarity even now between those areas designated
as part of the "Sotadic Zone" and tolerant erotic traditions,
Burton's essay dealt primarily with tolerance for pederasty
rather than the full range of homosexual behavior.
Different parts of the world seem to be characterized by
different erotic traditions, or complex systems of norms regulating sexual behavior, operating somewhat independently of
the formal religious and political systems. The Philippines is
part of the Southeast-Asian erotic tradition, which tends to
be quite tolerant of homosexuals. The Western world is rough-
ly divided into two major erotic traditions--the Anglo-Saxon
and the Latin. Both North American and Latin American
societies are part of what is commonly called the "Western
world." However, when we examine the sexuality of these
two areas, there are significant differences between them,
and these differences are of sufficient magnitude as to suggest different sexual cultures or erotic traditions.

A COMPARISON OF THE ANGLO-SAXON AND
THE LATIN EROTIC TRADITIONS

Men have more sexual license in Latin countries than men
in Anglo-Saxon countries; women have less. Consequently,
certain elements appearing in the Latin erotic tradition vary
considerably from those in the Anglo-Saxon. For example,
the use of sexual language is quite different in the two traditions. Jokes and ribald stories are told by males over the
family table after Sunday dinner in Guatemala City or São
Paulo which would shock even the most liberated housewives
in Portland or Chicago. For example, in Brazil there is often,
even in respectable middle-class homes, explicit allusion to
anal intercourse between men and women or to bestiality.
Such topics are considered inappropriate for general conversation in middle-class North American homes. There is widespread public urination by males in all parts of Latin America,
a habit regarded as unsavory by North Americans, who sometimes indulge in public urination along a dark freeway, behind
their vehicles. In contrast, the Latin male urinates when and
where he chooses. The sidewalks of the downtown area of

Guatemala City by 9 o'clock in the evening are literally covered with urination puddles, and the pedestrian must take
care where he or she steps. The darker walkways of São
Paulo and Salvador reek with smells of urination. The men
and teenage boys of Belo Horizonte, Brazil's third largest
city, do not hesitate to urinate in full view of large crowds
pouring out of an afternoon soccer game, although they
usually turn their backs to the crowd.

Prostitutes have a very different social position in Latin
countries than in Anglo-Saxon countries. In Latin countries,
generally speaking, they are treated as a normal part of the
social fabric rather than as a social aberration or criminal
class. This is probably a result of the power of males who
derive pleasure from the presence of prostitutes. As in Jorge
Amado's (1977) wonderful portraits of life in northeast Brazil,
respectable women scorn the prostitute as they pass her
house on the way to mass without questioning her right to
exist as a part of the normal social fabric of the town. In
contrast, Anglo-Saxon countries regard prostitution as aberrant behavior and usually criminalize it. The famous Wolfenden report, which was widely heralded as a progressive
document because it advocated consenting-adult statutes for
homosexuals, refused to recommend legalization for prostitution in England. In most Anglo-Saxon countries, prostitutes
are still subject to police surveillance and arrests in a way
which is regarded as barbaric by Latin Americans.

One of the most striking differences between the two
traditions is found in the area of homosexuality, especially in
the relationships between heterosexual and homosexual men.
Because these relationships are so different in the two traditions, they are likely to be easily misunderstood. Informal
norms of conduct control, to a considerable extent, relationships between heterosexual and homosexual males. This relationship is fundamental to an understanding of the treatment
of homosexuals in any society, for it is invariably the heterosexual males who make and enforce sex laws. Women, who
probably would treat homosexuals with far more leniency
than do men, generally do not determine society's treatment
of homosexuals.

From early on, homosexuals have a difficult time with
heterosexuals. As we have seen, children who later become
homosexual frequently report that as children they were considered sissies or effeminate boys. From a very early age
these children were bullied about by children who will later
become heterosexual males. At the same time prehomosexual
children are bullied about, they admire, envy, and may even
feel sexual attraction for the more masculine boys. Thus, in
adulthood many homosexuals are sexually attracted to masculine men, often to heterosexuals. Even though little sexual
contact may take place, especially in the Anglo-Saxon tradi-

tion, the ideal masculine object choice often is the heterosexual male. In the uniform bars of the large American cities
such as New York, San Francisco, and Los Angeles, this
theme is played out as homosexuals imitate heterosexual im-
ages to enhance their sexual attractiveness by the wearing
of the uniform and costume of policemen, cowboys, motor-
cyclists, and marines.

There appears to be some connection between homophobia and racism. Brazil, the Western society which is the least
racist, is also the most tolerant and least repressive toward
homosexuals. One important element in the relative lack of
racism in Brazil is undoubtedly the fact that the Portuguese
settlers defined blacks as sexually desirable, hence, there
is widespread interracial marriage. The mulatto woman in
Brazil is regarded as a sex symbol in much the same way as
the blond sex goddess is regarded in Anglo-Saxon countries.
While interracial sexual and marital liaisons have occurred
and do occur in Anglo-Saxon countries, such contact has
been highly romanticized and exaggerated in novels of the
"Old South." Compared to Brazil, the United States is characterized by a low level of interracial sexual contact and
marriage.

While homosexuals in the Anglo-Saxon world have little
exotic significance for heterosexual men, Guatemalan homosexuals contend that any heterosexual male, under the right
conditions, can be seduced. Through interviewing, it became
apparent that there are probably large numbers of heterosexual Guatemalan males who occasionally use homosexuals for
secondary sexual outlet. Effeminate and passive homosexuals
are defined by Latin males as appropriate sexual objects under certain circumstances. While no specific statistics are
available for Guatemala, a study by the Portuguese government found that 80 percent of heterosexual males regularly
have such secondary homosexual contact (Vayle 1979). This
is much higher than Kinsey's estimate of 37 percent of American males who have had homosexual orgasm after puberty.
A few of the males who engage in homosexual activity probably are genuinely bisexual, in the sense that a bisexual
pattern will continue throughout life. Most are probably predominantly heterosexual in that they prefer heterosexual
contact, they will marry, and their predominant sexual interest will be with women.

Such secondary sexual contact usually, but not always,
takes place during adolescence and up to the mid-twenties.
This is also consistent with Kinsey's findings that a good
deal of homosexual contact after puberty occurs during adolescence. The most important specific social conditions of such
sexual encounters are that the macho not be regarded as a
homosexual by the homosexual partner, and that he take the
active sexual role in anal intercourse, or that he is fellated

by the homosexual. Sometimes a small payment is demanded as further confirmation of the macho's heterosexuality. Such sexual activity is not taken seriously by the macho, who usually treats it with considerable levity. A Brazilian taxi-driver in Belo Horizonte with strong heterosexual interests was induced by three loucas or queens to perform anal inter-course with them in exchange for money. This was considered of so little importance that the taxi-driver good-humoredly told his wife about the incident at dinner the same evening. Some homosexual respondents in Guatemala were interested exclusively in masculine heterosexual or bisexual men (machos activos) who performed anal sex with them. The homosexuals drove around public parks and streets flirting, gesturing, and consciously acting effeminate in order to attract the men. They sometimes picked up four or five at a time and drove off to a secluded spot to have sex, without fear of being beaten or abused. Sometimes they gave parties and invited machos, who were fussed over, served drinks, waited on, and otherwise made to feel important. Such parties were re-garded as failures if the machos didn't appear. The following story was told by a member of a Guatemalan theater company:

> Our company, comprised of 35 male members,
> 32 of whom were homosexual, went to San
> Salvador, the capital of El Salvador, to give
> a performance of a play. By coincidence, we
> stayed at the same hotel as did members of
> several high school soccer teams. We began
> to flirt with the soccer players, commenting
> on their beautiful bodies or otherwise making
> suggestive remarks, letting the soccer play-
> ers know that we were homosexual and avail-
> able. During the course of the first evening,
> nearly all the soccer players had been se-
> duced by members of the theatrical group.

The activo-pasivo theme is frequently found within the Latin homosexual world itself, reflecting sexual patterns of larger society. This is especially apparent in São Paulo, where the homosexual population is quite large. Gay Paulis-tas are immensely curious, in a way that American gays are not, in who penetrates and who is penetrated. The first question asked about a sexual liaison is "who gave ass?"-- that is, which partner was receiving and which penetrating? A Paulista often lies if he was the passive partner, falsely declaring that he was the active partner. American homo-sexuals generally regard the activo-pasivo relationship as private and unimportant, manifesting little curiosity about the passive and active sexual roles.

As we have seen, informal norms in the Latin erotic tradition tend to be more permissive of homosexual behavior, permitting the heterosexual or bisexual male to make use of the homosexual, moving in and out of the homosexual world if he chooses. The formal norms, or the legal and political structure, and similarly more permissive. The Anglo-Saxon countries, such as Great Britain, the United States, Canada, and Australia, have traditionally prided themselves on their "strong democratic tradition." Upon close examination, however, they are repressive where homosexuality is concerned.

In Great Britain, consenting homosexual relations were decriminalized in 1967, following the well-known Wolfenden report. The adoption of consenting-adults laws in 1967 applied only to England and Wales. Consenting-adults laws applying to Scotland were approved in 1980, and those applying to Northern Ireland in 1982. However, under these laws the age of consent for homosexuals is 21 while it is 18 for heterosexuals. Despite the adoption of consenting-adults laws, homosexuals in Great Britain, as elsewhere in the Anglo-Saxon world, are still subject to police surveillance, harassment, and even raids. For example, in 1983 the Arizona Gay News reported:

> The biggest mass arrests of gay men since the mid-1970s took place during two recent raids on bathhouses in England and Wales. On January 23rd, 32 men were arrested when the police swooped on the Albion Sauna in Wallasey, near Liverpool. On March 27th, 54 men were taken into custody after a similar raid on the Pump House in New Port, South Wales. Both raids were reminiscent of those carried out by the Metropolitan Police some years ago in a determined--and successful--effort to close down all gay baths in London [Taylor 1983, p. 2].

Homosexual relations have been decriminalized in only three of Australia's eight states and provinces. Altman (1982, p. 101) observes: "the Australian state of Victoria, where the conservative government effectively decriminalized homosexuality in 1980 . . . wrote into the legislation that 'the Parliament does not intend by this act to condone immorality' and under pressure amended its own legislation to prohibit 'soliciting for immoral purposes.'"

In Canada the 1969 Code Amendments decriminalized homosexual activity between consenting adults in private in all of Canada. Nevertheless, age of consent laws in Canada are somewhat confusing though clearly discriminatory toward homosexuals. The age of consent for females in a heterosexual relationship is 16 years but in "homosexual and certain

kinds of heterosexual relationships [it is] twenty-one years.
. . . In heterosexual relationships there seems to be no age
of consent specified at all for males, yet for a homosexual
act it is . . . twenty-one years" (Vanderbelt-Barber 1972,
p. 504). Sexual acts involving more than two persons are
criminalized and homosexuals are prosecuted under this and
other statutes. Body Politic, the Canadian gay newspaper
whose own offices were raided on December 30, 1977, and
whose documents and manuscripts were confiscated in a controversial move by the Canadian police, reports: "Police
are violating individual privacy by raiding homes, bars,
baths, and private clubs. Massive raids, justified as enforcement of the bawdy house laws, have led to the arrest of
nearly 400 gay men in Toronto and hundreds of other people
in Montreal, Ottawa, Edmonton, Hamilton-Wentworth and other
cities" (Body Politic 1982).

Homosexuality remains criminalized in New Zealand, perhaps the most conservative of the Anglo-Saxon countries with
respect to homosexual relations. The editor of Spartacus
International Gay Guide reports that "homosexuality is completely illegal in New Zealand. The law carries heavy penalties. However, at the present most clubs, bars, saunas,
etc., are left alone by the police due to recent public outcry
against heavy-handed police actions. Recent attempts to
change the laws relating to homosexuality were defeated but
new moves could mean a change in the near future" (Stamford 1983, p. 515).

According to a count by the authors of an American Civil
Liberties Union handbook, 22 states of the United States have
decriminalized homosexual acts by legislative statutes (Stoddard et al. 1983). These states are Alaska, California, Colo-
rado, Connecticut, Delaware, Hawaii, Illinois, Indiana, Iowa,
Maine, Nebraska, New Hampshire, New Jersey, New Mexico,
North Dakota, Ohio, Oregon, South Dakota, Vermont, Washington, West Virginia, and Wyoming. Stoddard et al. summarize the somewhat complex and constantly changing issue of
criminalization and decriminalization of homosexual acts through
court rulings as follows:

> The Supreme Court of Florida has declared
> that state's sodomy law unconstitutional. Florida
> still has a prohibition against "unnatural and
> lascivious acts with another person," which has
> been interpreted to cover acts formerly pro-
> hibited by the sodomy provision. The Massachu-
> setts Supreme Court has ruled that a statute
> prohibiting unnatural and lascivious acts that
> had been used to prosecute acts of sodomy and
> oral copulation, does not apply to private sex-
> ual conduct between consenting adults. The high

courts of Iowa and Pennsylvania have held
that there consensual sodomy laws are inap-
plicable to private adult consensual conduct,
although the Iowa decision was limited to
heterosexual conduct. And a federal district
court in Texas recently invalidated that
state's criminal prohibition on 'homosexual
conduct.' Most importantly, New York's highest court, in a major decision on the constitu-
tionality of sodomy laws, has held that the
state's consensual sodomy law is unconstitu-
tional [1983, pp. 109-10].

The legality of criminalization of homosexual relations in
the remaining states has been upheld de facto by the United
States Supreme Court. In the case known as Doe vs. Commonwealth, the Supreme Court let stand a ruling of a lower
court (in 1977) that sanctioned the legality of criminalization
of homosexual relations in Virginia, using the weight of the
Supreme Court to maintain criminalization of homosexual relations. Thus, homosexuality in the United States, as in most
of the Anglo-Saxon world, remains criminalized to a considerable degree.

The Nazi era was characterized by virulent homophobia,
including the incarceration of homosexuals in concentration
camps. It is sometimes believed that there is a connection between Nazism and homosexuality because of the well-publi-
cized homosexuality of Ernst Rohm, the leader of the SS.
Rohm and a group of his followers were assassinated by Hit-
ler in 1934. On June 28, 1935, to celebrate the first anniversary of Rohm's murder, the Nazis enacted the "Law for
the Protection of German Blood and German Honor," under
which thousands of homosexuals, together with Jews, Gypsies,
Poles, handicapped persons, and labor organizers, were summarily exterminated. There is no evidence of any linkage between Nazism and homosexuality, other than the fact that
some Nazis, like some Democrats and some Republicans, were
homosexuals. Nazi Germany and the Soviet Union, represent-
ing two political extremes, have produced the two regimes
most repressive of homosexuals in the twentieth century.

Actually, all political systems, including the police and
military apparatuses that accompany them, tend to be primarily male heterosexual creations. This in part accounts for the
fact that many modern societies, with their highly developed,
well-trained police and military cadres, are repressive of
homosexuality.

Many people are under the impression that authoritarian
regimes inevitably repress homosexuals. For example, Altman
(1982, p. 90) writes, "It is no accident that all authoritarian
societies, whether Argentina and South Africa or the Soviet

Union and Cuba, are extremely puritanical sexually and, one should note, almost always strongly homophobic."

In many societies, homophobia is likely to lie just beneath the surface, even if not expressed openly. The extent to which homophobia surfaces depends upon many factors: social conditions, cultural traditions, and unique circumstances. However, upon closer examination, it is clear that there is no necessary connection between authoritarian regimes and repression of homosexuals. Certain societies define homosexuals as a dangerous and criminal class, others do not. Brazil and the Philippines are governed by right-wing dictatorships, yet their treatment of homosexuals is far more benign than in the English-speaking world.

THE LATIN TRADITION OF TOLERANCE

While the Anglo-Saxon countries began to decriminalize homosexuality, as we have seen, with the initiation of the Wolfenden committee in the late 1960s, homosexual acts between consenting adults in private were never criminalized in most of the Latin American countries. The early part of the nineteenth century saw the reforms in French criminal law known as the Napoleonic Code. Among the reforms under Napoleon was the decriminalization of homosexuality, and throughout the nineteenth century French homosexuals enjoyed considerably more personal freedom than did the English. For example, Oscar Wilde, at the outset of his famous trials, was urged by his friends to flee to France where homosexuality was not criminalized, but he stubbornly refused.

As the various Latin American countries achieved their independence from Spain and began to formulate their own legal codes, they looked to the French statutes, which were regarded as exemplary for their time. At that time, most of the Latin American countries followed the recently adopted Napoleonic Code, which had deleted consenting homosexual behavior from its list of criminal offenses. Thus, most Latin American countries never criminalized homosexual behavior. The legal status of homosexuality is a fundamental issue in societies which observe "due process." A Brazilian journalist, Celso Curi, who wrote a daily column in one of the general daily newspapers of São Paulo in which he gave bits of news about the homosexual community in Brazil or elsewhere, was charged with violating the public decency in Brazil. On March 12, 1979 he was absolved of the charges by Judge Regis de Castilho Barbosa, who pointed out that since homosexuality is not a crime in Brazil, publishing news about homosexuals cannot be considered against the public decency (Body Politic 1979, p. 18). While the Brazilian government exercises political censorship of the press, theater, television, and radio as a matter of course, it is interesting that both Great Britain and Canada, widely regarded as exemplary democracies, have actually been far more repressive of the homosexual press than Brazil, which is widely regarded as a "repressive right-wing military dictatorship." In Great Britain, the gay newspaper Gay News was almost closed down in 1977 in a widely publicized case in which Mary Whitehouse, an antigay crusader, brought heresy charges against the newspaper, under an archaic British law, for publishing an erotic poem about Christ.

Great Britain has a long tradition of suppression of literature about homosexuality. One of the first important modern scientific works about homosexuality, Havelock Ellis' Sexual Inversion was subjected to an obscenity trial in 1898. Both D. H. Lawrence's novel, The Rainbow, and Radcliffe Hall's lesbian novel, Well of Loneliness, were prosecuted because of homosexual material. Such activities are not merely a part of past history. More recently, John Rechy had difficulty publishing his 1977 novel, The Sexual Outlaw, in Great Britain. D. J. West (1977, p. vii), in the preface to Homosexuality Re-Examined, a revision of his earlier Homosexuality, writes: "When my first book about homosexuality appeared (twenty years ago) copies were confiscated as obscene by Australian customs officials and the American distributor, finding the title Homosexuality too blatant, bowdlerised it to The Other Man." West's work is a thorough, even-handed, scholarly review of the scientific literature on homosexuality.

In general, the public in the Anglo-Saxon countries reacts much more quickly to homosexual issues than does the general public in Latin America. In Latin America homosexuality is not generally regarded as a politically volatile issue. It is not one in which the public could be easily aroused, and it is doubtful therefore that Latin American governments or other organizations could use the homosexual issue politically as is frequently done in the United States. It is common practice in many American cities to raid gay bars or baths around election time to prove that an incumbent mayor is diligent in "protecting public morality." It is also unlikely that a political figure could successfully rally public support in Latin America for an anti-homosexual campaign such as that of Senator John Briggs in California in 1978. While many Latin Americans no doubt hold negative attitudes toward homosexuality, the homosexual issue is not seen as one of great social and moral importance. In general, Latin Americans are more sophisticated than Americans about homosexuality. They are aware that there are homosexual teachers in public schools and that there are even homosexual priests in boarding schools. Such behavior is widely accepted as a commonplace fact of life rather than as a controversial moral issue. A Brazilian mother, upon being reminded that there may be homosexual priests in her son's school, replied, "Yes, I know, and I have told Roberto to watch out for himself."

Brazilian tolerance for the homosexual seems to be part of a larger pattern of tolerance for sexuality in general. During four days of carnaval, Brazil is characterized by extraordinary relaxation of already permissive sexual attitudes, both toward homosexual and heterosexual behavior. During the 1984 carnaval, orgies in the major nightclubs of Rio de Janeiro were televised live on national television, an act which implies approval and cooperation from very high federal government officials. The following is exerpted from a letter describing the 1984 carnaval:

> There was no sense of decency anywhere in
> Brazil. Lots of nude people everywhere, women
> with no clothes on at all the bars, orgies in
> all the well-known nightclubs of Brazil, all
> shown on TV all over the country after mid-
> night. The schools of samba of Rio De Janeiro
> went crazy with incredible luxury and spending
> in these times of financial problems for Brazil.
> It was just amazing. Almost all the women went
> into the streets and parades topless. Sex was on
> everybody's mind [João Pinto, personal communi-
> cation, 1984].

In Brazil in 1981, a revealing incident occurred. An actor, Carlos Moreno, playing a timid, somewhat effeminate salesman, became popular on television commercials advertising a product "Bom Bril" for cleaning pots and pans. He was fired by the advertising agency because he was effeminate, and re-placed by a more machão actor. This announcer was not well-received by the Brazilian housewives and the advertising agency, DPZ, received thousands of telephone calls insisting that Carlos Moreno return to the advertisements. There was even a demonstration by the Association of Domestic Workers in Porto Alegre to protest the firing. As a consequence of protests all over the country, Carlos Moreno was returned to the television commercial (Folha De São Paulo 1981).

It may be argued that in Latin America law is not as im-portant as the informal enforcement procedures of police or arbitrary decisions of politically powerful persons. Nonstatu-tory power is important in all societies, and it is certainly important in Latin America. Informal police practices are on the whole far more important in the daily life of Latin Ameri-cans than of North Americans. It is true that there is con-siderable political violence in many countries of Latin America, but this violence is not usually directed against homosexuals. There does not exist in Latin America, either formally or informally, the systematic surveillance, entrapment, arrests,

and prosecution of homosexuals as in the Anglo-Saxon countries. For example, the surveillance of public toilets with
subsequent arrests and prosecutions is still common practice
in the United States, Canada, Great Britain, and Australia.
Although in Brazil there is some homosexual activity in public
toilets, bars, movie houses, or other places known to be
frequented by homosexuals, a more casual attitude toward
public sexual activity prevails, as was exemplified by the following anecdote. A respondent relates that he was in a public
toilet in São Paulo frequented by homosexuals. The custodian
entered to clean the toilet and, noticing a flurry of homosexual activity, instead of calling the police, said, "O.K., all
you queers, stop what you are doing for about an hour. Go
out and take a rest, I have to clean this damned toilet."

This is not to say that police never enter homosexual
establishments. They sometimes do, but when they do it is
not part of a general systematic surveillance of homosexuals.
Police are likely to enter a homosexual situation when it becomes political rather than purely sexual. An incident occurred in Guatemala in 1976 which illustrates this situation. An
American-style disco called "Pandora's Box," with a clientele
of primarily middle-class and upper-middle-class gay men,
opened in Guatemala City in 1976. Soon thereafter, two homosexual men, sons of highly placed political figures in Guatemala, entered the bar and checked their coats and packages
with an attendant in the outer lobby. Included in the items
checked were two pistols carried for personal protection.
When they finished dancing and went to collect their belong-
ings, one of the pistols was missing. They both became very
agitated. One of the men called his father, an influential
politician. In ten minutes the police arrived and lined up
everybody in the bar and searched them at rifle point. The
pistol was found, and the person who had taken it went to
prison. The pistol was important because of frequent political
assassinations, especially around election time, when rival
candidates are sometimes eliminated in this manner. A lost
pistol can be used for assassinations and blamed upon the
owner of the lost pistol rather than the real assassin. The
police intervened not because the bar was homosexual, but
for reasons unrelated to sexual orientation.

In Brazil, as in most of Latin America, documents are
very important. Citizens are subject to being stopped arbitrarily in the streets and having identification papers or
documentos demanded. In São Paulo a controversy involved
the drag queens or travestis who walk around near the Hilton
Hotel, some of whom are dressed in expensive gowns imported
from New York or Paris. The status of the travestis was
evaluated by São Paulo's chief of police, who ruled that they
could walk near the Hilton cross-dressed in public until any
hour of the night, as long as their documents were in order.

This epitomizes the Latin American view: sexual deviation is not as serious as political deviation, and homosexuality is not a political issue unless it becomes politicized.

This is precisely what happened in Argentina in the 1970s and early 1980s. No homosexual bars or cafes were allowed to exist. There was no public homosexual life as in most other Western countries. Homosexual gatherings, such as parties, were illegal, and while they did take place, they did so surreptitiously. In the early 1970s a rather strong gay liberation movement with a leftist orientation emerged in Argentina, Frente Liberación Homosexual. Many of the leaders of this movement were jailed. Most by now have left Argentina and are living in Spain, Australia, or other countries. While Argentina has a history of intermittent hostility toward homosexuals, the Frente Liberación Homosexual was prosecuted as much because it was leftist as because it was homosexual. Moreover, Argentina is at once the most homophobic of Latin American countries and the most Anglo-Saxon in terms of attitudes toward race and toward homosexuals. The political repression of homosexuals in the 1970s and early 1980s was triggered primarily because of the leftist orientation of the Frente Liberación Homosexual and homosexuals were prosecuted along with many other politically dissident groups. Political repression of homosexuals in the Anglo-Saxon countries tends to come about not because of the political orientation of homosexual groups--of which there are many--but because of homosexual orientation per se. In Anglo-Saxon countries homosexuals themselves, regardless of their political views, are regarded as a subversive and criminal group.

Cuba is another exception to the generally tolerant attitude of Latin American countries toward homosexuality. After Castro came to power, an official policy toward homosexuals was adopted, similar to that which existed in the Soviet Union. Homosexuals were regarded as a result of the decadence of capitalism and thus undesirable in the new communist order, and in 1965 they were placed in internment camps.

Allen Young, a member of the "New Left" and the Gay Liberation Front of New York City went to Cuba in 1970 and reported on his disillusionment with Cuba after his experience with their treatment of homosexuals:

> The oppression is not through sodomy laws, but rather through a commitment to creating a society which would have no homosexuals. Cubans involved in the Communist Party were more articulate in explaining Cuba's anti-homosexual position, though it has not been possible to find this position in public writings and speeches of the Cuban leadership. I was told that homosexuality was an aberration pro-

duced under capitalism, that the future
generations of Cuba would be free of homosexuals if only the youth of the country
could be kept from having contact with
acknowledged homosexuals. They admitted
that in an earlier period (1965, to be specific) homosexuals were interned by the thousands in special work camps known euphemis-
tically as Military Units to Increase Production
(UMAP). But, they said, the brutality which
marked these camps was a 'mistake,' and the
camps no longer existed. Instead, measures
were taken to insure that homosexuals were
excluded from contact with the youth. In
practice, this meant constant purging of homosexuals from schools, including the universities, and from many work centers. No one who
is gay, for example, may be employed in any
division of the Ministry of Education, though
enforcement is not perfect. One member of
the Cuban Communist Party told me how about
a dozen homosexuals of both sexes were quietly asked to leave their posts in the Foreign
Ministry [Young 1972, pp. 210-11].

At present, Cuba seems to be relaxing its treatment of
homosexuals and has considerably revised its criminal codes
dealing with homosexuality. In the new codes, which suggest
Cuba may be returning to a more traditional Latin attitude
toward homosexuals, the age of consent is 16 and there is no
law prohibiting consensual homosexual contacts between
adults (Stamford 1982). Thus, Cuba's laws regarding homosexuality are presently more tolerant than those in many of
the states of the United States. It is still to early to know
what Cuba's new stance toward homosexuals will mean in
terms of enforcement and prosecution.

Despite its 20-year attempt, Cuba was not able to eliminate homosexuality. Homosexuals still exist in significant
numbers. Like homosexuals everywhere, Cuban homosexuals
are active in cultural fields such as the dance, cinema, art,
and literature, and as Young (1972) observed, have enhanced
the international prestige of Cuba. Even drag queens continue to appear in Castro's Cuba. When police photographers
filmed the drag queens in their usual setting, they camped
and struck poses for the cameras (Young 1972, p. 213).

THE PHILIPPINE EROTIC TRADITION

The Philippines represents still another erotic tradition--
that of Southeast Asia, the most tolerant area of the world

with respect to variant sexuality. While in certain respects
the Philippines is westernized, it is strikingly different from
the Anglo-Saxon world in terms of its eroticism, and clearly
belongs to the Southeast Asian erotic tradition. For example,
Asian hand holding in public between males is common practice. That Philippine homosexuals are indigenous is suggested
by early reports. Father Juan de Plascencia, writing in 1589,
records that native Filipinos had among their native priests
"bayoguin . . . a man whose nature inclined toward that of
a woman" (Blair and Robertson 1903, p. 194). In a list of
"ministers of the devil" of the pre-Spanish religion practiced
by the natives, the Spanish friar-chronicler Juan Francisco
de San Antonio, writing in 1738, includes the bayoguin, who
was "an effeminate man . . . inclined to being woman and to
all the matters of this feminine sex" (San Antonio 1977, p.
156).

In the Philippines there has emerged a complex system
of social and sexual relations between heterosexual and homosexual males which is a permanent and dominant feature of
its social and sexual life. The Philippines, like all societies,
is a predominantly heterosexual society. (Its high birth rate
and population increase attest to this fact if no other evidence were available.) Like all societies, the Philippines produces a small (probably no more than 5 percent) population
of persons who are predominantly or exclusively homosexual.*
The reader will recall that in Cebuano the most widely used
and understood term for male homosexual is bayot. While the
term sward is used by a group of educated middle-class
homosexuals in Cebu to refer to themselves, bayot is the
most common term for homosexual, understood by homosexuals
and the general public as well. As in the case of the English
word "homosexual," bayot may take on various connotations
and may imply effeminate or transvestic homosexuality as well
as being merely descriptive of all persons of homosexual sexual orientation.

As is true generally of Southeast Asian and Polynesian
societies, the Philippines has maintained a longstanding tradition of tolerance for its homosexual populations. Homosexuals
are not regarded as aberrant, but as rather ordinary people,
well-treated by Western standards. There are no criminal
statutes dealing with consenting homosexual conduct, and
there is virtually no prosecution under other statutes. Pontēnila (1975) reports that in Dumaguete City an ordinance
against public cross-dressing was passed in 1952 but repealed
in 1971 by the city council itself because this ordinance was

*Excellent ethnographic works on homosexuality in the
Philippines are provided by a long and detailed article by
Hart (1968) and a valuable M.S. thesis by Pontēnila (1975).
Stamford (1979a) has written an authoritative guide to gay
life in the Philippines.

regarded as class legislation violating certain fundamental individual freedoms in the Bill of Rights. Even before its repeal, it was not enforced. Pontēnila's examination of the police logbook showed no record of arrests of bayot for sex-related offenses during this time. Homosexuals are not regarded as a dangerous and subversive group to be put under police surveillance as in the Soviet Union or the Anglo-American countries. There is little hostility or violence directed toward homosexuals--even toward transvestic homosexuals who frequently appear wholly or partially cross-dressed in a variety of public situations--at work, in beauty shops and dress shops, at the movies, on the streets, and at public social events. In Cebu some homosexual teachers at both grade school and university level teach in makeup without arousing hostility or fear that students will become homosexual. As in all homosexual communities, Cebuano bayot range from overtly masculine to overtly feminine in behavior. Because of the general tolerance of Philippine society with respect to sex and gender-related beahvior, the number of homosexuals who cross-dress or wear makeup is probably maximized, while in the Anglo-Saxon countries such behavior is probably minimized. Although there are both masculine and feminine homosexuals in the Philippines, it is the feminine bayot who occupy the most conspicuous place in the life of both the general community and the homosexual world.

Benign attitudes toward bayot are far-reaching, extending even to the highest political circles. The first lady, Imelda Marcos, is said to employ a coterie of bayot hairdressers and dress designers in Malacañang Palace. Both President and Mrs. Marcos appear publicly at organizations of fashion designers and hairdressers to present awards for the bayot's contributions to the Philippine economy. This sharply contrasts with the attitudes of President and Mrs. Kennedy, who reportedly chose Oleg Cassini as the first lady's dress designer because he was a "known" heterosexual, thus avoiding the possibility of scandal in the White House (Kelley 1978). What causes public scandal is, of course, socially defined, and public tolerance for homosexuals in the Philippines makes such public scandals impossible.

THE CALLBOYS

Within the broader atmosphere of tolerance for homosexuals, one of the most conspicuous features of the life of the Philippine bayot is the complex and extensive network of sexual and social relations which homosexuals have with heterosexual men. While homosexual males are probably sexually attracted to heterosexual males in all societies, culturally variable norms regulate sexual access to them. In Anglo-Saxon countries, access is quite limited in that these societies have no culturally prescribed ways by which homosexuals may initiate and engage in sexual relationships with heterosexual males, and there is no legitimation of sexual use of homosexuals by heterosexuals. In the Philippines, however, access is easier. Sexual contact may be initiated by either bayot or callboy. Pontenila (1975, p. 102) reports: "Some men, who prefer a bayot for "kicks" or variation in sexual gratification, may also initiate the contact. He would ask the bayot, "Antigo ka ba nga mopa-ak, Dang?" (How do you bite, young lady?) The bayot would answer, "Ngano man, papa-ak ka ba, Dong?" (Why, would you like to be bitten, young man?)."

Most of the sexual relationships of the bayot are with heterosexual or bisexual men through the callboy system rather than with other homosexuals. Callboy is a loose term referring to adolescent males from about 15 to mid-20s who are willing to have sexual relations with bayot for money. Their predominant sexual orientation is heterosexual in that they are mainly interested in women and will eventually marry and have families.

Sexual liaisons with bayot are rather common in adolescence and are treated as peccadillos of the same order as drinking and smoking rather than as serious transgressions. The 15-year-old son of a middle-class Cebu family became prematurely "wild," drinking, smoking, and spending time with a well-to-do bayot physician who gave the young man clothes and use of his car. The family complained that "he was too young to start drinking, smoking, and running around with bayot." Many adolescent males have their first sexual contacts with bayot, and such contacts, if not encouraged, are viewed as an acceptable outlet for adolescent sexual activity, in some cases preferable to marring the virginity of "nice girls." A bayot related the story of a visit to Pilar on one of the Camotes Islands near the island of Cebu where eight bayot went together to visit friends: "When we were going to sleep, a group of high school boys came and serenaded us through the window and then we went outside and picked partners. There were two boys apiece for each of us. We had sex. The next day I was invited for lunch at the house of one of the boys I had sex with. His mother was very friendly, saying, 'Just call me mommy.' She knew what had happened the night before."

Relations between heterosexual and homosexual males cannot be fully understood without some understanding of the role of economics in adolescent male-female relations. While social custom does not separate adolescent males and females as in some societies, economics in the Philippines often do. For example, Lino is a waiter in a popular downtown restaurant in Cebu and a part-time callboy. He is bright and industrious, but still has yet to finish high school at the age of 20. Lino describes his financial situation in 1979:

> I recently quit another restaurant job to work
> at "Pete's Kitchen," where I am making 5 pesos
> a day, working eight hours a day, seven days
> a week. For the first six-month probationary
> period I will not receive even my tips, which all
> go into a common coffer. Eventually I will re-
> ceive about 100 pesos a week in tips, but for
> the time being I must get by on 5 pesos a day--
> the price of a hamburger or movie. I get my
> meals free at the restaurant, but must pay P1.30
> for my jeepney, leaving me P3.70 per day--the
> price of a package of cigarettes. I would like a
> girlfriend but I don't have the money to take
> anyone out.

Many girls, as might be imagined, are also in difficult financial conditions and desperately want a good marriage as a way
out of poverty. Socially, these girls cannot regard sex lightly,
but must hold together all their assets, including virginity,
in order to make a match which will lift them out of poverty,
or at least not drag them down further. Naturally, romances
flourish despite poverty, but sex is not always the natural
culmination of romance, as might be the case under other
more affluent economic conditions. Sometimes adolescent males
will joke, "Girls just want to kiss, but bayot will work you
over. I think I will go back to bayot." It is in this sexual
hiatus that the bayot and heterosexual male serve each other
sexually. The bayot flatters the callboy, tells him he is guapo
(handsome), performs a variety of sexual acts, including
fellatio, and then pays him, too. This, at least temporarily,
offsets the callboy's frustration of not achieving the real object of sexual desire--females.

The extent to which the callboy's activities are professionalized varies widely. Some callboys go to Manila for a few
weeks to make money and then return to the provinces.
Others work as callboys steadily for periods of months or
even several years, later marrying heterosexually. Some are
schoolboys who seize an occasional opportunity for making money. While callboys are to be found everywhere in the Philippines,
and while there is a more or less professionalized group of
callboys in Manila, Cebu, and other large cities, the term is
amorphous, referring to almost any adolescent male who will
on occasion have sexual relations with homosexuals for money.
While precise figures are impossible, estimates by several
adult heterosexual males are that from 75 to 90 percent of all
adolescent males, especially from the urban working classes,
have at some time been paid for sexual relations. These estimates may be high, but they do suggest that the callboy
phenomenon is quite common. Heterosexual males frequently
report their first sexual experience to have been with bayot

in their home towns. In certain towns the callboy system has become highly institutionalized. In the sugar cane capital of Bacolod, a city of about 300,000 people, also in the Visayas, some 300 callboys are said to work in or near the area of the central plaza. In addition to having sexual relations with the local homosexual population, as many as a dozen boys will offer their services to any single male strolling through the park at high noon. The boys have free access to the main hotel in Bacolod, are known to guards and other hotel personnel, and move freely in and around the hotel as long as they behave themselves. Most hotels in the Philippines politely regard the sexual activities of their guests as private matters. While guests are usually well-protected in terms of security guards, roomboys are ubiquitous.

Some Bacolod callboys are led by a young "tourist-guide," who serves as a kind of pimp, but most operate on their own. Parents in Bacolod are generally aware of the callboy activities, but their attitudes are generally those of toleration and amusement: "Boys will be boys." Moreover, they feel that it is the client who is being taken advantage of. "Who but a crazy person would pay 50 pesos to have sexual relations with a scrawny 16-year-old boy?"

In the resort town of Pagsanjan on Luzon, practically all adolescent males in the town of some 3,000 inhabitants work as callboys (Stamford 1979a). These sexual activities are well-known to parents, of course, but again attitudes tend to be tolerant with relatively little moral indignation. In many cases the boys are the primary source of income for hard-pressed parents, brothers, and sisters who find it easy to ignore the source of their daily sustenance. Recently, the Kiwanis Club in Pagsanjan expressed concern over the callboy situation, not so much because of sex, but because of allegations having to do with drugs. Generally speaking, the poorer families are both aware of and tolerant of callboy practices. Such attitudes have their counterpart in the heterosexual world, where the female "hostess" is likely to be a nice girl from a poor family who is helping to feed her family rather than a highly professionalized prostitute. A favorite theme in Tagalog movies is that of the "hostess" who is forced to juggle her love for the boy-next-door and her need to sustain the family.

The callboy system does not appear to "turn boys into homosexuals," and callboys usually enter into heterosexual marriages by their early or mid-twenties, directing their attention to their wives, families, and jobs at the end of adolescence. Filipinos, long accustomed to the callboy system, do not share the Anglo-Saxon folk belief that sexual orientation is contagious, precariously balanced, or that a boy at a certain critical time can be "pushed into" homosexuality. Neither the general public nor the boys themselves fear that callboys will become <u>bayot</u>.

In Manila, along with the proliferation of female prostitution, there are houses with callboys and rooms, the most famous of which is the Retiro 690 Club, where each night some 40 different boys are available. Boys work only one or two nights a week. Some 200 boys in all are loosely connected with the Retiro 690 Club. A boy who receives about $15.00 U.S. per client can make as much as $45.00 U.S. in one night, while his father has to drive a jeepney long hours each day for a month to make the equivalent.

While the callboys in Manila and resort areas like Pagsanjan now cater to foreign tourists as well as Filipino, the callboy system is deeply rooted in traditional relations between homosexuals and heterosexuals in all areas of the Philippines. It is the heterosexual male willing to enter into a relationship with a bayot who is likely to capture the bayot's heart, either for a few months or for a fleeting sexual relationship. Sexual relations between the callboy and the bayot are not characterized by the rigid activo-pasivo relations which tend to be found between homosexual and heterosexual in Latin America. While bayot report that callboys prefer the active role, they do not rigidly insist upon it, and the nature of the sexual contact largely depends upon the financial arrangement worked out by the partners.

There tends to be a fixed price, depending on the desired activity, with the bayot paying according to his wishes. In Cebu, according to a knowledgeable bayot, the price scale at the beginning of 1980 (at an exchange rate of about 7.5 pesos to the dollar was:

5 to 20 pesos: hugging, kissing, and oral sex performed by the bayot

15 to 25 pesos: hugging, kissing, anal insertor role played by the callboy

30 to 100 pesos: "The works;" the bayot calls the tune for this price. The callboy will fellate or even allow the bayot to play the active anal insertor role

For even larger sums of money, 1,000 pesos for example, actors and television celebrities are said to be available, but such a fantasy is beyond the reach of most Cebuano bayot and remains a topic for gossip only.

Despite the normal preoccupation with and conversation about sex, the Philippine bayot does not have as extensive sexual contacts as his American counterpart has. The effect of the callboy system is to limit sexual relations with the possible exception of the wealthy bayot. Since the bayot is mainly interested in heterosexual men and not in other bayot, and since callboys only have sex for money, the frequency of sexual relations is directly dependent upon availability of money. Some bayot save for weeks for enough money to pay a callboy. Sexual encounters are further limited by the lack of privacy. As in most third world countries, unmarried people usually live with their families, and finding a time and place for sexual relations can often be a problem. The net effect of the callboy system is to attenuate the frequency of sexual outlet of both bayot and callboy.

Of course, bayot sometimes fall in love with callboys, creating financial pressure for the bayot. A professor reported that she had a heart-to-heart talk with Danilo, her hairdresser, about his carelessness with money. "Why don't you hang on to your money, Danilo?" "Because I am in love with my boyfriend, and he won't love me unless I give him money. He eats first and then I eat what is left over." Unlike Latin machos, Filipino callboys are sometimes seen in public nightclubs or restaurants on "dates" with bayot. This does not diminish the masculinity of the callboy, for the callboy-bayot relationship is generally understood by the public.

The beauty contest is an occasion for contact between callboys and bayot, bringing out the stage-door johnnies who hang around the improvised dressing rooms and stages. By tradition, the prize money, which may be no more than 100 pesos, is spent on callboys. Some of the contestants have "husbands" or "misters" whom they are maintaining, in which case they are "accompanied." Those who don't have misters "scout around" or entertain the stage-door johnnies. Sexual relations between bayot and heterosexual men occur in all social classes. In the poor barrios, where the bayot do not have money to go out on Saturday night, they sometimes sponsor Saturday night dances within the barrio, inviting bayot from other poor barrios to join in. They dress in whatever female finery they have and are treated as women by the men in the barrio, who also dance with them. Sexual encounters often ensue as the bayot spends his meager week's saving on a man. Even in the squatter areas, bayot are to be found where they often serve as launderers, manicurists, pedicurists, and household helpers, sometimes maintaining sexual relationships with men in the area.

Many bayot are to be found in the highest social circles, such as the movie industry in Manila. It is said that in the movie industry one has to have bayot sponsorship in order to achieve success. A well-known "bold star" or male sex symbol was reported to have been a well-paid callboy before his rise to stardom. Still another famous "action star" was previously a stunt man who allegedly achieved stardom through proper bayot connections. Gossip columns in the Manila press abound with such stories. Whether all these reports are literally true is not so important as the fact that the reports are not regarded as particularly scandalous or detrimental to an

actor's career. Unlike American stars, Filipino actors do not
agonize over whether homosexual roles will be detrimental to
their careers.

SOCIAL RELATIONS

The sexual relations between bayot and heterosexual
males are extensive and placed, characterized by a lack of
the hostility and violence toward the homosexual that often
accompany the relations between the American hustler and
his client. Similarly, the social relations between heterosexual and homosexual in the Philippines are relatively devoid of
hostility and conflict. Heterosexual men do not see bayot as
menacing, but as amusing and entertaining, even if they do
not consort with them. To have social contact with a bayot
does not mean that one is a bayot or even that one is having sexual relationships with bayot. For example, young
heterosexual males in Cebu frequently get their haircuts in
the beauty shops of the bayot, who have the reputation of
giving better haircuts than ordinary barbershops. The bayot
also busses over and flatters the heterosexual customers.
Bayot frequently appear in Filipino films, where they are
portrayed in a friendly and comic light. They are often
shown as companions of main characters or in other ways
part of the ongoing social scene. They are not portrayed as
dangerous psychopaths or murderers as is frequently the
case in American movies (such as Cruising, American Gigolo,
and Looking for Mr. Goodbar).

In the University of San Carlos in Cebu the relations
between heterosexual and homosexual students tend to be
jocular and cordial. For example, a group of heterosexual
engineering students sponsored a symposium for the entire
university on homosexuality in which two bayot, also students, represented the homosexual point of view. While American homosexual groups are often careful to present only
"straight appearing" homosexuals in such public relations
undertakings, it is the effeminate bayot who may represent
the homosexual point of view on such occasions in the Philippines. The symposium was characterized by considerable
good-natured, ribald interaction between the students and
the bayot. An effeminate bayot who uses makeup, a kind of
unisex outfit, and a fluffy hairdo--typical bayot street garb
--is sometimes greeted by flirtatious or salacious remarks
and whistles, but never hostility.

In the Philippines, all university students must complete
four semesters of ROTC in order to graduate. While the bayot
are expected to go through the ROTC program like everyone
else, effeminate bayot are not expected to march or handle
weapons if they don't want to, and they are allowed to work

in the office or to clean the officers' quarters. At the ROTC
parties they take a prominent role in planning the parties,
entertaining, dancing, and serving food.

While most of the public attention in the Philippines is
focused upon the effeminate or transvestic homosexuals, who
often are hairdressers and beauticians, it should be emphasized that Filipinos are also aware of the fact that many
homosexuals are masculine, and occupy, as in other societies,
a wide variety of occupations, including traditionally masculine occupations ranging from jeepney driver to politician.
While little public attention is paid to masculine homosexuals,
tolerance for effeminate homosexuals is not achieved by the
price of intolerance for masculine homosexuals; that is, while
effeminate bayot are found amusing, there is little hostility
expressed toward masculine homosexuals, whose lives tend to
be considerably more subdued than those of the effeminate
bayot. There is little public concern for masculine bayot, nor
is there criminalization of his activities. While there are few
places in a city like Cebu where homosexuals meet other than
on the street, certain movie houses serve as meeting places.
A masculine homosexual was asked what would happen if he
were caught having sexual play in a movie house. He responded, "It would be disastrous; the manager would ask me
to leave and never come back." Similar cases in the United
States are often criminally prosecuted. Thus, for both masculine and feminine homosexuals there is widespread social
tolerance and no criminalization or organized surveillance of
sexual activities, as is found in Anglo-Saxon societies. The
same can be said for lesbians or "tomboys," whose existence
is considerably more private than that of bayot. While the
general public is aware of lesbians, they evoke little concern
and certainly no moral indignation.

SOURCES OF TOLERATION

There is, of course, no definitive answer to the question
of why attitudes toward homosexuals in the Philippines are
so tolerant, any more than there is any definitive answer
why attitudes in the Anglo-Saxon world are so negative and
repressive. Longstanding attitudes connected with sexual
cultures or erotic traditions undoubtedly are of considerable
importance. Attitudes in the Philippines are part of the Southeast Asian erotic tradition, which tends to be quite tolerant
of all forms of consenting sexuality, including homosexuality
and prostitution. All societies regulate personal autonomy but,
of course, differ in the ways in which they do so. While the
Anglo-Saxon countries in some respects have achieved a high
degree of personal freedom, in other respects they restrict
personal freedom. For example, the United States is well-

known for its lack of censorship and its freedom of movement without documentation, yet historically it has greatly restricted personal freedom of racial and sexual minorities. Altman's generalization that "many Third World countries impose far more rigid morality than does the United States" (Altman 1982, p. 90) is not borne out by examination of Third World attitudes toward sexuality and variant sexuality. While there is wide variation with respect to the ways in which societies control sexual behavior, it is clear that the United States and other Anglo-Saxon countries enforce codes of sexual morality to an extent and in ways unknown in much of the Third World.

In the United States, certain sexual activities, particularly those of sexual minorities, are regarded as potentially dangerous and therefore as concerns of the state. While Philippine society, like many other societies, exercises indirect censorship of the press and requires extensive documentation, the regulation of private sexual activity, except in the case of rape or other types of forcible sexual relations, is not considered important to the state.

Filipino toleration of homosexuals may well be related to the broader attitudes toward gender-related behavior. There is a good deal of truth in the Filipino quip, "We don't need women's liberation in the Philippines--we've had it for years." Traditionally, women have occupied places of considerable importance in Philippine commerce and industry. More than half of the physicians in the Philippines are women. Women are very prominent in the universities, are apt to be in administrative positions, and are often chairpersons of departments such as physics or mathematics which have traditionally been considered "male departments." Since women appear to be more generally accepting of homosexuality than heterosexual males, the prominence of women in Philippine society may exert a softening effect on societal attitudes toward homosexuals.

Filipino mothers tend to be tolerant of emerging homosexuality in the form of early cross-gender behavior. Mothers sometimes collaborate with bayot children, giving them lipstick or letting them play with dolls, while concealing this behavior from the fathers. The Filipino view is similar to that of the native-born Hawaiian that "every family will have a mau (homosexual)." While all societies socialize children into sex roles appropriate to anatomical sex, the Filipino mothers are rather tolerant of effeminate behavior in bayot children once it appears (see Tables 2.14 and 2.15, pp. 53-54).

Surely economics are tied into this broader cultural pattern of toleration. As a bellhop in Bacolod put it, "Everybody in the Philippines is working." In a country which has serious problems in feeding its 50 million people, the daughter who works as "hostess" and feeds a family of six provokes little moral indignation. When the sexual activities of a call-boy make the difference between a family's eating and not eating, nocturnal comings and goings are not subject to scrupulous parental attention. While economics alone cannot explain the sexual tolerance of the Philippines, it may also be true that only well-fed societies can allow themselves the luxury of moral outrage over the millions of sexual acts and the great variety of sexual expression in any given society. Boswell's allegation that homosexuality is usually tolerated in highly urban societies (Boswell 1980, p. 35) is debatable. Toleration for homosexuals seems to be quite common in some traditional societies in contrast to some modern urban societies. This may well have to do with family size. One homosexual child in a family of ten is not seen as a tragedy. However, where families have only two children, one homosexual is likely to be much more upsetting. Unlike American society, Filipinos appear to know the sexual orientation of their children, and while they may not be delighted, they do not consider it a major disgrace to have a bayot child.

Knowledge of an toleration for the sexual orientation of one's neighbors may well be related to the density of the Philippine population. The density for the Visaya region is 203 persons per square kilometer; for the Island of Cebu it is 355 persons per square kilometer; for Cebu City the density is more than 800 per square kilometer. One of the most striking aspects of Philippine life is the presence of people--everywhere. If one walks through a lower-class or even middle-class neighborhood, there are people walking on the streets, gathered around "sari-sari" (variety) stores, clusters of teenage boys talking, men playing dominoes, women doing household chores. A kiss is rarely private; someone is always nearby. Privacy is a luxury only the well-to-do can afford. The Filipinos see the "tomboy" courting a neighborhood girl and gossip about it. Filipinos see a bayot making a pass at a neighborhood boy and joke about it. The visibility of these activities has the effect of demystifying them. The neighbor is likely to observe at first hand at least some of these activities and in turn sees their resemblance to his or her own heterosexual activities. The sexual activities of bayot and "tomboys" are not bizarre activities enacted in faraway places by strangers, but mundane activities acted out by acquaintances, friends, and relatives in one's own neighborhood.

Perhaps most important of all is the Filipino's belief in the naturalness of the bayot. The bayot is not mentally ill or criminal, but is part of the natural social order. Bayot constitutes a third sex or a "third creation," a term that is often invoked by bayot themselves as well as the general public. Filipinos are shocked that bayot are treated as insane and criminal in the United States, since they are regarded as part of the very ordinary Filipino world. Just as there are men and women, jeepney drivers, and lottery ticket vendors, there are bayot and callboys--all part of the ongoing, mundane social scene. In fact, Hart (1968) has suggested that societies which regard homosexuality as a natural, biological occurrence may be more tolerant than societies which view homosexuality as socially derived.

In an era of growing repression and intolerance of homosexuals in the English-speaking world, the careful examination of contemporary societies which are tolerant and the social-structural conditions which make for tolerance takes on special significance. The Philippine case is especially instructive. The antagonistic relations between heterosexual and homosexual males in the Anglo-Saxon world do not appear inevitable; instead, they emerge from particular social arrangements. The Philippine callboy system provides a socially acceptable way of dealing with the increase in genital arousal of males after puberty and of bridging the sexual hiatus between male and female sexual response in early and middle adolescence. At the same time, the system provides a socially acceptable way of simultaneously fulfilling the homosexual's erotic needs and providing for the callboy's genuine economic needs. The net effect of the system does not appear to turn heterosexuals into homosexuals; rather, it helps prepare heterosexual males for adult sexuality. The sexual relations between bayot and callboy appear to have the effect of softening the potentially harsh and antagonistic relations between heterosexual and homosexual males, frequently found in Western societies.

THE SOCIOLOGY AND
POLITICS OF HOMOSEXUALITY

It may now be obvious that the view presented in the preceding chapters is one which challenges many of the traditional social-scientific and psychiatric views of the origins and nature of homosexuality. As we have seen, homosexuals emerge in all societies. These persons do not choose their sexual orientation, nor is it created by the societies in which they live. A small group of about 5 percent of male homosexuals appears in all societies, as they have probably always appeared. No scientific evidence to the contrary has been established.

Unlike most social-scientific formulations, which view homosexual orientation as socially learned in origin, the present view suggests not only that homosexual orientation has a biological basis but that some aspects of gender behavior may also be biologically derived. While biological views have come to be viewed as inherently "illiberal," and social learning views have come to be regarded as inherently "liberal" with respect to the subject of homosexuality, this assumption needs reexamination. Although neither social learning nor biological explanations are inherently "bad" or "good," biological explanations of homosexuality have long had close connections with the struggle for gay rights. In practice social learning explanations, primarily through the psychoanalytic movement and indirectly through sociological formulations influenced by psychoanalytic thought, have had close connections with homophobia.

THE INFLUENCE OF FREUD

It is commonplace to note that although sociologists tend to be anti-Freudian, they nonetheless continue to be influenced by Freud's ideas. This is especially true with respect to Freud's ideas about homosexuality. It is unfortunate for the present state of the sociology of homosexuality that Freud became the starting point for our thinking about homosexuality, for we have not yet succeeded in freeing ourselves from the Freudian dogma. In other areas of sociology (for example, criminology) we have done so. A strong, empirically derived sociological criminology in the form of the Sutherland School emerged in the 1940s, to restrain the perpetuation of outlandish Freudian ideas in criminology. Such a movement never emerged in the sociology of homosexuality and thus Freud and Kinsey remain the two major intellectual influences.

It is unfortunate and ironic that Freud's ideas became so influential in sociological interpretations of homosexuality because, whatever the merits of Freud's more general formulation of sexuality, Freud lived and worked in a highly conventional, heterosexual world and had little understanding of homosexuals. It is doubtful that Freud even knew much about the homosexual subculture of his day, as he rarely treated homosexual patients, and despite his famous and rather sympathetic letter to the mother of an American homosexual, it appears that Freud found homosexuals personally distasteful. At one point he suggested that some homosexuals of his acquaintance be shipped "across the ocean, with some money, let's say to South America, to find their destiny" (Roazen 1971, p. 149). He confessed to Wortis that he found the sexual habits of Magnus Hirschfeld disgusting (Wortis 1963, p. 41). Wortis, who underwent a didactic analysis with Freud and kept a diary of his sessions as part of a fellowship to study homosexuality, provides us with a revealing summary of Freud's attitudes and opinions about homosexuality. It is clear from a reading of Wortis's diary that Freud held inconsistent and rather naive ideas about homosexuality. For example, he told Wortis that children raised by their fathers without the presence of their mothers would become homosexual. When Wortis suggested that the problem might be investigated empirically, Freud answered that research on this topic "is not necessary. We know how they will work out without that" (Wortis 1963, p. 91).

It is of course easy to judge historical figures from the point of view of present-day knowledge. However, even from the point of view of his contemporaries, Freud's ideas about homosexuality were untenable. Havelock Ellis, already a well-established sex researcher and writer, published Sexual Inversion in 1896 with coauthor John Addington Symonds. Through his wife, Edith Lees, a writer, feminist, as well as a lesbian, Ellis was able to explore homosexuality in a way far different from Freud's. John Addington Symonds, a well-known literary figure of his day, became interested in the study of homosexuality late in his life because of his own homosexuality. He collaborated with Ellis and supplied him with case histories, obtained with a crude questionnaire, of many of his friends and acquaintances who were living and working in the everyday world. Thus, Ellis and Symonds produced in Sexual Inversion what is probably the first study of homosexuality derived, if not from random samples, certainly from homosexuals outside prisons, asylums, and clinics.

Magnus Hirschfeld, a contemporary of both Freud and Ellis, is without a doubt the most important twentieth century researcher of variant sexuality. He has left a legacy of research on that topic, which will be difficult to duplicate. Hirschfeld interviewed thousands of homosexuals, transvestites, and transsexuals. He established the first modern institute where both research and therapy were conducted. The homosexuals, transvestites, and others who came to the institute were treated like guests rather than patients. He founded the first journal dealing with homosexuality. He fought doggedly for the decriminalization of homosexuality under German statutes. Despite a monumental contribution made by Hirschfeld--nearly 200 books and articles--his work is virtually forgotten in contemporary social scientific circles. His institute and its extensive and valuable collection were burned by the Nazis in 1933, and his staff imprisoned. Kinsey dismissed Hirschfeld's work out of hand, in part because Hirschfeld was a homosexual and in part because he was too much involved in political issues, particularly the fight to decriminalize homosexuality (Pomeroy 1972, p. 66). In many respects Hirschfeld's work on homosexuality is far more systematic and enlightening than Kinsey's.

The work of Ellis, Symonds, and Hirschfeld ought then to have represented a logical beginning point for the sociological investigator. In terms of both method and theory, both bodies of work are far more congenial to contemporary sociological thinking than the work of Freud. Unfortunately for the contemporary study of homosexuality, both bodies of work were rejected because they incorporated a view that homosexuality was innate. It is also important to note that despite the fact that the work of Ellis, Symonds, and Hirschfeld thoroughly rejected the notion that homosexuality was pathological, Freud's view that homosexuality was acquired and pathological became the dominant position. No doubt social scientists influenced by these ideas were more offended by the notion that homosexuality might be innate than by the idea that it might be pathological.

By the 1940s, under the influence of Freud and of Kinsey, the idea that homosexual orientation was biological, long associated with the struggle for homosexual rights, fell into almost irretrievable oblivion and disrepute. Kinsey held the view that homosexuality was acquired and nonpathological, a view which many sociologists also found congenial.

Kinsey's work, like Freud's, was primarily aimed at understanding sexuality in general, not homosexuality specifically, and his treatment of homosexuality suffers from some of the same problems as did Freud's. It seems ironic that much of the publicity that Kinsey received and much of the controversy in which he became entangled arose from the publication of his statistics on homosexuality. Kinsey came to the study of human sexuality rather late in life, and he apparently had little knowledge of homosexuality before undertaking his research. It is to his credit that once he had undertaken his research he did go into the homosexual community and make direct observation of homosexual life, including at least one occasion the observation of "sex in public places" at the Coliseum in Rome. On the whole the interpretation of homosexuality which emerged from Kinsey's work was not profound, and at points bordered on the naive. For example, he believed that homosexuality could result from teenage acne or obesity. Referring to Kinsey, Pomeroy records:

> Asked about a possible connection between
> acne and homosexuality, he could cite a number
> of cases where severe cases of acne so inter-
> fered with a boy's social adjustment that he
> found it difficult to make approaches to girls
> and was thrown back on his own sex. There
> was no physiologic connection, of course, as he
> was careful to note, but he could point to sev-
> eral cases in which acne, along with obesity,
> crippling, or other handicaps were physical
> factors in the development of homosexual pat-
> terns [Pomeroy 1972, p. 19].

At the most general level, his view is an acquired, non-pathological interpretation. Kinsey rejected any kind of physiological or hormonal explanation. Kinsey's own findings that a relatively large percentage of males had had homosexual experiences led him to embrace the notion that there is no such thing as a homosexual. In Kinsey's perspective, there are no behavioral elements connected with homosexuality. Rather, homosexuality is a point on a continuum. Kinsey sixes are behaviorally the same as Kinsey zeroes except in their sexual practices. Kinsey did not make a conceptual distinction between people who are exclusively homosexual and those who engage in homosexuality during adolescence or under some special circumstances (Kinsey 1956).

While Kinsey had many homosexual informants, he did not engage homosexuals as resarchers, insisting that his professional staff be "happily married" men, that is, heterosexual (Pomeroy 1972, p. 101). The implication is that heterosexuals could objectively study both homosexuals and heterosexuals,

but that homosexuals were incapable of studying either.
Pomeroy describes Kinsey's explanation of homosexuality as
follows:

> The physical basis, he believed, of both homo-
> sexual and heterosexual behavior was a touch
> response. When an individual had a pleasurable
> first experience, of either kind, he looked for-
> ward to a repetition of the experience often
> with such anticipation that he could be aroused
> by the sight or mere thought of another person
> with whom he might make contact. Unsatisfac-
> tory experience, on the other hand, built up a
> prejudice against repetition. Whether one built
> a heterosexual or homosexual pattern depended,
> therefore, partially on the satisfactory, or un-
> satisfactory nature of one's first experience
> [Pomeroy 1972, p. 76].

What has come into contemporary social science as an interpretation of homosexuality is likely to have its origins in
either the Freudian or the Kinseyian tradition. Both interpretations are variants of social learning theory, and place the
origins of homosexuality in the nexus of early social relationships. Contemporary social scientists generally have embraced
some variation of this position, assuming that there is something automatically humanitarian in the social learning position, without carefully examining the origins and consequen-
ces of that position.

While doing little empirical research on the topic of homosexuality throughout the 1960s and 1970s, sociologists perpet-
uated--without empirical evidence--the longstanding Anglo-
Saxon idea that sexual orientation is fragile, delicately balanced, easily modified, social behavior. While no doubt appearing innocent to the sociologists of the past two decades, this
position inadvertently provided the philosophical foundations
for the virulent homophobic movements that emerged in the
late 1970s with Anita Bryant's crusade, and that continue
unabated into the mid-1980s with the Moral Majority movement.

SOCIOLOGICAL EXPLANATION

The explanation of homosexual orientation most popular
with sociologists is simplistic social learning theory. For example, Thio writes in a deviant behavior text:

> Only through constant interaction with parents
> and other socializing agents of society, are
> they conditioned to narrow, focus, and restrict

> their sexual interest to the sexual object
> choice approved by society--and simultane-
> ously conditioned to kill off their interest in
> other object choices disapproved by society.
> Since there is a powerful taboo against homo-
> sexuality and strong support of heterosexuality
> in our society, most American adults have been
> conditioned to heterosexual activity.
>
> But some individuals may have been condi-
> tioned toward homosexuality by their sexual
> experience with same-sex others during their
> childhood or adolescence. They may have en-
> gaged in homosexual acts as an experimentation
> to satisfy their curiosity. . . . Whatever the
> reason that first led the youngster into homo-
> erotic society, if he or she repeatedly engaged
> in it and enjoyed it, he or she becomes homo-
> sexual [Thio 1978, p. 218].

On the surface this seems a reasonable position. However, it should be remembered that sexual orientation is fixed before many children have an opportunity to have childhood sex play, and some children do not have childhood sex play at all. Some children have homosexual sex play and become heterosexual. Some children have heterosexual sex play and become homosexual. Erotic imagery, including homosexual imagery, often precedes childhood sex play. Children who as adults will be homosexuals often experience strong homosexual attractions before any sexual contact. Furthermore, the social scientist must not only explain sexual activity per se but complex behavioral components which accompany sexual orientations and which begin to emerge quite early (see Green 1974, 1976; Whitam 1977). The persistent appearance of homosexual orientation presents the researcher with a difficult question: How do people become homosexual when, from the moment of birth, enormous efforts are begun to socialize children into a heterosexual orientation and a gender identity consistent with the cultural expectations for their anatomical sex?

A slightly different version of social learning theory emphasizes pathological family relationships. For example, Julian (1973, p. 231) writes that "certain pathological situations do seem to appear with significant frequency in the case histories of homosexuals: the family drama often includes a dominant or seductive mother, and a weak, detached, or overly critical father, factors which prevent the male child from identifying with the masculine role."

This is clearly Freudian and includes the role model notion. Even Money, who rejects the idea of biologically determined sexual orientation, holds that sexual orientation--either heterosexual or homosexual--becomes apparent as early as two or three years old (Money and Ehrhardt 1972; Money and Tucker 1975). As discussed in Chapter 2, a much more plausible explanation is that parents' attitudes are a reaction to emerging homosexuality, not its cause. Prehomosexual children, especially boys, who often exhibit feminine tendencies, incur the disappointment, hostility, and neglect of their fathers and find their mothers more supportive. Parents are usually surprised by the emerging homosexuality of their children. They react to it, frequently with considerable agitation, but do not create it.

McCaghy and Skipper (1974, p. 155) regard situational factors as crucial in the development of homosexual orientation. They suggest that "because sexual behavior, deviant or not, emerges out of the context of social situations, it would seem that the structure of certain situations might contribute to becoming involved in homosexual behavior and to the formation of homosexual self-concept."

Such situational ideas lend themselves nicely to interpretation by homophobic elements. If homosexuality emerges out of social situations, then it might be possible for teachers to make homosexuals out of students in the teacher-student situation. Sexual behavior is such a complex topic that no easy generalization can be made that sexual behavior emerges out of the context of social situations. While it is certainly true that all sexual behavior is acted out in a cultural context, it is also true that some sexual behavior is closely related to the body and its functions; other sexual behavior is related to social structure, and still other sexual behavior is related to social situations. Perhaps the most implausible sociological explanation of all is that of Robertson (1977, p. 205), who writes: "A new approach to the problem avoids many of these difficulties. It sees homosexual identity as the result of a false self-definition that people impose on themselves. This definition can be made consciously or unconsciously, voluntarily or involuntarily, but it is made in accordance with the prevailing beliefs of the cultures concerned."

This notion, widely disseminated in a best-selling introductory textbook, is preposterous. The idea that one can consciously and voluntarily think oneself into becoming homosexual is simply out of the question. The notion that one can unconsciously and involuntarily do so should strain the credulity of even the most naive undergraduate. Again Robertson writes: "Some people, including some homosexuals, assume that homosexuals are simply "born that way." But since we know that even heterosexuals are not "born that way," this explanation seems unlikely. . . . Homosexuality, like other sexual behavior, is learned" (1977, p. 204).

Robertson goes so far as to declare the idea of innate drives to mate with the opposite sex as a "myth," and writes

in the 1981 edition of Sociology (p. 8) that "Human beings
do not have an instinct to mate with the opposite sex. Our
sexual preferences are entirely learned." Even somewhat
unorthodox sociological theorists tend to follow rather ortho-
dox sentiments regarding explanations of sexual orientation.
Douglas, an ethnomethodologist and an influential figure in
the sociology of deviant behavior, writes:

> Current evidence seems to suggest that while
> the biological existence of sexual impulses is
> certain, the object of those impulses is not bio-
> logically specified in any fixed and determined
> way. The choice of sexual object--of the oppo-
> site sex, same sex, or even of nonhuman ob-
> jects--seems to be influenced in important ways
> by individual experiences and social contexts
> [Douglas and Waksler 1982, p. 166].

Social scientists cling tenaciously to social learning explanations of sexual orientation; yet as Diamond (1978) has
pointed out several important empirical studies raising serious questions about social learning explanations have been
available for quite some time, some as early as the 1950s.
These studies have been widely ignored or even repressed
by social scientists. This material consists of several types:
twin studies, follow-up research on the well-known penec-
tomized twin reared against biological sex, research on a
group of male children with 5-alpha reductase deficiency
reared against biological sex in the Dominican Republic, and
studies of the children of transsexuals and lesbians.

TWIN STUDIES

The best known and most widely cited study on homosexuality in twins is that of Franz Kallman. Although his
work has been systematically criticized on methodological
grounds and although there are, to be sure, methodological
problems with his work, it seems that his work has been
undeservedly dismissed and repressed--not because of methodological shortcomings, but because it supports a biological
view of sexual orientation which is unpopular with most social
scientists. For example, referring to Kallman's work, the
authors of a widely used textbook in human sexuality write:

> There is thus no evidence to date that bio-
> logical factors determine object choice. The
> author of one large-scale study of identical
> twins has claimed a genetic basis for homo-
> sexuality. He has shown that all the identi-

cal twins studied were concordant for homosexuality (that is, if one twin was homosexual,
so was the other). Among fraternal twins the
degree of concordance for homosexuality was
not statistically significant. This study has
been criticized on the grounds that similarities
in environment were not taken into considera-
tion, and other investigators have failed to
replicate its findings [Katchadourian and Lunde
1972, p. 277].

Albert Ellis (1965, p. 27) criticizes Kallman's study on
the following grounds: "In other words, Kallman's study
was not really an investigation of homosexuality in monozygotic twins, but of homosexuality in basically psychotic
twins. And it hardly comes as a surprise, to anyone who is
familiar with the behavior of psychotics, that when one of
them is overtly homosexual the other one is also most likely
to display distinct homosexual behavior."

Factually, Ellis is incorrect because, as Kallman has
written, only 22 cases are classifiable as "schizoid, severely
unstable with obsessive-compulsive features, or excessively
alcoholic." Therefore, 58 of the 80 monozygotic twins were
neither psychotic, neurotic, or alcoholic. Further confusing
the issue is the fact that Kallman included subjects from
"psychiatric, correctional, and charitable agencies" with
those obtained "through direct contacts with the clandestine
homosexual world" (Kallman 1952, p. 287). Some of Kallman's
twins, then, were derived from the general population. Regardless of source, there was high concordance among all
monozygotic twins sampled. These findings are consistent
with twin studies reported before and after Kallman. Unfortunately, Kallman does not include sufficient data for closer
examination, and the identification of specific twin sources
cannot be properly assessed. Although a reassessment of
Kallman's work is in order, his findings cannot be summarily
dismissed. A summary of the correlation of the Kinsey
ratings of Kallman's monozygotic twins is shown in Table 7.1
where Pearson's r = .64. The sexual orientation of the
cotwin in three pairs of 40 monozygotic twin pairs is unknown.

All available studies on twins to date are consistent in
showing a high concordance of homosexuality among monozygotic twins and a low concordance of homosexuality among
dizygotic twins. Predating Kallman's study, Hirschfeld in
1928 reported on complete concordance in seven monozygotic
twin pairs. He did not find such concordance in an unre-
ported number of dizygotic twins. Sanders reported in 1934
that six of seven pairs of monozygotic twins were concordant
for homosexuality (Schlegel 1962). At the same time, Sanders

TABLE 7.1 Kinsey Rating of Kallman's Monozygotic Twins

Pair number	First twin's rating	Second twin's rating
1	6	6
2	6	6
3	6	6
4	6	6
5	6	6
6	6	6
7	6	6
8	6	6
9	6	6
10	6	6
11	6	6
12	6	6
13	6	6
14	6	6
15	6	6
16	6	6
17	6	5
18	6	5
19	6	5
20	5	6
21	5	6
22	5	6
23	5	5
24	5	5
25	5	5
26	5	4
27	5	3
28	5	3
29	4	5
30	4	4
31	4	4
32	4	3
33	4	3
34	3	5
35	3	5
36	3	4
37	3	4

*Pearson's r = .64.

Source: Franz J. Kallman, M.D., "Comparative Twin Study on the Genetic Aspects of Male Homosexuality," The Journal of Nervous and Mental Disease 115 (1952):290.

also reports on four monozygotic twin pairs concordant for homosexuality which were studied by Siro (Schlegel 1962). Habel in 1950 reports on ten pairs of twins, five of which were monozygotic and five dizygotic. Three of the five monozygotic pairs were concordant for homosexuality, while none of the dizygotic pairs was concordant (Schlegel 1962).

The most frequently cited study since Kallman is that of Heston and Shields (1968) done in London between 1948 and 1966, using the Maudsley Hospital Twin Register, which was maintained by the Psychiatric Genetics Research Unit. These researchers report a high rate of concordance--between 40 percent and 60 percent--for homosexual orientation in 12 pairs of monozygotic male twins and a much lower rate of concordance--14 percent--for seven pairs of dizygotic male twins. It should be noted that this research was conducted with patients referred for psychiatric treatment.

Since Kallman, there have been numerous reports of one or two pairs of monozygotic twins, usually reporting only findings of discordance. Most of these are actually case studies or isolated cases of one or two pairs known at the outset to be discordant. Such studies include Lange (1931), Rainer et al. (1960), Klintworth (1962), Mesnikoff et al. (1963), Parker (1964), Koch (1965), Holden (1965), Davison et al. (1971), Green and Stoller (1971).

It seems ironic that Kallman's work has evoked such hostility from social scientists, since his view is that homosexuality is a nonpathological variant, a view which is now popular in the social sciences. For example, Kallman writes: "It seems advisable to view overt homosexual behavior in the adult male as an alternative minus variant in the integrative process of psychosexual maturation rather than as pathognomonically determinative expression of a codifiable entity of behavioral immaturity" (1953, p. 294). In the same vein he continues: "Overt homosexual behavior in the adult male may be viewed as an alternative minus variant in the integrative process of psychosexual maturation, comparable in the sexually reproductive human species to the developmental aspects of the left-handedness in a predominantly right-handed human world" (1953, pp. 118-19).

CHILDREN REARED AGAINST GENETIC SEX

Several recent studies emphasize the importance of the fact that "nature sets limits to sexual identity and partner preference and that it is within these limits that social forces interact and gender roles are formulated" (Diamond 1982, p. 183). Even some social learning theorists recognize that biology plays a part in the development of sexual orientation and gender behavior, but attribute to this a merely passive significance in human sexual behavior. For example, Money and Tucker (1975, p. 87) state, "Whatever the status of your chromosomes, hormones, sex organs, and individuality, their directional push was no match for societal pressures when it came to differentiating your gender identity." However, recent studies which may be considered natural experiments that test labeling theory suggest this is not true.

One of these recent studies deals with a highly publicized case in which the penis of one of two seven-month-old identical twin boys was accidentally burned off during a circumcision procedure done with an electric cauterizing needle (Money and Tucker 1975). Obviously quite concerned and upset, the parents sought help from medical specialists. On consultation with a plastic surgeon who knew of the surgical procedures then being done at Johns Hopkins to help hermaphroditic children, the parents were made aware of the possibility that the twin could be sexually reassigned. When the child was 17 months old the parents consulted specialists at Johns Hopkins, and at the age of 21 months the child underwent the first surgical procedure for sex reassignment. Subsequent to the penectomy the twin was castrated to remove the source of male hormones and then given female hormones. Thus, as Diamond has since pointed out in The Humanist (1978, p. 18), "It must be emphasized that as much as possible was done to defeat the male biological realities and enhance female biological maturation." When the twin was age 12, John Money and his colleagues directly involved with the case indicated that both the twin and the parents had made a successful adjustment to the reassignment decision. Social learning and feminist theorists seized this as evidence to support their contention that sexual identity is basically learned, and the case was widely cited in the social scientific literature as a success. However, it now appears the assessment of the twin's successful change from male to female was premature. "Instead of a successful switch to life as a female, the twin in 1976, when 13 years of age and first seen by a new set of psychiatrists, was said to be beset with problems" (Diamond 1982, p. 183). Diamond also reports that in 1979 psychiatrists familiar with the case have questioned the ability of the twin, then 16, to make a successful adjustment to life as an adult woman. Furthermore, the teenager was reported to walk with a very masculine gait, was called "cavewoman" by her peers because of apparent masculinity, and aspired to become a mechanic, a traditionally masculine occupation.

Another study which elucidates the significance of physiology relative to that of socialization was done in the Dominican Republic by Imperato-McGinley et al. (1979) on genetic males with an inherited deficiency of an enzyme known as 5-alpha-reductase. This enzyme deficiency causes a subsequent reduction in dihydrotestosterone, a hormone necessary for the differentiation of the male genitals while the fetus is developing within its mother's womb. The genitalia of male infants born with this enzyme deficiency look so much like female genitalia that they are routinely raised as girls. However, with the onset of normal testosterone (a male hormone) levels at puberty, these individuals undergo changes which include deepening of their voice, growth and development of their male genitals, and ability to achieve erections, although they are incapable of insemination. The condition does not cause breast development, and at puberty their bodies become more muscular.

Imperato-McGinley et al. identified, studied, and reported on 18 individuals who had been unambiguously raised as females and on whom they had obtained adequate postpubertal psychosexual data. Sixteen of the 18 spontaneously changed from thinking of themselves as girls to thinking of themselves and living as boys. Between the ages of seven and 12, these boys began to realize they were not ordinary girls and became concerned about their true sex. The researchers describe this change as follows:

> A male-gender identity gradually evolved
> over several years as the subjects passed
> through stages of no longer feeling like girls,
> to feeling like men, and finally, to the con-
> scious awareness that they were indeed men.
> The change to a male-gender role occurred
> either during puberty or in the post-pubertal
> period, after the subjects were convinced that
> they were men (male-gender identity) and were
> experiencing sexual interest in women. The
> gender-role change took place at 16 years of
> age, on the average, with a range of 14 to 24
> years [Imperato-McGinley et al. 1979, p. 1234].

Fifteen of the 18 males have adopted a male heterosexual orientation, and have lived with or married women. The sexual orientation of one individual is not known. One of the remaining subjects continues to dress as a woman and "has the affect and mannerisms of a man and engages in sexual activity with village women." This individual seems to resemble a heterosexual transvestite. The remaining individual is the only one of the 18 subjects having a same-sex orientation. According to these researchers: "At 16 years of age, she "married" a man in village B who left her after one year. She left the village, has been living alone and working as a domestic and has not been sexually involved with other men. She wears false breasts, yet her build and mannerisms are masculine. She denies any attraction to women and desires

surgical correction of the genitalia so that she can be a normal woman" (Imperato-McGinley 1979, p. 1234). This individual seems to be a transvestic homosexual or transsexual and
is the only one of the 18 subjects with same-sex orientation.
If labeling theories of sexual orientation are correct, then
we should expect more than one out of 18 subjects to have a
same-sex orientation. One out of 18 is consistent with chance
if we use the 5 percent figure for the occurrence of homosexual orientation in males in the general population.

CHILDREN REARED IN ATYPICAL FAMILIES

Social scientists frequently use role modeling to explain
the development of sexual orientation. However, two important and recent studies indicate that role modeling does not
determine sexual orientation. Richard Green (1978) studied
16 children being raised by transsexual parents and 21 children being raised by lesbian parents. The amount of time
children had lived in families comprised of parents with
atypical sexual orientations ranged from one to 16 years for
transsexual households and two to six years for lesbian
households. The ages of children raised by transsexuals
ranged from three to 20 years, and ages for children raised
by lesbians ranged from five to 14 years. Green (1978, p.
692) writes:

> Sexual identity of the younger children was
> assessed on gross measures found in previous
> research to best reflect emerging sexual iden-
> tity. These include toy and game preference,
> peer group composition (which is typically same-
> sex in grade-school-age children), clothing
> preference, roles played in fantasy games
> (which are typically of the same sex as the
> player), vocational aspiration, and the Draw-
> A-Person test (sex of the first person drawn
> is considered reflective of sexual identity;
> males typically draw males first, and females
> draw females first). For adolescents, informa-
> tion was obtained regarding romantic crushes,
> erotic fantasies, and interpersonal sexual be-
> havior.

Green divided the children into three groups for purposes of analysis. These groups included "Children Raised
by Female-to-Male Transsexuals" (nine children from four
families), "Children Raised by Male-to-Female Transsexuals"
(seven children from three families), and "Children Raised
by Female Homosexuals" (21 children from seven families).

In the female-to-male transsexual families, the sexual
orientation of seven of the nine children (five females and
two males) is known to be heterosexual. In one family, the
two children at the time of the research were ages seven
and eight, and their sexual orientations are as yet unknown.
However, the "children are content being female and male,
respectively. Her favorite toy is a set of dishes; his is a
walkie-talkie. She prefers girls as playmates, he prefers
boys" (p. 694). This is suggestive of later heterosexual
orientation.

In the first of the male-to-female transsexual families,
only one male has reached adolescence, and he is reported
to have a heterosexual orientation. The two girls are reported to be behaviorally feminine and the two boys to be
behaviorally masculine. In the second family, the only child,
an 11-year-old boy, "has no desire to be a woman, cross-
dress, or have an erotic relationship with a man. His mas-
turbatory and nocturnal dream fantasies are heterosexual"
(p. 695). In the third family, a four-year-old boy and
three-year-old girl were too young to ascertain sexual orientation. However, the girl states she wants to be a mommy
when she grows up, and the boy states he wants to be a
daddy when he grows up. Such childhood desires are usually
associated with later heterosexual orientation.

Of the 21 children raised in female homosexual families,
only four had reached puberty at the time of the study. All
four appear to be heterosexual, as assessed by Green's indicators of "favorite toy," "vocational aspiration," and "erotic
fantasies." Of the 17 children who had not reached puberty,
there are no data to suggest later homosexual orientation.

As Green points out, "both psychoanalytic and social-
reinforcement of role-modeling views would predict that having a transsexual or homosexual parent should have a striking effect on a child's sexual identity development (1949,
p. 696). However, as we have seen this is not the case in
the families evaluated by Green.

Similar results have emerged from a more systematic
study directed by Green using more sophisticated method-
ology. His associates Hotvedt and Mandel (1982) matched 50
lesbian mothers and their 58 children with 20 heterosexual
single mothers and their 25 children, who were "collected
from approximately 500 responses to requests for single-
mother subjects." A heterosexual mother and her family were
matched to a lesbian mother and her family on age (plus or
minus five years) and race of mother, age and sex of children, length of time separated from father, marital status of
mother (never married, divorced, separated, widowed),
income level of family, educational level of mother, and (when
possible) mother's religion of upbringing.

Participants in the study were from ten states in the Northeast, Midwest and South; families from both rural and urban areas in those states were visited at home by the researchers. For inclusion in the lesbian sample, women had to be self-designated as homosexual, had to have custody or joint custody of at least one child between ages 3 and 11, and had to have been living with no adult male in the home for at least two years [p. 280].

As measured by several behavioral correlates of later adult sexual orientation, the boys in the lesbian mother and heterosexual mother families were very similar and "consistently chose traditional masculine preferences in play activities, toys, dress, role models, and careers" (p. 283). With respect to the daughters, it was reported that "the two groups of daughters differed somewhat. First, girls in each group showed a wider range of scores than did boys, indicating possibly more flexible sex roles than boys are encouraged to have. Second, daughters of lesbian mothers scored as less traditionally feminine, but still not masculine" (p. 283). In conclusion, "analysis of the children's data has not revealed any sexual identity conflict or homosexual interest. Relationships with fathers and other males do not differ significantly. No examples of child neglect or abuse were discerned" (Mandel et al. 1979, p. 10).

POLITICS OF HOMOSEXUALITY

Social science and politics are closely interwoven, particularly in times and places where sex and gender are politicized. In recent decades the role-labeling perspective has been seen as aligned with such causes as the fight against racism and sexism. Much resistance to biological views of sexual orientation has to do with the mistaken conception that role-labeling theory is politically helpful to homosexuals as well as to blacks and women. We regard the application of the social learning perspective to the explanation of homosexual orientation not only as scientifically untenable, but politically detrimental to the achievement of "gay rights." The view that homosexuals are socially created is one which, beginning with the Freudians, has been linked to efforts to "cure" homosexuals. Sociological concepts such as role modeling and labeling, perhaps politically useful to the feminists, have been used by antihomosexual figures such as Anita Bryant and John Briggs. While sociologists may declaim against the use of sociological concepts by homophobic groups, it is nonetheless true that the view that homosexual orientation is malleable, superficial, and learned, feeds the long-standing fears of the Anglo-Saxons that homosexuals are dangerous people ready to recruit others.

The April 1978 issue of Footnotes carried an announcement that the American Sociological Association affirmed its support of the civil rights of homosexuals and encouraged research in this field. The Sociologists' Gay Caucus had wanted a stronger statement dealing with some of the substantive issues related to the homosexual question which were carefully skirted by the ASA resolution. A resolution adopted by the Sociologists' Gay Caucus in 1977 implied that "sociological concepts have been distorted and sociological research falsified" (SGC Resolution 1977) by homophobic groups and individuals such as Anita Bryant. In another source, the Sociologists' Gay Caucus states: "There is no sociological evidence that children exposed to homosexual role models will acquire homosexual orientations" (SGC pamphlet 1977).

While the resolution adopted by the council of the American Sociological Association and the efforts of the Sociologists' Gay Caucus seem laudable enough, the most fundamental problem raised by the ASA position remains virtually untouched: the nature of sociological research on the subject of homosexuality and its relationship to the rise of powerful homophobic elements in American society in the late 1970s. While most sociologists undoubtedly favor equal rights for homosexuals, they have popularized a view of homosexuality through the variations of social learning theories about the origins and nature of homosexuality, that is neither helpful to homosexuals nor based upon a firm empirical foundation. This view is not so much derived from careful observation of homosexuals and the homosexual world as it is an ideology left over from the black civil rights and feminist movements.

Feminists tend to strongly resist and reject any biological interpretation of homosexual orientation, and they sometimes do so at the expense of homosexuals. For example, in the highly publicized 1975 case of Sergeant Leonard Matlovich, his lawyers argued that since his homosexuality was innate, it could not be spread to nonhomosexuals and that homosexuality constituted no cause for dismissing him from the Air Force; yet from a feminist perspective, Faderman objects to this potentially effective legal strategy. She writes:

> [T]he congenital theory has of late been adopted
> by many gay militants because they believe
> (speciously) that it is politically expedient; that
> is, if homosexuality is an inherited condition, it
> can in no way be considered immoral. If people
> are born homosexual, then those not so born can-
> not "catch" homosexuality; therefore, there is no

> reason to make laws limiting the rights of
> homosexuals to teach, serve in the armed
> forces, and so forth [Faderman 1976, p. 76].

It has been widely assumed, without careful analysis,
that the scientific and ideological positions appropriate for
the issues of racism and sexism are also appropriate for the
analysis of homosexuality. While there are some similarities
between the issues, to be sure, it cannot be assumed that
the same social scientific position--namely social learning
theory--which was both scientifically correct and politically
helpful to other minorities--is scientifically correct and
politically helpful to homosexuals. By embracing the
notion of acquired homosexuality, sociologists have popularized the idea that homosexual orientation is a relatively
superficial aspect of human sexuality. Moreover, sociologists
frequently give the impression that to adhere to or explore
other explanations is somehow morally wrong or illiberal.
However, it is precisely around this and related points that
much of the homophobic rhetoric turns: that homosexuality
is learned and can thus be unlearned; that homosexuality
is a more superficial aspect of human sexuality than heterosexuality and so homosexuals can be treated differently from
heterosexuals; sexual orientation results from role modeling
and thus can be acquired in childhood or adolescence from
others; that improper role models (for example, homosexual
teachers) can lead children into homosexuality through their
mere presence. While sociologists have not consciously sup-
ported homophobic elements, they have popularized a view
that homosexual orientation is rather easily acquired through
interaction (a view which, apart from political considerations,
is not even consistent with the best research available).
Homophobic groups have been quick to see a connection between their aims and these social learning assumptions that
pervade much of the sociology of homosexuality and that
have been taught to countless undergraduates in courses
like "Introduction to Sociology," "Deviance," or "Social Psychology." For example, the Briggs initiative, intended to
prevent homosexuals from teaching in California schools,
utilized the role model concept in the text of the initiative
as it appeared on a ballot in California: "As a result of continued close and prolonged contact with school children, a
teacher, teacher's aide, school administrator, or counselor
becomes a role model whose words, behavior and actions are
likely to be emulated by students coming under his or her
care, instruction, supervision, guidance, and protection"
(California Initiative Measure to be Submitted Directly to the
Voters, Section 44837.5).

While the Briggs initiative was voted down in a general
election, the state of Oklahoma was successful in passing

similar legislation. This law allowed the firing of teachers for "advocating, soliciting, imposing, encouraging or promoting public or private homosexual activity" (Western Express 1985, p. 16). As may be seen from the language of the law-- "advocating, soliciting, imposing, encouraging, and promoting" --the philosophical basis of the law rests on the notion that homosexual orientation comes about through interaction with those already homosexual. The United States Supreme Court has since let stand a lower court decision striking down the law.

Outpost, Inc., in a recent bulletin, enthusiastically reported on two articles appearing in the Journal of Homosexuality which reject the notion that homosexuality has a biological basis. The Outpost News states:

> Two articles in the Spring 1984 Journal of Homosexuality (Vol. 9, No. 2&3), both written by Ph.D.'s catigorically [sic] reject the theory of an "inborn" homosexuality. Dr. Thomas Ford Hoult in his article "Human Sexuality in Biological Perspective: Theoretical and Methodological Considerations" states that "The claim that biological factors have an immediate, direct influence on such things as sexual identity, behavior or orientation remains unproven." Dr. Hoult reviews several of the studies often quoted in support of biological or hormonal basis for homosexuality and points out the flaws and inconsistencies in these works and cites examples of other works that fail to replicate their "so-called" results.
>
> In another article by Douglas J. Futuyma, Ph.D. and Stephen J. Risch, Ph.D. entitled "Sexual Orientation, Socio-biology and Evolution," the authors conclude that "for homosexuality to constitute an evolved trait, it must have a genetic basis. However, there is no reliable evidence that homosexual and heterosexual orientations are caused by genetic differences. On these and other grounds, we find socio-biological explanations of homosexuality to be implausible and unsupported by evidence."
>
> Both of these articles lend a great deal of support to the belief that homosexuality is a learned preference shaped and acquired by the interactions between an individual and his or her environment. These articles take a lot of the "punch" out of the pro-gay argument that homosexuals are "born that way". It simply isn't true [Outpost News July 1984, p. 1].

Outpost News is published by Outpost, Inc., whose goals are to "disciple believers in such a way that they may walk in the freedom from homosexual sin promised to them in I Cor. 6:11 and II Cor. 5:17, to evangelize the gay community with the Gospel of Christ, and to educate the church to its responsibility and capability to minister to a group of people largely ignored due to the nature of their sin" (Outpost News 1984, p. 1)..

In connection with the 1984 presidential election the Arizona Republican State Convention adopted a stand against gay rights based in part on the assumption that homosexual orientation is not biological. This resolution states:

Whereas, the Republican Party has always stood for the fundamental principles upon which this great nation was founded; and, Whereas, the principles and values of this nation are based on basic Judeo-Christian concepts; and, Whereas, the idea of and practice of homosexuality is in complete variance from the basic founding principles of this nation; and, Whereas, homosexuality is NOT a lifestyle forced upon any person by birth or social or economic pressure, but is instead an illness; BE IT THEREFORE RESOLVED that we, the people of the Arizona State Republican Party do hereby reject the idea of "Gay Rights" and, we urge that the homosexual community NOT be granted the status of a legitimate minority such as Blacks, Hispanics, Indians, etc., as is currently being considered by the United States Congress, and we urge all elected Republican Members of Congress and State Legislatures to reject all such claims from the homosexual community and their supporters [The Western Express 1984, p. 20].

SOCIAL TOLERANCE AND BELIEFS ABOUT ORIGINS OF HOMOSEXUALS

It has been generally assumed in social scientific circles not only that homosexual orientation is learned but also that there is a connection between social tolerance of homosexuals and the belief that homosexuality is socially learned. Not only is there no empirical evidence to support this view but, in fact, the opposite may well be true. Toleration may be connected with the belief that homosexuality is natural and biological.

With regard to surveys of the general population, Levitt and Klassen (1974) have reported on interviews with a nationwide probability sample of 3018 adults regarding their attitudes on various aspects of homosexuality. This sample, according to the authors, "represented with reasonable accuracy the noninstitutionalized adult population of the United States, according to the full range of variables usually considered to be fundamental in describing a population" (p. 29). The examination of attitudes reported here suggests that the American public generally takes a voluntaristic view of causation and cure of homosexuality. For example, 61.9 percent of the respondents believed that for most homosexuals "homosexuality is a sickness that can be cured;" 40.4 percent believed that most "homosexuals can stop being homosexuals if they want to;" 42.5 percent believed that most "young homosexuals become that way because of older homosexuals;" 30.3 percent believed that most "homosexuals are born that way." These categories are not mutually exclusive (p. 39).

A 1982 Gallup poll found that 52 percent of Americans think that homosexuality is caused by environment, while 17 percent believe that one is born with a homosexual orientation (Western Express 1982). In analyzing data from 89 Phoenix respondents in a survey of attitudes toward homosexuals done by Whitam, Milton (1983) found that 39 percent believed homosexual orientation was learned, 23 percent chosen, and 22 percent believed it was inborn (see Table 7.2).

These studies are consistent in their finding that most Americans believe homosexual orientation is learned or chosen, not inborn. In contrast, the general public in the Philippines --probably the contemporary society most tolerant of homosexuals--tends to believe that homosexual orientation is inborn. Donn Hart (1968, p. 237) has suggested, "In countries where heredity or biological factors are assumed to produce homosexuality the attitudes toward homosexuality are more tolerant." This impression, derived from Hart's research experience in Southeast Asia, particularly in the Philippines, is compatible with the survey data collected by Whitam in Cebu City, Philippines, in 1981. Male and female Filipinos (N = 173) in both lower-class and middle-class neighborhoods were interviewed with regard to their generalized attitudes about homosexuals (Table 7.3). When asked whether they thought homosexuality was inborn, chosen, or learned, the modal response was inborn with 46 percent; 15 percent thought it was chosen; and 39 percent thought it was learned.

In order to measure the relationship between beliefs about the origins of homosexuality and tolerance for homosexuals, a gamma ordinal measure of association was calculated for the Phoenix (Table 7.2) and Cebu City (Table 7.3) samples. Ex-

TABLE 7.2 Beliefs About Origins of Homosexuality and Homophobia: Phoenix Sample

Beliefs about origins of homosexuality:	Low Homophobia		Moderate Homophobia		High Homophobia		Total	
Born	12	40%	10	30%	5	19%	27	30%
Learned	11	37	16	48	12	46	39	44
Chosen	7	23	7	21	9	35	23	26
Total	30	34%	33	37%	26	29%	89	100%

Gamma = .23; p < 1.5.

TABLE 7.3 Attitudes Toward Homosexuals and Beliefs About Origins of Homosexuality: Philippine Sample

Belief about origins of homosexuality:	Positive Attitude		Neutral Attitude		Negative Attitude		Total	
Born	32	52%	29	45%	18	38%	79	46%
Learned	22	36	25	39	21	44	68	39
Chosen	7	11	10	17	9	19	26	15
Total	61	35%	64	37%	48	28%	173	100%

Gamma = .43; p < .01.

amination of Table 7.2 reveals a slightly positive association between the belief that homosexuality is inborn and low homophobia among the Phoenix respondents. Inspection of Table 7.3 shows a moderate and statistically significant (p < .01) relationship between the belief that homosexuality is inborn and positive attitudes regarding homosexuality among Cebu City respondents. The samples in both cases were small and not strictly random, so these findings are more suggestive than definitive. However, these data do seem to call into question the widely assumed connection between social learning explanations of homosexual orientation and tolerance for homosexuals.

HOMOSEXUALS: THE PERMANENT MINORITY

The description of homosexuals as has been outlined in this book clearly suggests that homosexuals are an authentic minority group. Until now, under the influence of both psychiatric and sociological thought, homosexuals have been widely conceived of as an aberrant, accidental creation rather than an inherent permanent manifestation of human sexuality. In a sense there are not only two sexes in the world, but several--male and female heterosexuals, male and female homosexuals, transvestic homosexuals, and transsexuals. The world of sexual orientation is far more complex than currently conceived in the social sciences. Homosexuals do not now constitute an authentic minority in the minds of most Americans. Even groups which traditionally support the extension of civil rights to minorities show little interest in the minority status of homosexuals. For example, the National Council of Churches was quite active in the black civil rights movement in the 1960s, but recent efforts by the largely homosexual Metropolitan Community Church to be admitted to the National Council of churches met with considerable hostility and rejection by that body. Black Protestant denominations have long been members of the National Council of Churches.

Perhaps no group within U.S. society has such serious civil rights problems as homosexuals. Homosexual behavior is still criminalized in half the United States. The criminalization of homosexuals by many states and the refusal of the United States Supreme Court to invalidate such laws set the stage for harassment by law enforcement agencies and for violence by elements in the general population, particularly "queer bashing" by young heterosexual males. A recent case in Maine is not unusual. Three teenagers, aged 15, 16, and 17, in Bangor, Maine, have been charged with the July 7, 1984 murder of Charles O. Howard, a Bangor gay man:

> They told police they chased Howard across
> a downtown street, beat and kicked him when
> he fell to the ground and then threw him over
> a bridge railing into Kenduskeag Stream. How-
> ard drowned in the stream; his body was
> recovered by police about three hours later.
> The youths claimed they attacked Howard,
> an effeminate obviously Gay man, because he
> had made a pass at one of them a few weeks
> earlier [Observer 1984, p. 1].

In the fall of 1984 in Tucson, there were three murders of
gay men believed to have been committed by teenagers. These
cases are still under investigation (Western Express 1985).
Two youths, aged 13 and 16, have been accused of the stab-
bing to death of one of the three gay men, Charles Bush,
in his mobile home in St. David, Arizona (Observer 1984, p.
1). Such attacks are commonplace in all American cities. The
attackers often go unpunished or receive light sentences
because the victims are homosexual. Such events are similar
to lynchings of blacks in the Deep South before the civil
rights movement, yet they evoke little public reaction even
from groups normally sensitive to civil rights issues.
    Despite the vote of the American Psychiatric Association
to delete some homosexual behavior from its list of pathologies,
many (perhaps even most) psychiatrists still feel that homosexuality is pathological. In 1977, the magazine Medical Aspects
of Human Sexuality, read largely by physicians and psychiatrists, sent questionnaires to 10,000 psychiatrists. Of the
2,500 psychiatrists who responded, some 69 percent still think
that homosexuality is a "pathological adaption (as opposed to
a normal variation)" (Medical Aspects of Human Sexuality 1977,
pp. 110-11). Transsexualism, transvestism, and childhood
cross-gender behavior are still regarded as pathological in
DSM-III (American Psychiatric Association 1980).
    Not only are homosexuals criminalized, victimized, and
labeled pathological, they are also regarded by some religious
groups as sinners deserving to be put to death, a view rem-
iniscent of the Inquisitions. For example, Dean Wycoff, a
spokesman for the Santa Clara, California Moral Majority movement, was quoted as saying, "I agree with capital punish-
ment, and I believe homosexuality could be coupled with murder and other sins" (Arizona Gay News 1981, p. 1). There
are very few, if any, groups in American society which
evoke more hostility than homosexuals.
    Despite the fact that homosexuals have far more serious
civil rights problems than women, in the past few years most
of the attention and energy of groups and individuals interested in sexual and gender freedom has been directed toward
the problems of women. While it is commonplace for sociologists

to regard women as a minority group, homosexuals comprise only about 5 percent of the population and experience far more deprivation of civil rights than women.

Using either sociological or legalistic criteria for minority status, homosexuals would clearly qualify as an authentic minority group. Bassis, Gelles, and Levine (1984) paraphrase Louis Wirth's classic 1945 statement on criteria for minority status as follows:

> First, minority groups are disadvantaged groups. Their members are excluded from full participation in society. . . . They often do not receive equal treatment under the law (indeed they may be subject to special laws). . . .
>
> Second, minority groups are held in low esteem, and they often become objects of suspicion, contempt, hatred, and violence. The physical or cultural characteristics associated with minority groups are devalued by the majority. The way their members look, act, and dress are ridiculed. . . .
>
> Third, membership in a minority group is involuntary--it is an ascribed status, not an achieved one. Individuals are born into the group. They do not choose to join and are not free to leave. . . .
>
> Fourth, minorities are self-conscious groups. Their history, their values and beliefs, and the unequal treatment they experience make them see themselves as "a people apart" [Bassis, Gelles, and Levine 1984, pp. 306-07].

Homosexuals, biologically derived, at predictable rates in all societies, certainly have as legitimate a claim to minority status as that of blacks, Hispanics, Native Americans, Jews, and other racial and ethnic minorities who, to be sure, still have many unresolved problems. Racial and ethnic groups are at least recognized as minority groups and are protected by law against discrimination and violence because of their minority status. The status of homosexuals in American society resembles in significant respects the status of blacks in the 1940s, and in some aspects homosexuals constitute a caste in much the same way that blacks were a caste before 1954.

Neither social learning nor biological explanations will ultimately protect the civil rights of homosexuals. That can only be accomplished through changes in legal statutes and court rulings. However, prevailing social-scientific descriptions of homosexual behavior and explanations of their origins have thus far failed to provide the basis for a major change in the way the public and the law view homosexuals. In examining the underlying rationale of Supreme Court cases dealing with the granting of minority status to "suspect classes" (potential minority groups), Dawson (1980, p. 7) writes that "in order for a group to be declared suspect it must be politically powerless, have experienced a history of discrimination, have a high degree of visibility, and have traits which are immutable." While a case could be made that homosexuals qualify on all four criteria, it is the principle of immutability which appears to be the most serious impediment at present for homosexuals. As presently conceived in the social sciences and translated into public attitudes, homosexual orientation is learned or chosen and therefore mutable. The formulation of homosexual orientation as biologically derived and therefore immutable, appearing in all societies at about the same rate, characterized by similar elements in different societies, and serving as the basis for significant contributions to society, is not only more scientifically accurate, it is also far more politically promising for homosexual rights than other contemporary formulations.

BIBLIOGRAPHY

Adam, Barry. The Survival of Domination: Inferiorization and Everyday Life. New York: Elsevier, 1978.

Akers, Ronald L. Deviant Behavior: A Social Learning Approach. Belmont, California: Wadsworth, 1977.

Altman, Dennis. "An Interview with Gore Vidal." Christopher Street, January 1978, pp. 4-10.

---. The Homosexualization of America. Boston: Beacon Press, 1982.

Amado, Jorge. Dona Flor and Her Two Husbands. New York: Avon Books, 1977.

American Psychiatric Association. Diagnostic and Statistical Manual of Mental Disorders. 3rd ed. 1980.

Apperson, Louise Behrens and W. George McAdoo, Jr. "Parental Factors in the Childhood of Homosexuals." Journal of Abnormal Psychology 73 (1968):201-06.

Arizona Gay News. Vol. 5, issue 38, 1980, p. 2.

---. Vol. 6, issue 7, 1981, p. 1.

Bancroft, John. "The Relationship Between Gender Identity and Sexual Behavior." In C. Ounsted and D.C. Taylor, Gender Differences, pp. 63-64. London: Churchill Livingstone, 1972.

Bassis, Michael S., Richard J. Gelles, and Ann Levine. Sociology: An Introduction. 2nd ed. New York: Random House, 1984.

Bates, John E. and P.M. Bentler. "Play Activities of Normal and Effeminate Boys." Developmental Psychology 9 (1973): 20-27.

---, P.M. Bentler, and Spencer K. Thompson. "Measurement of Deviant Gender Development in Boys." Child Development 44 (1973):591-98.

Bell, Alan P. and Martin S. Weinberg. Homosexualities: A Study of Diversity Among Men and Women. New York: Simon and Schuster, 1978.

---, Martin S. Weinberg, and Susan K. Hammersmith. Sexual Preference: Its Development in Men and Women. Bloomington,Indiana: Indiana University Press, 1981.

Bene, Eva. "On the Genesis of Male Homosexuality: An Attempt at Clarifying the Role of the Parents." British Journal of Psychiatry 111 (1965):803-13.

Berube, Allan. "Coming Out Under Fire." Mother Jones (February-March 1983):24-29, 45.

Bieber, Irving, Harvey J. Dain, Paul R. Dince, Marvin G. Drellich, Henry G. Grand, Ralph H. Grundlach, Malvina W. Kremer, Alfred H. Rifkin, Cornelia B. Wilbur, and Toby B. Bieber. Homosexuality: A Psychoanalytic Study. New York: Basic Books, 1962.

Blair, Emma H. and James A. Robertson, eds. The Philippine Islands: 1493-1898, Vol. 7. Cleveland: Arthur H. Clark, 1903.

Bloch, Iwan. Die Prostitution, Bd. i. Quoted in Havelock Ellis, Sexual Inversion, p. 61 (1942).In Studies in the Psychology of Sex. New York: Random House, 1942.

Body Politic. June 1979, p. 18.

---. April 1982, insert.

Boswell, John. Christianity, Social Tolerance, and Homosexuality. Chicago: The University of Chicago Press, 1980.

Bouge, M. Journal de la Société des Océanistes 11 (1955): 147.

Bray, Alan. Homosexuality in Renaissance England. London: Gay Men's Press, 1982.

Brown, Daniel G. "Transvestism and Sex-Role Inversion." In Albert Ellis and Albert Abarnel, Encyclopedia of Sexual Behavior, pp. 1012-22. New York: Hawthorne Books, 1961.

---. "Homosexuality and Family Dynamics." Bulletin, Meninger Clinic 27 (1963):227-32.

Buhrich, Neill and Neil McGonaghy. "Parental Relationships During Childhood in Homosexuality, Transvestitism and Transsexualism." Australian and New Zealand Journal of Psychiatry 12 (1978):103-08.

Bullough, Vern L. Sexual Variance in Society and History. New York: Wiley, 1976.

Burg, Richard. The Perception of Evil: English Sea Rovers in the Seventeenth Century Caribbean. New York: New York University Press, 1983.

Burton, Sir Richard. The Sotadic Zone. Special edition. New York: The Panurge Press, 1885-1886.

Carpenter, Edward. Intermediate Types Among Primitive Folk. London: George Allen, 1914.

Childs, M. "Japan's Homosexual Heritage." Gai Saber 1 (1977):41-45.

Churchill, Wainwright. Homosexual Behavior Among Males. New York: Hawthorn Books, 1967.

Clinard, Marshall B. and Robert F. Meier. Sociology of Deviant Behavior. 5th ed. New York: Holt, Rinehart and Winston, 1979.

Collins, John P. "Nihon No Nanshoku." Ed.D. dissertation, Institute for Advanced Study of Human Sexuality, 1983.

Crisp, Quentin. The Naked Civil Servant. London: Fontana, 1968.

Davison, Kenneth, Harry Brierley, and Colin Smith. "A Male Monozygotic Twinship Discordant for Homosexuality." British Journal of Psychiatry 118 (1971):675-82.

Dawson, Steve. "Analysis of Suspect Classifications and Its Application to Homosexuals." Paper, Arizona State University, College of Law, 1980.

Devereux, George. "Institutionalized Homosexuality of the Mohave Indians." In Hendrick M. Ruitenbeek, The Problem of Homosexuality in Modern Society, pp. 183-226. New York: E. P. Dutton, 1963.

Diamond, Milton. "A Critical Evaluation of the Ontogeny of Human Sexual Behavior." Quarterly Review of Biology 40 (1965):147-75.

---. "Sexual Identity and Sex Roles." The Humanist (March-April 1978):16-19.

---. "Sexual Identity, Monozygotic Twins Reared in Discordant Sex Roles and a BBC Follow-up." Archives of Sexual Behavior 11 (1982):86.

--- and Arno Karlen. Sexual Decisions. Boston: Little, Brown, 1980.

Douglas, Jack and Francis D. Waksler. The Sociology of Deviance. Boston: Little, Brown, 1982.

Ellis, Albert. Homosexuality: Its Causes and Cures. New York: Lyle Stuart, 1965.

Ellis, Havelock. "Sexual Inversion." In Studies in the Psychology of Sex. New York: Random House, 1942.

Evans, Ray B. "Childhood Parental Relationships of Homosexual Men." Journal of Consulting and Clinical Psychology 33 (1969):129-35.

Evans, T. and M. Evans. Shunga: The Art of Love in Japan. New York: Paddington Press, 1975.

Faderman, Lillian. "The Morbidification of Love Between Women by 19th-Century Sexologists." Journal of Homosexuality 4 (1976):73-90.

Farrell, Ronald A. and James F. Nelson. "A Causal Model of Secondary Deviance: The Case of Homosexuality." The Sociological Quarterly 17 (1976):109-20.

Folha De São Paulo. Quarta-fiera, May 6, 1981, p. 34.

Footnotes. April 1978.

Ford, Clellan S. and Frank A. Beach. Patterns of Sexual Behavior. New York: Harper, 1951.

Free Spirit Newsletter. "Are Homosexuals Easy to Identify? By Appearance? Behavior? Choice of Profession? The Gay Activist Responds." May 8, 1978, p. 8.

"G". "The Secret Life of Moscow." Christopher Street (June 1980):15-22.

Gagnon, John H. and William Simon. Sexual Conduct. Chicago: Aldine, 1973.

Garner, Brian and Richard W. Smith. "Are There Really Any Gay Male Athletes? An Empirical Survey." Journal of Sex Research 13 (1977):22-34.

Gartrell, N.K., D.L. Loriaux, and T.N. Chase. "Plasma Testosterone in Homosexual and Heterosexual Women." American Journal of Psychiatry 134 (1977):1117-18.

Gebhard, Paul H. "Incidence of Overt Homosexuality in the United States and Western Europe." In John M. Livingwood, ed., National Institute of Mental Health Task Force on Homosexuality, pp. 22-29. Rockville, Maryland: NIMH, 1972.

Goffman, Erving. The Presentation of Self in Everyday Life. Garden City, New York: Anchor Books, 1959.

Goodich, Michael. The Unmentionable Vice: Homosexuality in the Later Medieval Period. Santa Barbara, California: Ross-Erickson, 1979.

Green, Richard. Sexual Identity Conflict in Children and Adults. New York: Basic Books, 1974.

---. "One-hundred Ten Feminine and Masculine Boys: Behavioral Contrasts and Demographic Similarities." Archives of Sexual Behavior 5 (1976):425-46.

---. "Sexual Identity of 37 Children Raised by Homosexual or Transsexual Parents." American Journal of Psychiatry 135 (1978):692-97.

---. "Childhood Cross-gender Behavior and Subsequent Sexual Preference." American Journal of Psychiatry 136 (1979):106-08.

--- and John Money. "Stage Acting, Role-taking and Effeminate Impersonation During Boyhood." Archives of General Psychiatry 15 (1966):535-38.

--- and Robert Stoller. "Two Monozygotic (Identical) Twin Pairs Discordant for Gender Identity." Archives of Sexual Behavior 1 (1971):321-27.

--- and Marielle Fuller. "Family Doll Play and Female Identity in Preadolescent Males." American Journal of Orthopsychiatry 43 (1973):123-27.

---, Marielle Fuller, Brian R. Rutley, and Jared Hendler. "Playroom Toy Preferences of Fifteen Masculine and Fifteen Feminine Boys." Behavior Therapy 3 (1972):425-29.

Greenblatt, David Robert. "Semantic Differential Analysis of the 'Triangular System' Hypothesis of 'Adjusted' Male Homosexuals." Ph.D. dissertation, University of California at Los Angeles, 1966.

Haddad, M. George. "Catherine Deveuve." Blueboy (September 1978):14, 90-91.

Harry, Joseph. Gay Children Grown Up. New York: Praeger, 1982.

---. "Defeminization and Adult Psychological Well-Being Among Male Homosexuals." Archives of Sexual Behavior 12 (1983):1-19.

Hart, Donn V. "Homosexuality and Transvestism in the Philippines." Behavior Science Notes 3 (1968):211-48.

---. Personal communication, 1979.

Helbing, Terry. "Gay Theater Issue: An Introduction." Christopher Street, June 1978, pp. 5-8.

Herdt, Gilbert H. Guardians of the Flute: Idioms of Masculinity. New York: McGraw-Hill, 1981.

Heston, L.L. and James Shields. "Homosexuality in Twins: A Family Study and a Registry Study." Archives of General Psychiatry 18 (1968):149-60.

Hirschfeld, Magnus. Sexual Anomalies and Perversions. New York: Emerson Books, 1944.

Holden, H. "Psychotherapy of a Shared Syndrome in Identical Twins." British Journal of Psychiatry 111 (1965): 859-64.

Hotvedt, Mary E. and Jane Barclay Mandel. "Children of Lesbian Mothers." In William Paul, James D. Weinrich, John C. Gonsiorek, and Mary E. Hotvedt, eds., Homosexuality: Social, Psychological, and Biological Issues. Beverly Hills: Sage, 1982.

Hughes, Preston. "Coffee, Tea, or He?" Christopher Street, January 1978, pp. 29-31.

Humphreys, Laud. Tearoom Trade: Impersonal Sex in Public Places. New York: Aldine, 1975.

Hyde, H. Montgomery. The Love that Dare Not Speak its Name. Boston: Little, Brown, 1970.

Imperato-McGinley, Julianne, Ralph E. Peterson, Teofilo Gautier, and Erasmo Sturla. "Androgens and the Evolution of Male-Gender Identity Among Male Pseudohermaphrodites with 5-alpha-Reductase Deficiency." New England Journal of Medicine 300 (1979):1233-37.

Jonas, C.H. "An Objective Approach to the Personality and Environment in Homosexuality." Psychiatric Quarterly 18 (1944):626-41.

Julian, Joseph. Social Problems. Englewood Cliffs, New Jersey: Prentice-Hall, 1973.

Kallman, Franz J. "Comparative Twin Study on the Genetic Aspects of Male Homosexuality." Journal of Nervous and Mental Disease 115 (1952):283-97.

---. Heredity in Health and Mental Disorder. New York: W. W. Norton, 1953.

Kando, Thomas. Sex Change. Springfield, Illinois: Charles C. Thomas, 1973.

Karlen, Arno. Sexuality and Homosexuality: A New View. New York: W. W. Norton, 1971.

---. "Homosexuality: Its Scene and Its Students." In James M. Henslin and Edward Sagarin, eds., The Sociology of of Sex. New York: Schocken Books, 1978.

Katchadourian, Herant A. and Donald T. Lunde. Fundamentals of Human Sexuality. New York: Holt, Rinehart and Winston, 1972.

Katz, Jonathan. Gay American History. New York: Thomas W. Crowell, 1976.

Kelley, Kitty. Jackie Oh! New York: Ballantine Books, 1978.

Kinsey, Alfred C. "Criteria for a Hormonal Explanation of the Homosexual." In Donald Webster Cory, ed., Homosexuality: A Cross-Cultural Approach, pp. 370-83. New York: Julian Press, 1956.

---, Wardell B. Pomeroy, and Clyde E. Martin. Sexual Behavior in the Human Male. Philadelphia: W. B. Saunders, 1948.

Kitsuse, John I. "Societal Reaction to Deviant Behavior." In Earl Rubington and Martin S. Weinberg, eds, Deviance: The Interactionist Perspective, pp. 15-24. New York: Macmillan, 1978.

Kleeman, James A. "The Establishment of Core Gender Identity in Normal Girls." Archives of Sexual Behavior 1 (1971):103-29.

Klintworth,G.K. "A Pair of Male Monozygotic Twins Discordant for Homosexuality," Journal of Nervous and Mental Disorders 135 (1962):113-25.

Koch, G. "Die Bedütung Genetischer Faktoren Für Das Menschliche Verhatten." Aryliche Praxis 17 (1965):823, 839-46.

Kolodny, R.C., W.H. Masters, Julia Hendryx, and G. Toro. "Plasma Testosterone and Semen Analysis in Male Homosexuals." New England Journal of Medicine 285 (1971):1170-74.

Kopay, David and Perry Deane Young. The Dave Kopay Story. New York: Arbor House, 1977.

Lange, J. Crime as Destiny. London: Allen and Unwin, 1931.

Lauritsen, John and David Thorstad. The Early Homosexual Rights Movement 1864-1935. New York: Times Change Press, 1974.

Lebovitz, Phil S. "Feminine Behavior in Boys: Aspects of Its Outcome." American Journal of Psychiatry 128 (1972):103-09.

Leser, Hedwig. "The Hirschfeld Institute for Sexology." In Albert Ellis and Albert Abarnel, eds., Encyclopedia of Sexual Behavior, pp. 967-70. New York: Hawthorn Books, 1961.

Levitt, Eugene E. and Albert D. Klassen, Jr. "Public Attitudes Toward Homosexuality: Part of the 1970 National Survey by the Institute for Sex Research" Journal of Homosexuality 1 (1974):29-43.

Levy, Robert I. "The Community Function of Tahitian Male Transvestitism: A Hypothesis." Anthropological Quarterly 44 (1971): 12-21.

Lorrimer, Jon. "Israel's Gay Colonies: Sex Life in a Kibbutz." QQ Magazine (December 1975):26, 41-43.

McGaghy, Charles H. and James K. Skipper. "Lesbian Behavior as an Adaptation to the Occupation of Stripping." In Clifton Bryant, ed., Deviant Behavior: Occupational and Organizational Bases. Chicago: Rand McNally, 1974.

Maccoby, Eleanor E. and Carol N. Jacklin. The Psychology

of Sex Differences. Stanford, California: Stanford University Press, 1974.

Mandel, Jane Barclay, Mary E. Hotvedt, Richard Green, and L. Smith. "The Lesbian Parents Comparison of Heterosexual and Homosexual Mothers and Their Children." Paper presented at the Annual Meeting of the American Psychological Association, September 4, 1979, New York.

Margolese, M.S. "Homosexuality: A New Endocrine Correlate." Hormones and Behavior 1 (1970):151-55.

--- and O. Janiger. "Androsterone/etiocholanolone Ratios in Male Homosexuals" British Medical Journal 3 (1973): 207-10.

Mead, Margaret. Sex and Temperament in Three Primitive Societies. New York: William Morrow, 1935.

Medical Aspects of Human Sexuality. "Sexual Survey #4: Current Thinking on Homosexuality." November 1977, pp. 110-11.

Mehan, Hugh and Houston Wood. The Reality of Ethnomethodology. New York: John Wiley and Sons, 1975.

Mejia de Rodas, Idalma. Unpublished field notes, 1976.

Mesnikoff, A.M., J.D. Ranier, L.C. Kolb, A.C. Carr. "Intrafamilial Determinants of Divergent Sexual Behavior in Twins." American Journal of Psychiatry 119 (1963): 732-38.

Meyer-Behlburg, Heino F.L. "Sex Hormones and Male Homosexuality in Comparative Perspective." Archives of Sexual Behavior 6 (1977):297-325.

---. "Sex Hormones and Female Homosexuality: A Critical Examination." Archives of Sexual Behavior 8 (1979):101-19.

Miller, Paul R. "The Effeminate Passive Obligatory Homosexual." American Medical Association Archives of Neurological Psychiatry 80 (1958):612-18.

Milton, Gloria J. "Social Beliefs, Social Background and Tolerance of Homosexuals." M.A. thesis, Department of Sociology, Arizona State University, 1983.

Mitzel, John. "Sports and the Macho Male." Gay Sunshine: A Journal of Gay Liberation (June-July 1973):16-17.

Money, John and A.J. Russo. "Homosexual Outcome of Discordant Gender Identity/Role in Childhood: Longitudinal Follow-up." Journal of Pediatric Psychology 4 (1979):29-41.

--- and Anke A. Ehrhardt. Man and Woman, Boy and Girl. Baltimore: Johns Hopkins Press, 1972.

--- and Patricia Tucker. Sexual Signatures. Boston: Little, Brown, 1975.

Morrison, James. The Journal of James Morrison. London: Golden Cockerel Press, 1935. Quoted in Robert I. Levy, "The Community Function of Tahitian Male Transvestitism: A Hypothesis," Anthropological Quarterly 44 (1971):12-21.

Mott, Luiz. Gay Books Bulletin, September 1984a.

---. Personal communication, 1984b.

Murray, Stephen. Newsletter of Anthropological Research Group on Homosexuality 1 (1979):3.

Newton, Esther. Mother Camp: Female Impersonators in America. Englewood Cliffs, New Jersey: Prentice-Hall, 1972.

Observer. "Murder of Arizona Gay Legal?" December 27, 1984, p. 1.

---. October 24, 1984, p. 1.

O'Connor, P.J. "Aetiological Factors in Homosexuality as Seen in R.A.F. Psychiatric Practice." British Journal of Psychiatry 110 (1964):381-91.

Outpost News. July 1984, pp. 1-2.

Paluszny, Maria, Benjamin Beit-Hallahmi, John C. Catford, Ralph E. Cooley, Cecila Y. Dull, and Alexander Z. Guiora. "Gender Identity and Its Measurement in Children." Comprehensive Psychiatry 14 (1973):281-90.

Parker, Neville. "Homosexuality in Twins: A Report on Three Discordant Pairs." British Journal of Psychiatry 110 (1964):489-95.

Penteado, Darcy. A Meta. São Paulo: Edições Simbolo, 1976.

Phillip. "Behind the Gay Curtain." Campaign, April 1980, p. 17.

Pinto, João. Personal communication, May 1984.

Pomeroy, Wardell B. "Homosexuality, Transvestism and Transexualism." In C.E. Vincent, ed., Human Sexuality in Medical Education and Practice, pp. 367-86. Springfield, Illinois: C. C. Thomas, 1968.

---. Dr. Kinsey and the Institute for Sex Research. New York: Harper and Row, 1972.

Pontēnila, Maria Simeona J. "An Ethnographic Study of the Overt Bayots in Dumaguete City." M.A. thesis in Anthropology, Silliman University (Dumaguete, Philippines), 1975.

Rainer, J., A. Mesnikoff, L. Kolb, and A. Carr. "Homosexuality and Heterosexuality in Identical Twins." Psychosomatic Medicine 22 (1960):251-59.

Rekers, G.A. and C.E. Yates. "Sex-typed Play in Feminoid Boys Versus Normal Boys and Girls." Journal of Abnormal Child Psychology 4 (1976):1-8.

Roazen, Paul. Freud and His Followers. New York: New American Library, 1971.

Robertson, Graham. "Parent-Child Relationships and Homosexuality." British Journal of Psychiatry 121 (1972):525-28.

Robertson, Ian. Sociology. New York: Worth, 1977.

---. Sociology. New York: Worth, 1981.

Rosen, David H. Lesbianism: A Study of Female Homosexuality. Springfield, Illinois: Charles C. Thomas, 1974.

Saghir, Marcel T. and Eli Robins. Male and Female Homosexuality. Baltimore: Williams and Wilkins, 1973.

San Antonio, Juan Francisco de. The Philippine Chronicles of Fray San Antonio. Manila: Historical Conservation Society, 1977.

Schlegel, Willhart. "Die Konstitutionsbiologischen Grundlagen der Homosexualität." Z. menschl. Vererb.-u. Konstitutionshlehre 36 (1962):341-64.

Schneebaum, Tobias. Keep the River on Your Right. New York: Grove Press, 1969.

Schofield, Michael. Sociological Aspects of Homosexuality. London: Longmans, 1965.

Schur, Edwin. Crimes Without Victims. Englewood Cliffs, New Jersey: Prentice-Hall, 1965.

Schuvaloff, George. "Gay Life in Russia." Christopher Street, September 1976, pp. 14-22.

Shewey, Don. "Gay Theatre: Gays in the Marketplace vs. Gays for Themselves, Part I." Blueboy, May 1978(a), pp. 68, 81-83.

---. "Gay Theatre: Gays in the Marketplace vs. Gays for Themselves, Part II." Blueboy, June 1978(b), pp. 63-66, 92-97.

Siegelman, Marvin. "Parental Background of Male Homosexuals and Heterosexuals." Archives of Sexual Behavior 3 (1974):3-18.

Simmons, J.L. "The Nature of Deviant Subcultures." In Earl Rubington and Martin S. Weinberg, eds., Deviance: The Interactionist Perspective, pp. 280-82.

Sociologists' Gay Caucus Resolution. 1977.

Stamford, John D., ed. Your Spartacus Holiday Portfolio: Philippine Provinces. Amsterdam: Spartacus, 1979(a)

---. Spartacus International Gay Guide, 9th ed. Amsterdam: Spartacus, 1979(b)

---. Spartacus International Gay Guide, 11th ed. Amsterdam: Spartacus, 1981.

---. Spartacus International Gay Guide, 12th ed. Amsterdam: Spartacus, 1982.

---. Spartacus International Gay Guide, 13th ed. Amsterdam: Spartacus, 1983.

Stephan, Walter G. "Parental Relationships and Early Social Experiences of Activist Male Homosexuals and Male Heterosexuals." Journal of Abnormal Psychology 82 (1973): 506-13.

Stoddard, Thomas B., E. Carrington Boggan, Marilyn G. Haft, Charles Lister, and John P. Rupp. The Rights of Gay People. New York: Bantam Books, 1983.

Stoller, Robert. Sex and Gender. New York: J. Aronson, 1968.

Taylor, Lindsay. "British Raids on Bathhouses." Arizona Gay News, May 25, 1983, p. 2.

The Voice. May 8, 1980, p. 29.

Thio, Alex. Deviant Behavior. Boston: Houghton-Mifflin, 1978.

Thompson, Norman L., David M. Schwartz, Boyd R. McCand-less, and David A. Edwards. "Parent-child Relationships and Sexual Identity in Male and Female Homosexuals and Heterosexuals." Journal of Consulting and Clinical Psy-chology 41 (1973):12-27.

Thompson, Spencer K. "Gender Labels and Early Sex Role Development." Child Development 46 (1975):339-47.

Tripp, C.A. The Homosexual Matrix. New York: McGraw-Hill, 1975.

Vanderbelt-Barber, Gina. "Homosexuality in Canada." In Craig Boydell, Carl Grindstaff, and Pam Whitehead, eds., Deviant Behavior and Societal Reaction, pp. 501-23. Toronto: Holt, Rinehart, and Winston, 1972.

Vayle, Mandy. "Portugal." Blueboy, January 1979, pp. 64, 67.

Warren, Carol. Identity and Community in the Gay World. New York: Wiley, 1974.

Weeks, Jeffrey. Coming Out: Homosexual Politics in Britain, from the Nineteenth Century to the Present. London: Quartet Books, 1977.

West, D.J. "Parental Relationship in Male Homosexuality." International Journal of Social Psychiatry 5 (1959):85-97.

---. Homosexuality Re-examined. Minneapolis: The Univer-sity of Minnesota Press, 1977.

West, Mae. Goodness Had Nothing To Do With It. New York: Prentice-Hall, 1959.

Western Express. February 2-16, 1982, p. 4.

---. August 29-September 11, 1984, p. 20.

---. December 19-January 3, 1985, p. 1.

---. April 12-25, 1985, p. 16.

Westwood, Gordon. Society and the Homosexual. London: Gollancz, 1952.

Whitam, Frederick L. "Childhood Indicators of Male Homosexuality." Archives of Sexual Behavior 6 (1977):89-96.

---. "The Entendidos: Middle Class Gay Life in Sao Paulo." Gay Sunshine: A Journal of Gay Liberation (Winter 1979): 16-17.

---. "Childhood Predictors of Adult Homosexuality." Journal of Sex Education and Therapy 6 (1980a):11-16.

---. "The Prehomosexual Male Child in Three Societies: The United States, Guatemala, Brazil." Archives of Sexual Behavior 9 (1980b):87-99.

---. "Variant Sexuality: Ellis. Freud; Hirschfeld, Kinsey." In Romano Forleo and Willy Pasini, eds., Medical Sexology, pp. 295-304. New York: Elsevier/North-Holland Biomedical Press, 1980(c).

--- and Michael Zent. "A Cross-cultural Assessment of Early Cross-Gender Behavior and Familial Factors in Male Homosexuality." Archives of Sexual Behavior 13 (1984):427-39.

Wortis, Joseph. Fragments of an Analysis with Freud. New York: Charter Books, 1963.

Young, Allen. "The Cuban Revolution and Gay Liberation." In Karla Jay and Allen Young, eds., Out of the Closets: Voices of Gay Liberation, pp. 206-28. New York: Douglas-Links, 1972.

Zucker, Kenneth J., Susan J. Bradley, Carl M. Corter, Robert W. Doering, and Jo-Anne K. Finegan. "Cross-gender Behavior in Very Young Boys: A Normative Study." Paper presented at the Symposium on the Sexuality of the Child, September 7-9, 1979(a), Montreal.

---, Robert W. Doering, Susan J. Bradley, and Jo-Anne K. Finegan. "Sex-typed Play in Gender-disturbed Children and Their Siblings." Paper presented at annual meeting of the American Psychological Association, 1979(b), New York.

Zuger, Bernard. "Effeminate Behavior Present in Boys from Early Childhood: I. The Clinical Syndrome and Follow-up Studies." Journal of Pediatrics 69 (1966):1098-107.

---. "The Role of Familial Factors in Persistent Effeminate Behavior in Boys." American Journal of Psychiatry 126 (1970):1167-70.

---. "Effeminate Behavior Present in Boys from Childhood: Ten Additional Years of Follow-up." Comprehensive Psychiatry 19 (1978):363-69.

--- and Patsy Taylor. "Effeminate Behavior Present in Boys from Early Childhood: II. Comparison with Similar Symptoms in Noneffeminate Boys." Journal of Pediatrics 44 (1969):375-80.

INDEX

ABOUT THE AUTHORS

FREDERICK L. WHITAM is associate professor of sociology at Arizona State University. He holds a B.A. degree from Millsaps College and an M.A. and Ph.D. from Indiana University.

His principal area of interest is variant sexuality, particularly cross-cultural aspects of homosexuality. He has published numerous articles on variant sexuality and is a member of the International Academy of Sex Research.

ROBIN MATHY is a graduate student in the departments of sociology and anthropology at Arizona State University. He is a graduate of the Arizona State University honors program summa cum laude with a B.S. in sociology.

His principal areas of interest are deviant behavior and variant sexuality. He has also published short stories, poetry, book reviews, and articles, as well as having written several award-winning essays.